# THE
# BINMAN
# CHRONICLES

⊏⊐

# NEVILLE SOUTHALL

## THE BINMAN CHRONICLES

*In collaboration with*

# JAMES CORBETT

For Emma and Samantha.

Published by deCoubertin Books Ltd in 2012.
deCoubertin Books, PO Box 65170, London, SE18 9HB
**www.decoubertin.co.uk**

First hardback edition.
ISBN: 978-0-9564313-8-7 – Standard edition
978-1-909245-00-6 – 1984 FA Cup Winner Signed Limited Edition
978-1-909245-01-3 – 1985 European Cup Winners Cup Winner Signed Limited Edition
978-1-909245-02-0 – 1987 League Champion Signed Limited Edition
978-1-909245-03-7 – 1995 FA Cup Winner Signed Limited Edition
978-1-909245-04-4 – 92 Cap Welsh legend Signed Limited Edition

A CIP catalogue record for this book is available from the British Library.
Cover and typeset design by Allen Mohr.

The title, The Binman Chronicles, was conceived by Graham Bateman of Runcorn
via a competition on evertonfc.com and chosen by Neville Southall as the title of this book.

Printed and bound by CPI Group (UK) Ltd, Croydon, CR0 4YY

Every effort has been made to contact copyright holders for photographs
used in this book. If we have overlooked you in any way, please get in touch so
that we can rectify this in future editions.

# CONTENTS

FOREWORD *by Howard Kendall* — IX

INTRODUCTION — 1

*Chapter One* — BINMAN — 7

*Chapter Two* — SHAKER — 30

*Chapter Three* — TOFFEEMAN — 43

*Chapter Four* — VALIANT — 63

*Chapter Five* — SUPERNOVA — 73

*Chapter Six* — DRAGON — 88

*Chapter Seven* — LEGEND — 106

*Chapter Eight* — EXILE — 121

*Chapter Nine* — DISSENTER — 138

*Chapter Ten* — NEARLY MAN — 158

*Chapter Eleven* — STRUGGLER — 170

*Chapter Twelve* — VETERAN — 190

*Chapter Thirteen* — PATRIOT — 214

*Chapter Fourteen* — NOMAD — 227

*Chapter Fifteen* — TEACHER — 245

*Chapter Sixteen* — SAGE — 251

*Appendix* — Q & A — 259

ACKNOWLEDGEMENTS — 268

INDEX — 270

# F O R E W O R D
## BY HOWARD KENDALL

I FIRST GOT A WHISPER ABOUT NEVILLE SOUTHALL in 1980 from a very good friend of mine called Norman Jones, who had a public house in Llandudno. I was player manager of Blackburn Rovers at the time and Neville was playing for Winsford United in the Cheshire League. Norman said, 'I think you should come down and see this young goalkeeper at Winsford United and have a look at him. His father drinks in my pub, as well.' I asked him what the pub was called, and he said it was The Neville. I knew then that we were fated.

I went down to Cheshire to see Neville play. It's very rare that you see a goalkeeper that you're impressed with so much when watching them for the first time. I was fortunate this particular night; he was coming out for crosses, he was shot stopping, his kicking was good, his positional play was a little raw – but that was to be expected. In short he had all the qualities you love to see in a goalkeeper. I thought, there's not many times you see a goalkeeper for the first time and think 'he's the one'. So I contacted my chairman and told him that I'd found a goalkeeper. But the £6,000 fee was too much for Blackburn at a time when the club already had two senior keepers, and Bury snapped him up instead.

A year later I had moved back to Everton and was looking for another goalkeeper and thought of Neville straightaway. He had done well in his year at Gigg Lane and his price was a bit higher too. But at £150,000 he proved one of the best bargains ever.

At the same time I signed Jim Arnold from Blackburn as well. I knew it would be a bit much to jump from non-league to the First Division in barely a year and I saw Jim as a short-term answer to my problems. But I never doubted Neville.

I kept my contract as a player when I went to Everton from Blackburn because I thought I'd help the kids along. So I played with Neville in the reserve team and he was just so impressive, it was only a matter of time before he broke into the team. And when he did, of course, we all know what happened.

Neville became the world's best, for me, but it never changed him. There were none of the accruements of a famous footballer and he still cycled to training from his home in West Derby. But his success and recognition were all fully deserved.

When I returned to Everton for a third spell as manager in 1997, one of the hardest things I had to do was bring an end to his Everton career. We had just signed Thomas Myhre from Norway, and Neville I felt had started to lose some of the agility that had once made him such a great player. I didn't really want him to be extending the length of his career and having people point the finger at him, because he's too good for that. I remember bringing him up to my room on the morning of the Leeds game, and I was absolutely choked having to tell him I was leaving him out. I knew just how much it meant to him, but he took it well.

All the time that I was at Everton I never once pointed the finger at Neville for conceding a goal. I think, given how long he was there, that's the highest compliment you can pay him. He was a great, great player and crucial to me and Everton for many years.

Howard Kendall, July 2012

# INTRODUCTION

ON A FOOTBALL PITCH IN THE SOUTH OF ENGLAND, the tension is rising to boiling point. Something – I'm not sure what just yet – has happened and a young lad in a Chelsea kit is marching towards me, perspiring, his neck muscles strained in a paroxysm of rage. I knew that the situation was tense, but hadn't quite expected this.

'You fucking twat! You fat prick! Go and fuck off, you knobhead!'

He's a scrawny thing, no more than 17 years old. As he stands in front of me jabbing his finger and uttering every profanity he can think of, I tower over him, and think for a few seconds about how to respond. Across the other side of the pitch everyone has stopped and is looking to see what will happen next.

I listen, half expecting the angry roar of a crowd urging some sort of action. But there is nothing, just the sound of this upset and confused teenager and seagulls cawing overhead. Fog and a light drizzle blow in from the North Sea. I've played in some of the greatest stadiums in the world – Wembley, the Bernabeu, Munich's Olympic Stadium, as well as at Goodison Park more times than any other player – but today my surroundings are less salubrious. I'm standing in Ramsgate FC's charming but ramshackle ground, on a hill above the Kent town, with a group of disengaged teenagers.

I look down at the kid, and smile. All through my playing career one of my most important attributes was not letting people know what I thought. It's a quality I've brought into my new vocation.

'Is that the worst you can do?' I say. 'I've had fifty thousand people shouting far worse things at me. Is that really the worst that you can think of?'

'You dickhead! Fuck off!'

I shake my head to let him know that I'm not impressed with the standard of his insults. It'll take far more than this to upset me.

'Bastard!'

'No, try again,' I say, smiling and shaking my head once more.

I can see that his rage has hit its crescendo; that his anger will only subside from now on.

'Fucker!' he snarls, but now I'm just laughing.

'Oh, go and fuck off,' he snarls, and gives up, stomping off to join the other kids, who are in a huddle on the halfway line, shivering and curious.

It's a small victory, but I know that he could combust again at any time. But today's excitement is over and we get back to work.

⌶

FOR 25 YEARS I WAS GOALKEEPER for a variety of professional and semi-professional clubs, as well as my country. I played more games for Everton and Wales than any other player and am synonymous with them, but turned out for many other teams, ranging from Bradford City in the Premier League to Bull Fossils in the second division of the Dover & District Sunday League, for whom I played centre half and scored the deciding goal when we won the league title in 2003.

I won the League Championship twice, the FA Cup twice, the European Cup Winners' Cup and am one of only four goalkeepers to win the FWA Footballer of the Year award. I played nearly 900 matches as a professional footballer, plus almost a century of internationals. I was unlucky not to play at a World Cup or European Championship, but came close on several occasions. I turned out alongside some of the greatest players of my generation – Ian Rush, Mark Hughes, Gary Lineker, Trevor Steven and Graeme Sharp – and played against some of them too – Lothar Matthäus, Marco Van Basten and Ruud Gullit. For many years people said I was the best goalkeeper in the world, praise which I often struggled to deal with.

But now I do something very different and in many ways far more important. I teach.

For the last eight years I've worked with some of the most marginalised and disengaged youths in Britain. The acronym for these kids is NEETs – Not In Education, Employment or Training – but it doesn't really reflect the true myriad of issues they face. Beset by behavioural problems, learning disabilities and abuse, they have fallen by the wayside of mainstream education and, eventually, employment. In society they are often defined as chavs or trailer trash; lazy labels that stigmatise and marginalise them further. They are British society's forgotten minority; abandoned, ignored, but a problem waiting to happen. A life of poverty, petty crime and substance abuse usually lies ahead of them, but sometimes it can be more explosive – as witness the August 2011 riots that destroyed parts of London and led to running battles with police across major cities throughout Britain.

There are very few avenues out of this cycle of problems and self-destruction. Most people aren't interested in these kids and would sooner see them fade into their estates, unseen and unheard – even though they're just a problem waiting to happen. The government has, however, put some money into training, recognising that it's easier to turn someone's life around when they're 16 or 17 than when they're older and carry more baggage. Local colleges are empowered to provide basic skills training, and although the system has flaws it has the power to transform the direction of someone's life.

It's something that I fell into almost by accident, and after studying for two years, I qualified as a teacher. I work in partnership with local colleges near my home in Kent and provide a training programme, which uses football at its core. I take on kids who have nothing – excluded from school, sometimes kicked out by their parents, jobless, clueless about how to make their way in the world – and work through a programme that gives them qualifications, self-confidence and a second chance. Football is the hook that gets them interested and they work on coaching qualifications, while they also train in six other subjects that we arrange around football. After 26 weeks with me they go back into the world, hopefully with some meaning and purpose. While a few invariably fall through the net, it can be a life-changing experience.

But there are, of course, challenges along the way. These are troubled, volatile souls, who are usually struggling to make sense of a crazy world. All sorts of things are going on at home and among their friends. Things kick off and blow up all the time, as with the kid who went berserk with me that morning in Ramsgate.

When it does I take myself back to my playing days. I stop being a teacher for a few moments and I'm Neville Southall the goalkeeper again. Back then I never let anything bother me – not the crowd, not the opposition, not my own team-mates. It was one of the first and most important lessons taught to me as a professional footballer: don't let anyone know what you're thinking. Being dispassionate and staying calm are the hallmarks of a good goalkeeper but they're traits that serve me well as a teacher too. There are, of course, other aspects of my job that draw on my football background. I like to build a sense of team spirit and create a space where these kids can feel welcome, safe and wanted, and can go on and flourish.

I made a difference to the football history of Everton and Wales. I might not get headlines any more, but I'm very happy to make a difference to the lives of these kids.

$\mathbf{\pm}$

WHEN I STARTED WORK ON THIS BOOK I wanted to lift the lid on a different side of my life and show who I really am and the making of that person. Until now, very few people know the sort of work that I have done since I finished playing, and even fewer people know the real me. Because I was – and am – an outsider in the sport that made me famous, very few people knew or understood me, and over time I became a sort of caricature.

Over the years I've been cast as many things: grumpy, unsociable, obsessive, crank, lothario, genius, legend, miserable, idiosyncratic, troublemaker, rebel, oddity, maverick, patriot, sad, loner, sullen. I suppose I have at various times fitted all these descriptions, but I've also been many other things too: father, teacher, theatre buff, book addict, history obsessive, among many others. My former team-mate Pat Nevin once described me as 'The classic eccentric with a complex character.' He's right in a way, but also wrong. I'm at once more complicated and straightforward than anyone could ever imagine. Like most people I have some idiosyncrasies, but really I'm just a normal bloke.

This book charts my life story. It's a happy and sad tale, that takes you from a youth in the lovely but isolated town of Llandudno, where football defined my life, through non-league football and on to Bury, Everton, Wales and various other outposts leading all the way to Ramsgate.

It was my obsession to be the best player possible so that I could help Everton and Wales, and I sacrificed a lot through my single-mindedness and dedication to my craft. As a player I was quite insular and never happy with what I'd achieved, always thinking about the next game, the next challenge. Because I was so focused on what I was doing and on rectifying my perceived shortcomings there was never an opportunity to reflect on what I'd done and achieved. But looking back now I can see that it was all worthwhile.

It's nearly 15 years since I last defended the goalposts of Everton and Wales, but I can honestly say that those institutions have never left me. I've enjoyed looking back over my career and hope that those who supported me along the way enjoy my recollections of the highs and lows I traversed. But above all I hope that people understand the person who filled those gloves a little bit better and have a better appreciation of how I came to be.

# CHAPTER ONE
# BINMAN

THEY SAY THAT PEOPLE reflect the place they come from, and my upbringing in Llandudno certainly made me the person that I came to be.

Llandudno was a brilliant place to grow up. It wasn't a typical Welsh town at all and was full of Scousers and Irish, who had come to do holiday jobs. Yet there was no edge to the place and no atmosphere; I never saw any trouble there. There was a closeness and family atmosphere about the place. There wasn't much to do there: there were the beaches and the hills and inland were the Snowdonia mountains, although we never really went there.

My parents, Fred and Rose, had met in the late 1940s when my mum visited the town while on holiday from her home in Salisbury. It was an old-fashioned long-distance romance, kept up by letters, until they took the plunge and got married in the mid-1950s. Mum moved up from England and remained in Llandudno for the rest of her life.

My dad was lucky to be alive by then and had had a tough war. He had lied about his age so he could join the Paras and ended up fighting at the Battle of Arnhem in September 1944, the famous nine-day battle immortalised in the Richard Attenborough film A Bridge Too Far. The battle came after months of Allied victories in France and Belgium and as part of Operation Market Garden was intended as the first move to liberate the Netherlands. British, American and Polish paratroopers were dropped to try and secure key bridges, but the British troops landed some way from their objective, and in trying to make up lost ground met fierce resistance from SS troops. My dad had been wounded very badly and was shot in the leg and bayoneted in his lung, which was later removed. He spent a year recuperating in Switzerland, but the health problems caused by his injuries would always have an impact upon him. Down the centre of his chest was a huge ugly scar from where they'd operated upon him. I have a photograph of him taken not long after the fighting finished. In it, he looks like an old man, but he was only in his twenties. His injuries weren't the only thing he came back from the war with. He had a collection of souvenirs in the loft, including a Sten gun, which me and my brothers would look at with a sense of awe.

Dad did all sorts of different jobs. He drove a van for the local baker and all kinds of other odd jobs. His injuries meant he was never able to do manual labour and I think he got some sort of emergency benefit, although it wasn't much. It must have been very difficult for him, bringing up a young family and knowing there were all sorts of things he couldn't do. That said, only having one lung didn't stop him smoking, and it didn't stop him drinking or going out. He played footy sometimes and was always playing golf. I never remember him suffering. He just got on with what he had to get on with. He ended up working at the Hotpoint factory on the assembly lines there. My mum, who had stayed at home to look after me and my brothers when we were children, also worked there later.

My parents were very different. Dad was very gregarious and outgoing, probably what you'd describe as a bit of a character. He socialised a lot and people around town all knew him. He used to like an argument – you could lock him up in a room by himself and he'd start a row. He wasn't nasty, he just used to like winding people up and was constantly taking the piss out of everyone. Winding people up was his hobby; he'd get two people rowing and sit back and laugh. I suppose it's probably where I get it from. My mum, in contrast, was very quiet, although she couldn't get a word in edgeways with my dad around. She was a proper old-fashioned mother: she cooked and cleaned and looked after me and my brothers. Being English in a small Welsh town possibly set her apart as something of an outsider, although she had some friends. She was good-natured and kept herself to herself, and I never heard her say a bad word about anybody, ever.

I was born on 16 September 1958, the middle child of three boys. Steve is two years older than me and Jeff two years younger. We were close growing up, but then we had to be. Two of us shared a bed and whoever had the single bed was lucky. It worked well in winter, to be fair, because it was always so bloody freezing in our house. Often you had your coat on the bed just to keep warm. Yet we had a nice childhood. There was always food in the house, we always had clothes, my parents were always around. We never had much money, but then we didn't miss anything either. We were grateful for what we had, grateful for anything really. If we were given something at Christmas, we considered it a bonus.

Until I was about ten we lived at 6 Belle Vue Terrace, which is high above Llandudno town, on the peninsula called the Great Orme. It was a very small rented terraced house with no heating, no bath and no toilet, apart from outside. The Orme is a great hump and we were at the very top of it, so to get anywhere you had to walk down the hill and, of course, back up it to get home.

At the top there was a pub called The Summit, where my dad some-times went drinking with a boxer called Randolph Turpin, who was the licensee. Turpin was considered by many to have been the best European middleweight in the late 1940s and early 1950s, although it meant nothing to me at the time. The pub used to open and close sporadically, sometimes reinventing itself as a café, and Turpin ended up shooting himself dead after going bankrupt. But there was nothing else there besides a tram station and a farm, where we'd sometimes go and get milk and a few things. Wild goats roamed around the Orme and Welsh regiments used to come from time to time and take them as mascots. It was an old tradition that dated back to the American War of Independence for Welsh battalions to have goats and, bizarrely, that's where they got them from.

We were a close family and, I suppose, quite insular. Me and my two brothers were quite self-contained at the top of our hill and we just played among ourselves. There was a tram station halfway up the hill and the trams would go up again to the summit, but there weren't that many other kids around and nobody was going to walk up from town just to play with us. Because of where we lived I didn't even really get to know my extended family. My uncles were old fellows, but after they moved down the hill into Llandudno we never saw much of them. That was just the way it was. We went to stay with my mum's family every year in Salisbury. That's the only place we went to: there was no money for holidays, and – with one foot-balling exception – I never really went abroad until I joined Everton.

My brothers and I filled our days with football. These weren't 20-a-side free-for-alls, like many other kids would play. There were never enough bodies for that. Just me, Steve and Jeff, and sometimes there was another lad. That's how I ended up in goal in these games out the back. Steve was in charge, being the oldest, and Jeff was too young, so I got stuck in goal. The dynamics of our family and being the middle son probably shaped my destiny.

When I was ten we moved down from the Orme and closer to town. The long uphill walks were taking their toll on my dad and the council moved us to Cwm Place. It was a bigger and newer house, so there was no more bed sharing. In fact, sometimes we'd have our own bedroom, depending on who was getting on with who at the time. Me and my brothers were always fighting, so the two of us that were getting on shared the double bedroom, and the other one went in the single one.

Obviously it was brilliant not having to walk up that hill every day, but the move was great for playing more sport. Cwm Place is situated around a great oval of grassland, so we could play football there, play golf there, do everything that we wanted to do. My dad worked nights and would go bananas if he was disturbed while having his sleep during the day, so if we weren't in school we were sent out to play. There were far more kids there as well, including Joey Jones, who'd go on to play for Liverpool and Wales, who lived two doors down.

School for me was all about football. I'd started out at Great Orme School, then Craig-y-don and Ysgol John Bright, which was a comprehensive. I was never close to anybody at school, but I knew a lot of people through playing football. In that sense I don't think I've changed much, but I wouldn't have seen myself as a loner even then. There's no doubt I like my own company, but I like talking to people as well. I just have to get to know them quite well.

I hated school, absolutely hated it. I wasn't stupid, just totally out of my depth. The problem was my own making. In middle school when we'd done tests for streaming I'd got hold of the answers and simply copied them out. Because of that I was put in a higher grade than I should have been. We did French and Welsh and I just couldn't do it. We'd sit in the language lab with big earphones on listening to French tapes and we'd have to write stuff down. But how could I write things down if I didn't understand them? It made me feel like an idiot, even though I know I wasn't. I was just in the wrong place. My cheating basically killed my education and at times destroyed my self-confidence. When one of the teachers called me 'thick' I told my dad, who went ballistic. He was going to get his Sten gun and go up to the school and beat the teacher up, but there was absolutely no point in doing that as I was simply in the wrong place.

Because I was unable to do the work, I wasn't interested in any subjects other than history or PE. History and sport were my main things. In the end they let me out of classes and I played football continuously. There were no showers and by the time I got home I'd be stinking. We'd play five-aside, put our clothes on, walk a couple of miles home and stand in the sink to have a wash. Then we'd be off out again playing football. There was a youth club nearby and I'd go along and play there.

It's only in the last few years, since I qualified as a teacher myself, that I realised my unhappy experience in school has had some sort of positive outcome. I think it's given me a good affiliation with the type of kids I deal with now because I've been in a shit place myself. I know how hard it is when you just don't understand what's going on. Some of the teachers I had didn't give a shit about me. Or they saw me as a waste of space and concentrated on the good kids. Others might have cared, but didn't have the time to coax what potential I had out of me.

It sounds strange, but all I did was play football. I didn't have any other interests, even when I was older. I didn't listen to music. Discos I hated because I was so shy. If I went to a pub I'd play darts. I never drank or smoked, never even experimented with anything like that. I tried lager once, had two sips and didn't like the taste. Nothing stronger than tea has ever passed through my lips since. The only other thing I enjoyed was gymnastics in the youth club. I was good at that, and I think it helped with my agility as a goalkeeper.

I was enthusiastic about gymnastics for a couple of years. But there was a downside to that too. Someone at the youth club thought it'd be a good idea to do a show in Denbigh. Putting on a show was fine, but what we didn't know until we got there was that it was in the local asylum. That's right, they'd taken a load of teenagers to the loony bin. The patients were all rocking in their chairs and didn't have a clue what was going on. Walking in there in my vest and shorts while all these poor people were groaning in their chairs was one of the scariest things I had to do in my entire life.

Although I played football day and night, there was never a point where I remember thinking, 'I'm quite good at this.' I played for the school team and junior teams, usually a couple of years ahead of my age group, but I just went with the flow, did what I had to do.

＝

WHEN I WAS 12 I STARTED PLAYING in men's leagues, for Llandudno Swifts. It was quite an experience! Everyone thinks of me as a big man, but I was tiny until 15 or 16, in fact until I started doing gymnastics. My uncle, Johnny Roberts, ran the team. He was bonkers and his training sessions were bonkers too. He used to make us run up the Orme, and he'd race us on this old bus he'd bought. He would say, 'If you're not on this bus, that's it, I'm leaving you behind!' And he did – he did it all the time! You'd have to go all the way back down the hill, a good couple of miles.

I played for the Reserves there, and also for the Under-14s in the morning. But when I was still 12, Johnny called me up to the senior side. It was a big game and I was thrust into it. They were only a few miles apart but Llandudno and Colwyn Bay were two towns that just never got on. When you got the football teams from each side of the divide playing against each other it was, on a local level, a bit like Celtic and Rangers. Everyone just wanted to fight each other. When the Colwyn Bay players saw me – a tiny, scruffy 12-year-old – they must have laughed and thought they were going to smash the dwarf who was in goal. But I never had any problems. We won 2-1 and I enjoyed the atmosphere of the game. I didn't know what I was do-ing – in fact I didn't have a clue and would simply react to everything, instead of anticipating. But I didn't get smashed, in fact the opposite happened: I ended up accidentally breaking the ankle of their star player, a striker called Elvin Morris, when he tried to go around me.

My Uncle Johnny was a great influence on me. He probably wasn't the best of managers, because there was no organisation as such and our results were awful. But he let us play as we wanted and he put his heart and soul into running the club and giving us the opportunity to train and play matches, which as kids was all we wanted. He had been in the RAF and was extremely fit, which is where some of his eccentric training routines would come from. We'd be on the bus to Porthmadog or somewhere like that, and he'd stop a mile or two outside town and tell us to get off the bus and run the rest of the way there. That'd be our warm-up. We never had a team talk or anything like that. Occasionally he'd say something stupid like, 'Go out and enjoy yourselves.' He was one of those people who believed that it didn't matter what the score was, so long as you enjoyed yourself and weren't scared to try your best and play. That was the best thing about Johnny. You could make a million mistakes and he didn't give a shit.

Around the same time I started sneaking out on a Sunday morning to play for the local pub team, The Steam Packet. We had one huge lad from our street, a real giant, and he said to me, 'Right, you go in goal and I'll kill anyone who goes near you.' Nobody ever came near me because he'd have thumped them. They were good lads and just loved playing football. And so did I – I never got any money out of it or anything like that; I just played because it's what I did. Mind you, my dad would have killed me had he known I was playing with men in a pub league.

I was, by then, playing four matches every weekend. Saturday mornings were spent playing for the school team. Then I'd get changed and straight on the bus with the Llandudno Swifts first team. Sometimes if we were playing locally we wouldn't even have a bus; it'd be an open-topped truck, with two of the players sitting in the cab and the rest of us sat in the back. There were some older players, but we were mostly all the same age – 14 to 16 – and a bit of a joke team. Everyone used to laugh at us as we'd get hammered every week. Playing in a men's league meant that 12-0 was a victory. Losing 12-0, that is. If we only let in eight we'd go home and have a party. I think the most I ever let in was 21 goals. You'd have thought that as a goalkeeper if you let in 21 goals you'd be depressed. But I probably saved 21 others and was learning lots. Quite often there'd only be seven or eight of us playing and Johnny would go into the local pub and pull all sorts of numbskulls out to make up our numbers.

On Sundays I played for the pub team, and in the afternoon I turned out for another side. Monday, of course, was school, but I played footy all day there, and did the same when I came home.

We had a decent school team and in 1975, in my final year at school, we reached the finals of the *Daily Express* Schools Five-a-side Championship, and travelled down to Wembley Arena. A total of 1,673 schools had entered the competition and we made the last four as Welsh Champions after winning through heats at Deeside Leisure Centre, where I was named player of the tournament. We took a minibus down to Wembley, where we played Cornbank Boys Club from Edinburgh and took them to a penalty shootout, which we lost 3-2 – but only after a penalty I'd saved was ordered to be retaken for some reason, and converted. It was an outrageous decision! Afterwards the *Express* described me as an 'outstanding young goalkeeper'.

Llandudno Swifts was always an adventure. We'd go all over North Wales, up to remote villages in the hills and mountains. This was football at its most basic. We used to get changed in the pubs; sometimes in the bar with the drinkers! Or we'd get changed in a barn with only an old tin bath full of cold water. When we played a team called Mountain Rangers, they had a telegraph pole on one side of the centre circle. Once one of our lads, a guy called Brian Mackem, had been out the night before and had the shits, and had to run off every few minutes and relieve himself in a little stream that ran around the back of the pitch, and then run back on. You can't buy that, can you?

Another village, Llanrwst, was well known for its fantastic pitch and the fact that the villagers had a reputation for throwing referees in the river if they didn't agree with what he'd done. Another time we went to Penmachno, which was in a remote valley not far from Betws-y-Coed, and the whole village would come out to try and antagonise you. Players would be dribbling down the wing, and the old fellows would try and hit them with their walking sticks. One time we were playing there, one of our players, a guy known to me only as Hawkeye, broke his leg. It was absolutely horrible, listening to a grown man screaming in pain. There was nothing they could do – the hospital was two-and-a-half hours' drive away – so they splinted him with a corner flag, carted him off and we played on while he waited for an ambulance in complete agony.

These were the days before motorways had opened up North Wales to the outside world. It wasn't as easy to bugger off and go and see Manchester United or Everton or Liverpool unless you made a real effort and spent two or three hours getting there. Local football was the thing. Whole villages came out to watch some games, while other times there'd be just 50 or even 10 people. But there was genuine pride in what local teams did and a real will to win. Sometimes real battles were played out on the pitch and referees used to get absolutely hammered too. It was never intimidating for me though, even as a scrawny little kid. I loved it, it was just good fun.

In the summer of 1973, when I was 14, Johnny Roberts announced that we were going 'on tour' to West Germany. I have no idea where he got the idea from as we couldn't usually get a team together to play down the road, never mind a different country. But suddenly we were on our way to Germany. I'd never been anywhere at that stage of my life except Salisbury, and Manchester on a couple of occasions, and now I was headed to Dusseldorf.

I wish I could say my first overseas trip was revelatory or life-affirming, but it was just long. We piled onto our decrepit old bus and headed down to Dover, a journey of nearly 350 miles on a vehicle that could go no faster than 40 or 50 miles per hour. Johnny and his son, my cousin Ritchie, took it in turns driving, while in the back our arses numbed so that we could barely feel our legs. It was non-stop until we got on the ferry, then another 300 miles through France, Belgium, Holland and into West Germany, driving right the way through the night. The first thing we did on arriving in Dusseldorf was to crash into another bus. Johnny got involved in a big shouting match with the other driver before driving off and mercifully reaching our hotel, where we were able to sleep. We'd been on the road for nearly 30 hours.

That night we played one of Fortuna Dusseldorf's youth teams. I've no idea how Johnny swung it so that our ragtag team played one of the best in Germany, but he did. Fortuna would finish in third place in the Bundesliga the next season.

We saw nothing of Germany in our short stay, but I was unexpectedly offered the chance to extend my visit. The next morning we were up at dawn to go straight back to Llandudno, but on the way out of the hotel Johnny pulled me aside.

'Neville,' he said, 'do you want to stay here?'

I thought he was taking the piss, so asked him what he meant.

'Fortuna Dusseldorf want to sign you. Do you want to stay?'

I suppose you reflect on these moments in your life as a possible turning point and wonder what might have been. But you've got to picture me at that time of my life: I was 14; I'd never been anywhere or done anything, I didn't speak the language, and I had only the clothes on my back, my kit and a spare pair of socks and underpants. I thought for a few seconds.

'Sorry, Johnny, I can't be bothered,' I said.

Johnny shrugged his shoulders.

'Okay, let's go,' he said. And I got back on the coach and didn't get off it again until we arrived back in Llandudno a day later.

At the time I never thought about what I might be learning or where this might all lead to. There was no time to think as I was too busy playing. But it was always good fun, I saw a lot of action – particularly playing for Llandudno Swifts, where I'd be picking the ball out of my net every few minutes – and became very experienced, very quickly. I never got intimidated, nor did I worry about people trying to kick me. Because I was young I never sat down and thought, 'I tell you what, I'm really good at this, I'll carry on doing this.' I never thought that or thought of football as a career. Liverpool and Everton were less than 70 miles away, but to my mind they might as well have been on a different planet.

MY DAD WAS A MANCHESTER UNITED SUPPORTER, but he only took me to go and see them four or five times. I vividly remember, when I was about ten, watching George Best slalom past about six Chelsea players and score at the Stretford End. It was an incredible moment. But I wasn't a Manchester United fan, in fact I didn't really support anyone. I liked the way Chelsea, with players like John Hollins and Peter Osgood, played football in this era, but I suppose my team, if I had one, was West Ham. This was a time when they had the trio of players that were central to England's World Cup victory – Martin Peters, Bobby Moore and Geoff Hurst – but it was their style that I admired rather than the individuals: good passing, fluidity, attacking football.

The goalkeeper I admired most was Pat Jennings. That was when I was a bit older and could appreciate his qualities. I liked him because he was a bit different. He'd make a save with his face, or his knee, or his arse. And obviously he'd be in the right place at the right time, which is a skill in itself. But all the other goalkeepers of this era were a bit too robotic for me, while Jennings was more unorthodox. You have to make a save with different parts of your body, don't you? That's one of the reasons I liked him. He also used to boot the ball miles, turning defence into attack in an instant. A goalkeeper should be the first form of attack, but not everyone exploits that virtue. There was an air of calm about him too; nothing was ever any effort.

He'd catch it one-handed. It was all just nice and easy. I suppose that was his greatest virtue: he made it appear easy to play in goal. I'd see some of the others on Match of the Day and think, 'Why's he making a big panic over that? It's nothing. Be like Jennings.'

In Llandudno the only professional footballers were Gerry Humphreys, Joey Jones and, later, Gareth Roberts. Gerry was a talented forward and the son of the former Everton and Wales centre half, Jack Humphreys. He had played briefly for Harry Catterick's great Everton teams in the mid-1960s, before having a decent career with Crewe Alexandra and Crystal Palace. But by the mid-1970s he was back in Llandudno driving taxis. Joey Jones was one of our neighbours. He was three years older than me, bigger at the time, and hard. He was a bit of a tearaway in his younger days and part of a gang called The Parrots. He had braces and boots and all that and had a bit of a reputation for fighting, causing trouble. But underneath he was just soft as shit, the sort of person who would give you his last penny. He joined Wrexham in 1973, and later played for Liverpool and Chelsea, winning the European Cup in 1977. I played with him for Wales as well. Another one of my neighbours, Gareth Roberts, also went on to have a professional career with Wrexham.

But that was all later. At the time, there was no one locally who you could look up to and seek to emulate. Even when clubs started taking an interest, I never thought about the leap up to professional football. Wrexham were the local club and they used to come down and hold a tournament on the beach at Llandudno. I used to play in that all the time, so they knew who I was. I went for a trial at the Racecourse Ground once but they said no. Someone told me later that they thought I was too scruffy to sign for them. I went for a trial at Bolton when I was 14 or 15, but my side got beaten 6-0. Crewe gave me a trial when I was a little bit older but it was very haphazard. I played in goal in the first half, but the manager put me in with a load of little kids. We got to half-time and we had done all right, but then I was asked to play at centre half because they had another goalie they wanted to look at. I played okay, but never heard back.

My performances for the school team saw me selected to play for Caernarvonshire from the age of 12. I discovered then that I wasn't the only talented young goalkeeper in North Wales. Eddie Niedzwiecki came from Conwy, just along the North Wales coast, and like me would go on to play in the First Division (with Chelsea) and for Wales, before his career was ended by a succession of injury problems before he was 30. I played in goal the first year for the county and the second year Eddie went in goal and I played centre half. To be honest, it didn't bother me so long as I was playing. I was quite happy in or out of goal.

Many years later, after my parents died, I found a bin bag full of scrapbooks that my mum had kept charting my career from the age of eight until Everton's second title win in 1987. I had no idea that she'd kept this record and I found many things I'd never seen before. One of them was an article written by a former teacher, Stan Roberts, who ran the Llandudno District Primary Schools football team. My mum had had it translated from the Welsh and it's worth quoting from it here, because it offers an insight into what I was like as a schoolboy footballer. Certainly I wasn't aware of what was said at the time, including the notion that 'Some teachers believed I was paid for playing!'

'It was obvious,' wrote Mr Roberts …

> … that Neville wasn't going to pursue an academic career, playing for Manchester United was his chief aim. He played for Llandudno district Primary Schools Team and Eddie Niedzwiecki was the team captain. What did Neville learn as a 10-year-old in a team that became primary schools league champions for North Wales? Learning to mix perhaps, for Neville was a very shy boy. Learning to travel far from home to places like Wrexham, Holyhead and Deeside to play football. Learning to win against boys who one day

*would be household names themselves. Learning to look like a footballer on the field. Employing self-confidence when things looked bad. Receiving beautiful silver to start his collection of prizes in the football world.*

Although I excelled at sport, school was an unhappy experience and I left without qualifications. My last year was a bit of a farce. They changed the rules in my year, saying that you had to stay until you were 16, whereas before you could leave at 15. Being born in September I was one of the oldest in my year and was ready to go and enter the working world, but I was forced to stay. I wasn't interested in lessons or anything but sport. At the same time I wasn't prepared to skive off as my brothers did. So I had a strange situation where the school were happy for me to go in the morning, and just wander to whichever class was playing sport and join in. I didn't do any proper lessons at all. I'd go in the morning, get marked 'in' on the register, play footy with whoever was there, go home for my dinner. In the afternoons sometimes I went back and sometimes I didn't – it depended if there was a match on or not.

Looking back, I suppose I was naive. I had no plan or aspirations other than to keep playing and playing and playing; playing as much as I could because that's what I liked doing.

⊐⊏

MY AMBITION WHEN I LEFT SCHOOL was to be a postman. There were never any thoughts, not ever, that I could make a living from football. Remember, this was the era of The Black and White Minstrel Show, not X-Factor. This ridiculous idea that anyone can be a superstar in an instant was just not prevalent then. In fact, the whole idea of being a professional footballer seemed so far removed that I might as well have wanted to become a spaceman. The great football hubs of Manchester and Liverpool seemed very remote – before the motorways Manchester was two and a half hours by car – and the thoughts that many kids in those cities might have had about playing for Everton or United never crossed my mind. I didn't ever think about football that much, I just played the games and that was it. If I had a decent kit and a decent pair of boots I was happy. It wasn't like it is now. Football in the early 1970s wasn't shoved down your throat. There was no internet, of course, and newspaper coverage was a few pages – none of the big supplements you get now. Not that I'd ever have seen it: I can't remember ever seeing a paper in my house. Nor was there wall-to-wall TV coverage. *Match of the Day* was on Saturday, and occasionally on Sunday there was *The Big Match*, both of them highlights programmes. When football was on TV nobody went out until it was over. Then everybody used to go out and play footy after that and you'd pretend you were playing the games you'd just seen. But that was it.

Back then I'd rather have been a postman than a footballer, because I knew I could work outside. But when I went to the careers officer at school they didn't take me seriously. They asked me what I wanted to do and I said I wanted to play football and be a postman. Their response was 'Yeah, all right – next!' And so nothing became of my ambitions to become a postman.

My first job after I left school was at the Ritz. No, not the famous hotel on London's Piccadilly, but the Ritz Café, a greasy spoon in Llandudno that served tourists. I was an odd-job man and did anything and every-thing – peeled the potatoes, cleaned the floors, cooked the food if I had to. The fellow that ran it was the tightest man in the world: it was the sort of place where food was scraped up off the floor and thrown back in the fryer and later served to the customers. I was paid £18 a week for six days a week – 8.30am until 6.30pm – which were not good wages by any stretch of the imagination. It came to an end after about nine months. I put 24 chickens in the oven and buggered off to play football and forgot about them and they were incinerated. The boss wasn't too impressed, but by that stage I couldn't bear it any longer, so I walked out.

My next job was with the council. They brought in seven or eight of us and we did all sorts of jobs for them. We started off going around town looking for old lampposts to replace with fibreglass ones. Our next task was more arduous. The North Wales coast is dotted with old gun emplacements and forts dating back to the Second World War when they were built to repel a German invasion. They gave us sledgehammers and crowbars and sent us up the Great Orme to go and smash some of them up. But these things had been built to withstand missiles, so a crowbar wasn't going to get you very far. Next they gave us drills, but it was still all a bit hopeless; it was hard and sweaty and we'd strip off, people were falling over and accidentally smashing each other with hammers. Then they gave us diggers, but most of us had never driven so we were grinding these diggers up and down the hills. Finally the council sent up an explosives expert. The fellow who turned up hardly had any fingers, so he obviously wasn't that good with dynamite, but he did what a bunch of lads and an artillery of hammers, drills and diggers hadn't been able to and got rid of the old fort. These were good days, and I loved working outside, the camaraderie, heading down to the pub at lunchtime, where we'd have a pie, and the others would have a pint.

After we'd demolished the old fort, the council didn't know what to do with us, so they put me on a bin lorry crew. Being a binman is something people always remember me for, but I only actually worked the bins for a couple of months. Although the first few 4.30am starts were a struggle, and I had to get wise to the rest of the crew sending me to go and get the bins at houses with big dogs – I'd always be getting chased by dogs in the first few weeks – it suited me down to the ground. We'd stop for breakfast halfway through, and I'd be finished by 10am. Then I'd go home, sleep for a couple of hours and go and work for my uncle, who had a galvanising factory. I'd knock off there at 6pm and head straight back out to play football and then do it all again. I was earning about £75 a week – four times what I'd got at the Ritz – and playing plenty of football as well.

I'd started playing for Llandudno Town when I was 15, and it was a better standard than the Swifts. My team-mates were older lads and they were pretty decent players. They were the sort who would go out on a Friday night together, get absolutely wasted, turn up on Saturday, have a real good go at the game, and then go and do it all again on Saturday night. They grafted like mad and put absolutely everything into it. There were a few Scousers on the team, who gave it some real tenacity. I think Scousers must be descended from General Custer, because they never give up. We'd also actually win games, which made a nice change from the Swifts, although I was a bit of a fair-weather player and still shifted between the two teams. They had a nice ground, right in the centre of town, which was inexplicably sold off in the late 1970s so that an ASDA could be built over it.

By the time that had happened I was long gone. When I was 16 I joined Bangor City, a club with – by North Wales standards – an illustrious reputation. In 1962, under the management of the Everton legend T. G. Jones, a man they called 'the uncrowned Prince of Wales', as Welsh Cup winners they had ventured into the European Cup Winners' Cup for the first time. They were drawn against Napoli in the first round and a hammering was expected but, incredibly, they won the home leg 2-0 against the Italian giants. They lost 3-1 in Italy, but there was no away goals rule back then, and at the Highbury replay they fought gallantly, but lost 3-1 again.

There were no visits to London or Italy while I was there, and the club had fallen on hard times. Our player-manager was Dave Elliot, a former Sunderland and Newcastle defender, and although money was tight at the club we had some good players. There was Billy Telford, a former Manchester City forward, and defender John McClelland, who would have a long and successful career with Glasgow Rangers, Watford and Northern Ireland; I also played alongside Joe Fagan's son, Kit. Len Davies, the former Stoke goalkeeper who had played in Bangor's famous games against Napoli, was the kitman – the first of many I would encounter, and they were all the same: bonkers.

We were playing in the Northern Premier League and because I was only a youngster I was never sure of a place in the team. Peter Eales, an experienced former Wigan and Altrincham goalkeeper, was ahead of me in the pecking order. It was the first time I was playing for money and saw the impact that it could have in a dressing room. I was getting £10 a week, which I considered a bonus as I was just happy to be involved. But there were lads on the same as me, not happy that others were on £50 a week, or £100 per week. Some of the players were on £150, which caused more problems – particularly when the club ran out of money and couldn't pay them any more. I was carefree about the whole thing and my view was that you'd play first and get the money later, but there were players who would demand to be paid before they played. It wasn't a good place to be, although on reflection I suppose that money may have been the difference between them paying their mortgage or not.

Bangor was 20 miles away from home, and although there was a train, late at night, I was still reliant on my dad to pick me up from training. This, unfortunately, led to me spending a night at Bangor's decrepit old ground, Farrar Road. Training finished at 9pm and Dad had said he'd be there by 10pm. It was a freezing night and I waited and waited. Manchester United had been playing and I think he just got pissed and forgot all about me. I went to the train station, but I'd long missed the last train back to Llandudno. There were no mobile phones, of course, and my options were limited to going to the police station or bedding down for the night in the stadium, which I did. I lay in the dugout with an overcoat over me, but I didn't sleep much. Farrar Road was only a few hundred yards away from the Menai Straits between the Welsh coast and Holyhead, and the wind lashed in. It was a cold night and I was glad to be on the first train back the next morning. When I got home Dad just looked at me, and said, 'Oh shit, I forgot to pick you up. Sorry!'

Although I wasn't in the first team much at Bangor, this was when I first came to the attention of Everton. They were managed by Billy Bingham during this period and should have won the League Championship in 1975, and possibly a few years later as well. Dave Elliot told me about their interest and said that they'd like to take me on trial. But then Dave left shortly afterwards and that was the end of that.

I suppose that is one of those great 'what if' scenarios. Everton had such great players as Bob Latchford, Martin Dobson and Roger Kenyon; many people said that all they lacked to win the League title was a top-class goalkeeper and maybe they were right. I definitely wasn't ready for the First Division at that age, but a few years later? Who knows. Maybe had I signed then I'd have played a thousand matches for Everton and helped end a barren patch in which they were very much in Liverpool's shadow. Or maybe I'd have been forgotten in the A-team or reserve side and never have made it at all. I'm a great believer in destiny and the idea that things happen for a reason. Looking back now, I see that Everton and I were destined to combine, but that I might not have been the same player had I not followed the path I did to get there.

Instead of going to Goodison I went to Conwy, home to Llandudno's big rivals Conwy United. The money had run out at Bangor and to be honest it was a relief to get away. Peter Eales was owed £150 and we didn't hear the end of it. I was owed a tenner, but when they paid everyone off Eales got his money while my cheque bounced. Instead of earning a few quid to play, at Conwy we all paid £3 per week and it was great. It was a relief not to hear people complaining endlessly about money and what they had or hadn't got. Money can be the cause of so many problems.

By this stage I'd stopped working for the council and started work as a hod carrier on building sites. After I'd stopped working on the bin lorries they'd sent me and the lads out to count broken kerbstones and replace them. It was frankly just boring and a waste of time, so I left. It was hard work on the sites but relatively well paid, and lifting piles of bricks up ladders every day made me incredibly fit. It was probably the fittest I've ever been. In the evenings, if I wasn't training, I'd go and run for an hour on Llandudno beach. I didn't need to do anything else. Building sites also suited me better because I was self-employed and could suit myself to some extent. It gave me the flexibility to play more footy.

At 20 I joined Winsford United in the Cheshire League. Gwyn Williams, Conwy's manager, was friends with Johnny Williams at Winsford and recommended me for a trial, which I came through. They were keen to sign me, but the problem I had was over the logistics of playing for them. Winsford was over the other side of the English border and I had no way of getting there, other than by train via Chester for home games or Manchester for aways. With the connection it took the best part of a couple of hours. The compromise we reached was that the secretary, Peter Warburton, would pick me up and drop me off at the station and during the week I'd train on my own. It worked quite well, except for the time we were playing Stalybridge Celtic and someone decided to lob a brick through the cabin of our train. I didn't get there until half-time and our centre half had had to deputise in goal, none of which went down too well. Not least given that we were drawing at half-time and ended up losing 1-0!

Winsford was a great experience for me, and the standard was ten times as competitive as Llandudno or Conwy had been. We were playing in the sixth or seventh tier of English football and our team – in fact the whole league – seemed to be packed full of Scousers, who were incredibly aggressive and competitive. We were playing in front of a few hundred people, much like I had for Bangor, but it all seemed so much better to me. Playing in such an environment certainly raised my game. It was also something of an eye-opener and we visited all these places I'd never been before; some were great, some were diabolical.

Playing in places around Liverpool always made the biggest impression on me. Travelling there was like going to the other side of the moon. It was much more street-wise, much more aggressive, with everyone absolutely dying to win no matter what. We played somebody like South Liverpool and within five minutes a player had got sent off for head-butting an opponent. Manchester, by contrast, always seemed to be a lot calmer, a lot more controlled. Then you got to somewhere like Chorley and it would be different again – more of a villagey feel. Then Fleetwood, a fishing town out on the Lancashire coast, was just crazy. It was always windy, which for a goalkeeper is the worst kind of conditions. The time we played someone booted me in the ribs and cracked one. I had to finish the game but it hurt like hell. I went to the doctor's and he shoved it back into place with a crack and told me to stay off work for two weeks. I couldn't possibly stay off work for two weeks as I was self-employed – I wouldn't get any money. So I carried on hod-carrying and carried on playing, which was quite painful.

I had a good season with Winsford. I was player of the year and young player of the year and we won the league and the Cheshire Senior Cup in its centenary year.

Back in Llandudno playing for Winsford set me apart: I was playing at 3pm on a Saturday afternoon and nobody else did that unless they were a pro. I was quite happy about that; it was my own special thing. Not that it changed me at all. On a Sunday I'd still play football, outfield for a pub team. It's just what I did; I liked playing football. It was how I relaxed. It was my weekend.

━┮━

WHEN I STARTED AT WINSFORD my thought was that I'd give it a year and see where it took me. There was still never any expectation that I'd become a professional, even then. I liked playing football and just wanted to test myself by playing at the highest level I possibly could. But it wasn't easy. It was lonely, hard and tiring. If I played midweek I wouldn't get home until 2am and I'd be up again at 7am for work. It was hard sometimes when I'd been hod-carrying all day to go home, get changed and go out training again on my own, often on a dark and freezing cold beach. My motivation was to do myself justice. I liked being fit and didn't want to let myself down.

But the realisation I was doing well for Winsford never fully sank in until quite late on in my year there. At the start nobody knew who I was or had seen me play before. I was an unknown. We had a great team spirit, the whole team were playing well. People used to praise me individually, but I'd take it all with a pinch of salt: one person's good goalie is another person's crap one. As soon as one game finished I just thought about the next one, and I knew that no matter how well I was playing I was never guaranteed to be picked again. Maybe I was too unassuming, or naive, or maybe just a bit stupid, but I never felt like an aspiring professional.

That was until one day when I was on the train home to Llandudno, making the long journey back from Winsford. Joey Jones at this stage was playing for Wrexham, even though he'd won the European Cup just a few years earlier with Liverpool. His dad, Harry, had been to watch him and got on the train when it passed through Wrexham. Like all of Joey's family he was a cracking fellow, an absolutely brilliant dad who we all knew and liked. He came and sat down by me and we chatted a bit and suddenly he said something that always stuck with me.

'Don't worry about anything, Neville,' he said. 'Just keep going because you'll make it one day. I've got complete faith in you.'

At the time I was so unassuming that I thought it was just a nice thing for someone who'd never really seen me play to say. But looking back, I see it as a moment when, like a light being switched on, my mind became alert to my own potential and how far I might be able to go.

# CHAPTER TWO
# SHAKER

IT WAS COMING TO THE END OF THE 1979/80 SEASON. Winsford were flying high and I was enjoying myself. We were playing a midweek game and I was getting myself ready for the race over to Chester to get the last train home when John Williams, the manager, said there was someone waiting to have a chat with me.

'I've got to go home. I'll miss my train,' I said.

'You should talk to this fellow, Neville,' he insisted.

But I wasn't having any of it; I just wanted to get the train in time. I got my kit together and left the dressing room, and there in the corridor was this very forthright Mancunian.

'I'm Dave Connor. I'm manager of Bury and I'd like to have a chat with you,' he said.

Like the nugget that I was I told him that my time was very limited as I had a train to catch home. Dave took my naivety and brusqueness in his stride.

'I'll give you a lift home,' he said.

'I live in Llandudno.'

'I'll give you a lift.'

And that was it. From that moment I was never in doubt that I wanted to play for this man. I thought, 'You don't do that normally, do you, as a manager? You don't give some sort of nugget a lift home.'

It must have been very late when we got in to my house, and he turned straight back and went to Bury. There were no motorways and it must have taken him most of the night just to have a chat with me. It impressed me and I thought, 'Well, whatever happens, if anybody else comes in I'm going to sign for Dave, no matter what.' Just on the basis of him giving me a lift.

We didn't talk about how my life might change as a footballer. Instead we chatted in general terms about how he'd taken over and how he wanted to build the team and where he saw Bury moving on. He was more or less trying to convince me to join but he actually wasted an hour and a half talking, because once he'd dropped me off at the door that was it: he'd won me over by making sure I got back home. I suppose it was stupid in a way, him giving me a ride in his car and me saying, 'I'll sign, give us the paper.' No wages were talked about; nothing like that. I knew it was going to be probably lower than what I was on hod-carrying, and it was.

Bury weren't the only team that came in for me at the time. Somebody phoned me up from Wigan Athletic and tried to get me to sign for them. They offered me a council house as part of the deal. At the other end of the line, someone was saying, 'Don't worry, we'll get you a council house and we'll give you a decent …' But I wasn't listening, I just thought, 'I'm not going there … Dave Connor did what he did for me.' It might sound strange or naive that someone giving me a lift could make such a deep impression, but that was the way I thought. As soon as he left in the car, I thought, 'I'm going to sign for him, when I can.'

Although Joey Jones's dad had sown the idea that I might be good enough to play professionally I did have some doubts when it came to signing for Bury. Hod-carrying was hard work but it paid well. I was offered £150 per week to play for Bury, which was less than I was earning on building sites and taking home from Winsford. I know it might seem a bit daft now, but that was a dilemma: do I take the opportunity to play professionally or do I stay where I am hod-carrying?

In the end I thought I had to try it, had to find out for myself. Deep down I didn't want to be hod-carrying until I was 70. I loved football and I loved being fit. I had to have a go at it and see where it took me. If it didn't turn out well I could always go back to the building sites.

The lads at work were really happy for me. They knew I played foot-ball, that I was taking time off work to play, and they were more aware than most people of some of the sacrifices I was making. Being self-employed, the harder you worked the more money you got, but if I ever fell behind in my work they never gave me a hard time, but would give me a hand doing the bricks. It was a good little team and they probably helped me more than I realised at the time. But I also worked hard myself and would go in on Saturday and Sunday mornings to get the place set up for the forthcoming week. Anything that would buy me and my busy schedule of football and training an extra half-hour here or there.

Bury wasn't the most glamorous club in the world to go to, but there were some people in Llandudno who immediately assumed that I'd got above myself. I think 75 per cent of the people were chuffed for me, but the other 25 per cent were jealous and didn't want me to go. That's just how small places are. When I went back after I'd signed for Bury, there were a few people who never spoke to me again. Don't ask me why. I think in most places they either like you because you've done well for yourself, or they dislike you for it. There were people I knew – who I'd been to school with – and they walked the other way, or didn't look at me. They never said hello. When it happened the first few times, it was upsetting and a bit weird. It wasn't like I was on £50,000 a week or driving a Rolls-Royce (in fact, I still couldn't drive). But after a while I thought, 'Stuff them – it's their problem, not mine; I can't help doing what I do.'

Once the season was over with Winsford there was no great send-off. There was never any sense of 'I used to be a hod-carrier, now I'm a footballer.' It was strange in a way because I kept working. I worked pre-season as well some of the time because they gave me a day off and I went back to Wales and the sites.

Before I left for Lancashire I got married to Eryl Williams in Conwy on 21 June 1980. My brother-in-law, Iwan Williams, was the best man and we held the reception at the Uxbridge Hotel in Llandudno. We'd met a few years earlier on a blind double date with my brother and his girlfriend. The move to Bury and away from North Wales probably brought our wedding plans forward a bit.

But preparing for the world of professional football was my big thing. I worked really hard in the six or seven weeks between the end of Winsford's season and the start of pre-season training with Bury. I wanted to be up to the standard of my new professional team-mates when training began. I'd never trained with Winsford but then I didn't need to. Hod-carrying kept me naturally fit and I ran in the evenings. I was very fit, but I thought that pre-season as a professional was going to be really hard so I started doing even more. I ran and ran and ran as much as I could round the Great Orme, which is probably about five miles round, up and down hills. After I did that pre-season was easy for me. I've never found a pre-season anywhere hard because I've always trained all through the summer.

All these preparations might have counted for nothing though. Two weeks before I was due to start Dave Connor was sacked and they brought in Jim Iley. Iley was a straight-talking Yorkshireman who had played as a midfielder for Spurs and Newcastle in the 1950s and 1960s. He'd then gone on to manage Barnsley. It was never explained to me why Dave Connor was sacked just before pre-season.

I was massively concerned by this development. Firstly, because I wanted to play for Dave Connor, who was the reason I'd signed for Bury. Secondly, there was a new geezer in Jim Iley who I didn't know, who hadn't done anything for me and I'd done nothing for him. In short, he didn't owe me a thing.

I headed over to Bury to find out what was going on. I won't say Jim was the most welcoming person I've ever met in my life. He was quite blunt, which in another time would have been absolutely brilliant for me. If I'd have been a bit older and a bit wiser when he was my manger I think we would have got on all right, because we'd have worked out an understanding. But I was young and naive and rather demanding.

I think my first conversation went something like this: 'Dave Connor said the club would find me a house when I moved. I haven't got a house and I need one now.'

Jim just sat there, this bald unsmiling geezer, and probably thought, 'What have I got on my hands here? Who the hell is this?'

He told me in no uncertain terms that the club wouldn't be finding me a house and that I had to sort myself out. He was probably right, but coming from Llandudno it was a bit of a culture shock. I had an expectation – possibly a foolish one – that they would look after me, but I was out on my own.

At first I split my time between Llandudno and staying with Bury's young right back Benny Phillips and his family. Benny's family were the loveliest, most hospitable people and did everything they could to make me at home. But being the kind of person I am, I found it all a bit awkward as it wasn't my own space. I used to head back to Llandudno on a Thursday, which was our day off, and do my old routine: train on my own and even do a bit of hod-carrying. In the end we found a small place in the Lancashire village of Ramsbottom, which was a lovely place to live, and I'd get a couple of buses to training in Bury. If it was pissing down with rain you got soaked.

But I was always there early, by 9am.

Training was good but it wasn't quite what I expected. We'd get changed in the club, do some work in the gym, then play a bit of head tennis on the concrete, where Keith Kennedy, the left back, used to throw stones for his dog. He had one or two Alsatians he used to bring to training with him. Then we'd walk down the road, which was probably about 200 yards, and there was a steelworks and a field surrounded by a metal fence. It didn't belong to the club and was pretty basic. If you wanted to go to the toilet you'd have to nip behind the bushes. On the first session on my first day we gathered in the centre circle on this pitch. Jim Iley suddenly announced, 'Last one out the centre circle does doggies.' (Doggies are a series of short hard sprints.) Everyone bombed it away and I was left alone, consigned to doing sprints on my own. There was no warm-up or anything; it was ridiculous, real kids' stuff. I thought to myself, 'Is this it? Is this professional football?'

Bury was in a state of transition when I arrived. There were a few senior pros, strong characters, coming towards the end of their careers and a manager without the experience to properly handle them. There were also some good young players like Alan Whitehead. But there was something in the camp where you could tell it wasn't quite right. Once I'd seen the reaction of some of the older players to Jim Iley I realised it wasn't all going to be sweetness and light. But Jim was great with me. I wasn't his signing, but there was always a sense that he was going to have to use me.

John Forrest was the first-choice goalkeeper when I arrived and had been there for a long time by then, since the mid-1960s. He was approaching his mid-thirties so they were obviously looking for somebody younger, but John was doing okay. In fact he was a great goalie and wasn't the sort of person who viewed a young upstart like me as some sort of rival. He was very accommodating and tried to help me learn more.

But things didn't go right for the team. We were at the foot of the Fourth Division and Jim couldn't find the winning formula. He chopped and changed his side, but results wouldn't improve. A month into the season

I was supposed to make my debut against Mansfield Town in place of John Forrest. It was in all the local papers and hyped up, but I was ill on the morning of the game so I couldn't play. I'm sure Jim thought I'd bottled it, even after a doctor had been round to see me.

Next we were drawn to play Nottingham Forest in the League Cup the following Tuesday. Forest were the European Cup holders and under the reign of Brian Clough, but our preparation left a lot to be desired. It was a 7.45pm kickoff, but we were expected to be at Gigg Lane for 5.30pm. We had a doggies session then went back to the changing room to have a sit around, and then warmed up for the match. This was all after a morning training session too. Forest turned us over 7-0 and afterwards Jim wondered why we'd lost!

My first-team chance wasn't long in coming, but it was an inauspicious start. We played Wigan Athletic on 20 September . When I ran out to do the warm-up the Bury fans started booing me. 'You're fucking shit! Why don't you fuck off!' they yelled.

This was just the warm-up! They weren't happy at all that I was replacing John. I didn't panic, but I did think: 'I haven't even started yet.'

People always have their favourites and people don't like change, but that experience was something that stuck with me for a long, long time. I never told anyone this when I was a player, but sometimes it's difficult when there's four people behind the goal and they all want you to fuck off and they're telling you that you're shit. I thought, 'We haven't kicked off yet, give me a chance.' Some people – probably 99 per cent – gave me a chance, but there was always that 1 per cent who thought I wasn't going to make it. They obviously trusted John, and thought I was some sort of nugget out of non-league. They didn't know what I was like or what I was going to do, but we won 2-1 that afternoon and I did okay. My professional career was finally under way.

Jim hired the former Manchester United manager Wilf McGuinness as coach, which had a big impact on me. Wilf's time as United manager had not been a success, coming at a time when the great team of George Best and Bobby Charlton was falling apart. But this tends to overshadow his reputation as a brilliant coach and he certainly helped me. Wilf was just great, a brilliant lively fellow – and he still is. He used to take me out on a Tuesday afternoon on my own, train with me. At the age of 22 that was my first goalkeeper coaching, ever.

I am a great believer in clubs having specialist coaches for all training positions. It surprises me that no clubs really do this beyond the goalkeeping position. If I ran a club I would have a goalkeeping coach that did goalkeepers in the morning along with a defensive coach to take the defenders, a midfield coach to take the midfielders, and so on. The players would all then work on their own individual bits and come together later. That to me makes sense. If you did an hour a day focusing on your own position, plus a couple of hours match time, that's a lot of hours over the course of a season specialising, improving, achieving excellence.

At Bury I was introduced for the first time to this new world of specialised coaching. We used to do a good 90-minute session and it certainly improved my technique. Wilf's got an infectious personality and I came away from his training sessions with my confidence a mile high.

But it was the advice he gave me that had the most enduring impact. Wilf taught me that football and goalkeeping was not just about fitness and technique; it was a psychological battle too. He said: 'Look, when you get in this team you're going to have centre forwards who are going to smash you. For no reason; that's what they do. They want to intimidate you. If you just get up and laugh they won't know what's going through your head. Just get up and don't react; just laugh at them.' That was the best piece of advice I ever had. From that day onwards never would I let another player know what was going through my mind.

For all the perfectionism I would later display in my preparations there were times when I messed up. I went to Northampton and forgot my gloves, which didn't go down very well. I had to borrow a pair from Northampton and we got beaten 5-3, so the manager wasn't impressed with me. But then it probably wasn't surprising that I made stupid mistakes like that. I'd got to Bury and didn't really know what I was doing and suddenly I was in the team and still trying to figure out what I was doing. It was all part of a steep learning curve and from then on I never travelled without a ton of kit. I always had loads of spare gloves and at least two pairs of boots with me. I was always watching the older heads to see what I should be doing and it helped me lots later on in my career.

The team had plenty of characters and it was a good blend of all the players who'd been about and had some banter, and then some young ones coming through who were confident about what they could do. Pat Howard, a veteran centre back, was full of chat. Kevin Tully, a left winger, was bonkers; he would sit in the dressing room sucking his thumb while Jim gave his orders. Benny Phillips was always lively; Keith Kennedy was always talking. But it was a serious business too, much more so than it ever was with Everton; there was never any high jinks or messing around.

Life away from the pitch was never very glamorous. I was on less money than I had been at Winsford and it wasn't really enough to get by on. That winter was freezing cold and we brought in storage heaters to warm up the house. They were pretty old and because there was snow everywhere we kept them on. I had absolutely no idea what they were costing and when the electricity bill came in I was in shock. I didn't realise a bill could be so high and there was no way I could afford it. Because we didn't have any savings we had to sell all our furniture to pay the electricity board. It was a bit of an eye-opener.

It wasn't glamorous, but it was a good life. I loved Ramsbottom and it was a great place to live, very quiet and in the country. Our first place was a nice house and then we moved to this little cottage, where the bus stopped outside, and there was a pub probably 200 yards down the road. Dad used to stay weekends sometimes after the Manchester United match and go back on Sunday night or Monday and we enjoyed having him.

⊥⊤

THE TEAM STRUGGLED throughout the 1980/81 season to score goals, but I was progressing well. In fact there was a period when I was doing rather too well for Jim Iley's liking. We went for a period when he wouldn't let me train with the first team on a Friday morning because I was saving too many of their shots. He told me that the outfield players were losing confidence and that I was going to end up getting him the sack. How bizarre is that?

Jim was a decent fellow, but he didn't get on with the other lads and I felt he became a bit isolated. We played up in Scotland for an Anglo-Scottish Cup game and I think we might have lost, I can't quite remember. Jim sat in one room with his coaching staff and everyone else sat in the other. It was a sign to me that things weren't quite right. I used to room with Steve Johnson, a mixed-race lad from Liverpool who was massive; a real big powerful centre forward, who would score some beautiful goals from distance, but went through droughts where he couldn't find the net. I always found him very easy-going, but he fell out with Jim, and every time he scored he'd give him a bit of grief. He was a real nice lad, and I'm sure Jim got worse stick from the others.

The year I was there Bury were consigned to Fourth Division mediocrity. They were never going to get promoted, but they were never going to get relegated either. They ended the season winning 17 and losing 18 – they were that kind of side. But before getting hammered by Nottingham Forest we knocked Newcastle out of the League Cup, and we also made the third round of the FA Cup, which wasn't bad by Fourth Division standards. Back then lower-league clubs still competed against Scottish teams in the Anglo-Scottish Cup. We made the semi-finals of that before bowing out to Chesterfield over two legs.

But, as shown by Jim Iley's reluctance to use me in goal for Friday training, I was getting better and better. I think the more games you play the more confident you become. Bury wasn't the kind of place where everyone would tell you how brilliant you were. In fact it probably took me three-quarters of the season to win over the Bury fans. But we had some good old pros who would encourage you and give you advice.

John Forrest, as I've said, never saw me as a rival coming in to take his place. In fact he was great and helped me a lot. I was lucky and there was never any 'I'm not doing this, not doing that with you'. He was just good as gold. Years later at Everton I would use that experience myself when encountering young goalkeepers. When the club signed players I never said, 'Bugger off, you're a rival'; I tried to help them because of the way John – and later Jim Arnold at Everton and Dai Davies with Wales – treated me. If you're better than him, you're better than him; if he's better than you, he's better than you and will get his chance. That's the basis on which I used to work.

At the end of the season we had an awards night, or maybe it was an awards afternoon. Either way it was a nice occasion and I was named Bury's player of the year and young player of the year. I'd played 44 games, conceded 50 goals and kept 15 clean sheets. I was lucky, because suddenly I was seen as the main player, the main person in the team, and got all the attention. The *Manchester Evening News* even wrote a gushing profile of me in which they called me 'a future First Division star'. But we had some really good young players who I thought would go on and do well elsewhere.

As for me, even though I'd got some recognition I had no expectations of going anywhere. There was a story in the *Football Pink* that said Manchester United were having me watched. Stoke, Wolves, Leeds and Chelsea were also meant to be interested. But I used to read the paper sometimes and they'd say so-and-so has watched the game and I'd think, 'Yeah, but what does it actually mean?' Some days I thought they wrote it just because was nothing else to write about the game.

It's funny at the end to a professional season. We played our last game and got changed and everyone said, 'See you next season, then.' And that was it! There was no ceremony or fanfare, just 'see you in a few months!' I thought it was great at first, getting paid to do nothing for the first time in my life. But after about a week I was bored senseless. This would be the same throughout my whole career. I hated summers, absolutely hated them. I didn't really like going on holiday. I hated the nothingness. I yearned for pre-season to begin.

I went back to Llandudno in the summer to stay with my mum and dad. One day I went to the newsagents, and suddenly I saw myself on the back page. Apparently I was meant to join Everton but the deal had been called off because Winsford were owed a cut of the fee. Instead I was going to be sold to Newcastle. It was the first that I knew of any transfer, never mind to a First Division club. I was bewildered.

I went straight back to Bury and sought out Jim Iley to find out what was going on.

'Everton want to buy you,' he said. 'But Winsford are due a cut of the transfer and no one can agree. I don't think the deal is going ahead.'

I was slightly taken aback by this, but like a lot of things it was out of my hands. There was no point worrying about it, so I went home. It turned out that when I joined Bury for £6,000, they'd agreed to pass on 25 per cent of any future fee to Winsford. Someone at Bury had phoned the Winsford chairman Cliff Noden to offer £10,000 as a compromise, to which he'd agreed. But then he'd read in the paper that the fee was going to be £150,000 and the 'compromise' was barely a quarter of what they were entitled to. Understandably he wasn't happy at Bury pleading poverty and called the deal off. Suddenly Cliff and the Bury chairman, Ron Clarke, were trading digs in the press and I was stuck in the middle.

The next day Jim Iley phoned me in Ramsbottom. Winsford had agreed on £25,000 as their cut and everyone was happy.

'The deal's on, Everton want to sign you. Do you want to go and talk to them?'

There was only one answer to that.

'How are you going to get there?' he asked, like a concerned parent all of a sudden. He knew I didn't have a car, so he said, without waiting for my answer, 'Be at the ground at 10am and I'll drive you there.'

My career at Bury had started with the Bury manager Dave Connor giving me a lift home to Llandudno. Little could I have imagined then that it would come to a close a year later with a different Bury boss giving me a ride to one of the most famous clubs in British football.

# CHAPTER THREE

# TOFFEEMAN

JIM ILEY DROVE ME THROUGH A CITY IN TURMOIL. In July 1981 Liverpool was ravaged by some of the worst inner-city rioting seen in the 20th century, arising from long-standing tensions between the city's police and the local black community. In nine days of riots centred on Toxteth, hundreds were injured, more than 500 people were arrested and scores of buildings were razed to the ground. It was quite a change from sleepy Llandudno or Bury. When Jim drove me in to sign the city was literally on fire.

I had been to Goodison once before when I was a teenager; we'd been taken to see Everton after a junior game in the city when I was about 13 or

14 and Gordon West was still in goal. But it was still one of my first visits to Liverpool. I'd played at South Liverpool and on the non-league circuit, but nowhere like this. I didn't have a clue about the place.

Right away I was impressed by Howard Kendall, who was clearly a decent fellow and a real bundle of energy. His first words to me were, 'Do you want a drink?' When I told him I was a teetotaller he looked at me as if I'd landed from another planet.

He didn't have to sell the club to me, or try to either. The option was, 'Do you want to sign or not?' He offered to double my wages, which was nice, and there were a few nuts-and-bolts things to sort out. The medical was a formality. If Howard wants to sign you, he'll get you. You could have a hole in your head and if he wanted you badly enough you'd get through the medical.

Before I knew it we were posing for silly photographs in front of a press photographer. But Howard never explained the club to me, or how my life was about to change forever. I didn't know what Everton's training was going to be like – for all I knew it could have been the same as Bury's – or whether I would be second, third or first-choice goalkeeper. After I signed on the dotted line he just wanted to take me out and get pissed. That was his initiation, to show me the city over drinks. He still couldn't quite understand it when I said I was a teetotaller, but we went out anyway and had a few steaks.

There was no great ceremony or anything like that. I was just a lower-league signing, one of seven players Howard would buy that summer. There was hardly even anyone at Goodison, just Howard, Jim Greenwood the club secretary, and Jim MacGregor, the doctor. I don't think anyone else knew who I was.

There's a famous story about Tommy Lawton, the great 1930s centre forward, signing for Everton and getting the tram to Goodison. He was spotted by a conductor who came up to him and asked if he was Lawton, the new signing. 'I am,' said the young striker. 'You'll never be as good as Dixie,' came the blunt assessment. But afterwards when I got on the bus and went back home to Bury nobody even recognised me.

When pre-season training started a few weeks later it was Colin Harvey, who was then Everton's reserve team manager but would go on to be Howard's assistant through the glory years, who made the deepest impression on me. Straight away Colin reminded me of all the Scousers I'd played with at Winsford.

It's hard to describe Scousers, but all the way back to my childhood in Llandudno I've always felt great affinity to the people and their city and believe them to be a breed apart. They're a bit special. They've all got really good hearts. They're quite aggressive, because it's a hard city and you have to fight for what you want and sometimes just to earn a living. They're determined. They have a great humour, but a bit of class to go with it too.

This impacted on the pitch as well. There was an expectation and hunger for success that was innate in a Scouser's psychological make-up. Playing for Everton was not like playing for, say, Norwich, where you can have good game, a couple of mediocre ones and a stinker, and everyone thinks you're a good player. At Everton they want you to play your bollocks off every game. They don't care if you've had a row with your missus, or you don't feel that well, or if you're not quite fit. They don't care about any of that. You've got to be perfect, and if you're not they don't like you.

Colin, for me, epitomised what a Scouser is and personified that wide array of heavy expectation. Footballers have to be aggressive in the right way and Colin was just that: he was aggressive in his training, he was aggressive in his play, he was aggressive in chasing what he wanted. Off the pitch he was mild-mannered and charming, but on it he was different. He had been a great player but had been forced to retire through injury five years earlier. You could still see that style about him on the training pitch, that he had a good football brain in his head, that he could use both feet; that he was the sort of stylish player the club had once been synonymous with. He led by example. He trained and trained and trained. Players looked at him and were inspired by what he did. Even years later, when he was in his fifties and was having to get plastic hips put in, he'd get bollockings off the surgeon for training when he should have been resting.

As a coach Colin would always give you bits of advice; he'd always sit you down and say, 'Maybe you should have done that.' He'd push you to be as good as he was; that's what I liked about him. He was never satisfied about anything. Everyone said he's grumpy but Colin just set standards, and he set standards in training that were beyond some of our players at the time.

I always think grumpy people are cantankerous for two reasons – either they are actually just grumpy, or they simply demand more than anybody else, and Colin, I think, demanded more. He'd get frustrated even with himself in training if he did a bad pass or bad touch in head tennis. I'd look at him and think, 'Colin you're retired; it doesn't matter, mate.' But it did to him, and that's the difference. It's hard to describe; it was a real sense of not wanting to let his standards drop, even though he was no longer a player. But his personality was infectious too and he'd have a laugh with you as well.

For me, Everton was a test to see if I could handle playing at that level. It wasn't much of a gamble, because I knew that the worst-case scenario was that they'd send me back to Bury. But at the same time I knew I had to supplant two more experienced custodians. First there was Jim McDonagh, a big Yorkshireman who was an Ireland international because of his parentage. Howard's predecessor, Gordon Lee, had signed him a year before I came and he'd done pretty well, but Howard didn't fancy him and was trying to get rid of him. Jim knew he was on his way out and didn't play in the first team while I was there. Howard sold him back to Bolton from whom he'd joined.

There was also Jim Arnold, who had followed Howard from Ewood Park. Howard had 'discovered' him two years earlier playing non-league for Stafford Rangers when Jim was nearly 30. He went straight into the team and did really well for Blackburn, setting all sorts of clean-sheet records. Jim was well grounded, which probably came from combining a daily job with semi-professional football for more than a decade. He would have made a good policeman. He had high morals and if he didn't think something was right he'd say so. Like John Forrest at Bury, he never competed against me, he was there to help me. I never forgot that and always promised myself I'd do the same with other young goalkeepers when I was established.

Jim and I were part of seven new signings that summer. Howard had started his sweep of the old guard by selling Bob Latchford to Swansea City and John Gidman to Manchester United, and he invested the money widely and some would say wildly too.

From Bolton he bought Mick Walsh, a proper old-fashioned centre half. Mick was a good digger, a good talker and had been around a lot longer than me. He was the sort of player who could have put his face into everything, he was going to get hurt for you; a real proper rugged defender.

Winger Mickey Thomas brought a bit of energy and flair to the team. He could dribble with pace and you knew you could throw him the ball and he'd do something with it. Although he was sometimes frustrating I felt he was underrated and maybe didn't get the recognition he deserved, at least not at Everton.

Centre forward Mick Ferguson came in from Coventry for a decent fee. He had the smallest feet you'll ever see for someone that big. He was at least six feet tall, but his feet were probably only size 6. He had loads of injury problems with his ankles and I'm sure they were related to his feet. Mick went through a lot just to make his mark, but he wasn't in there long. I think sometimes it's hard to make an impression when a club is changing so much so quickly.

Howard signed striker Alan Biley after he'd had prolific spells in lower divisions with Derby County and Cambridge United. He was, I suppose, a bit of a gamble, but he'd always scored and always would score, though not at Goodison Park. I felt sorry for Alan because he used to get absolutely slaughtered by the fans because he couldn't score a goal. I've seen Alan cry after games; the stick that he got was hugely undeserved. He was an absolutely brilliant lad but I just think he realised from the start that Everton wasn't the club for him and he was desperate to get away. He reminded me a lot of Mo Johnston, who was also a good footballer, but it just didn't happen for him at Everton, maybe because it was the wrong time. Alan was probably very close to making it at Goodison. Maybe if he'd joined the season after he would have got lucky and it would have worked out. Luck has a lot to do with success and failure in football. I think I was incredibly lucky not to be in the team when I first joined, because things were changing all the time. When I got my chance I was probably given longer to make a mark than any of the other new signings.

Lots of things were different at Everton, not just the sense of expectation, the history, and the sheer size of the club. Training was very different. In truth it was a doddle to what had preceded it at Bury and in non-league. Howard was a football manager in the true sense of the word. He wanted everything done with the ball. On a typical day we'd arrive at Bellefield (Everton's training ground) between nine and half-past. We'd play some head tennis and go out. There'd be a warm-up, a little circle, a game of some sort; probably a bit of shooting, maybe a few little sprints, and that would be it.

We'd be finished by quarter-past or half-past twelve, maximum. Sometimes we did some running, but not very much. Howard believed that if you were successful you didn't need to run on the training ground. Playing 70 games a season was enough and you just needed to do enough to tick over. Sometimes there'd be a bit of messing around. In fact, with health and safety, you'd never get away with some of the things we did back then. Sometimes Howard would get all the apprentices and line them up in the goal. We'd all smash balls at them and they had to stop them going in. They'd all be trying to impress Howard by throwing their faces at the ball and all that. They'd be covered in blood or half knocked out and the first team would just be pissing themselves laughing.

For me, there was a big change in my life from my days in non-league. Only 15 months before I joined Everton I was working as a hod-carrier, training on my own on Llandudno beach, then playing Saturdays for Winsford and Sundays as centre back for the pub. All I did was work, train, play, or travel to games. Now as a professional footballer I had more time to myself than at any other period in my life.

A lot of it was just hanging about. I was never one for hobbies. I used to try staying at Bellefield until about two o'clock if I could. We stayed in Ramsbottom for a while, but that was too far away and because I didn't drive I was reliant on others for lifts. For a while Howard used to give me a lift in as he was still living out that way from his Blackburn days. I don't think he liked that at all, not that I liked listening to Terry Wogan on his car radio every morning either. But I think it shows just what an absolute nugget I was back then – the reserve goalie asking the boss for a lift home. Can you imagine?

Eventually I cottoned on that this wasn't the done thing, so it was a case of going back to the station, getting the train into Liverpool, then back out to Manchester, then a train to Bury and then a bus home. It was a fair old trek. Eventually we moved to West Derby, right by Bellefield. Once or twice I cycled in, which someone latched on to and for years people thought I cycled to training every day. (Even now people ask me if it was true that I used to cycle to Bellefield from Llandudno, never mind West Derby – I don't know if they think I'm Lance Armstrong or something!) After training it was a short walk home and I'd head out again and walk the dogs. Then it was teatime, after which I'd walk the dogs again. I'd watch TV for a while or read a book and then it was bedtime. I was never one for nightclubs or going out much. Football was the thing; I wasn't interested in that much else. Sometimes during midweek I'd even go and watch Liverpool and study Bruce Grobbelaar's play. It was football or nothing.

Being a footballer is an incredibly selfish profession. It never gave me any time for anything else. I had to give up a lot to play football the way I wanted to do it. I wouldn't do anything – going out with my wife, attending a school awards ceremony, meeting fans, whatever was on the agenda – that would adversely affect my preparations in any way. My view was that I had to do everything to the best of my ability and everything else had to go by the wayside to achieve that. It might sound a harsh or cruel outlook on life but I believed I needed to be completely focused and insular because no one else could play for me. Even though it's a team game, within that team you've got the individuals and you have to look after number one because there's nobody else to do it for you. Nobody's going to pat you on the back if you don't play well for three weeks; they just won't play you.

Whether the team's struggling or the team's doing well you still have to maintain your routine and do things right. That in itself means you have to be pretty selfish in lots of ways. As a goalkeeper there's even greater pressure: if you don't do your job then the next player can't do his job properly, because he'll be worrying about you messing up. You have to look after one person, and that's you. That's what football teaches you. You're the master of your own career, you've got to look after it the best you can, because as soon as a manager doesn't want you he'll let you know. I'd give up everything I could give up to do what I wanted to do, which was to play to the very best of my ability.

Jim Arnold went straight into the first team at the start of the 1981/82 season, but I wasn't surprised or disappointed. He was the experienced goalkeeper, the number one, although I was confident that wouldn't be the case for ever. Reserve teams also meant something in those days and played their home games at Goodison. When I first played in the reserves Howard was still playing. He was in his mid-thirties then, but you could still see the natural skill and elegance that had set him apart as one of the finest players of his generation. Wherever Howard was he'd call for the ball and everybody passed it to him, whether he was on his own or surrounded by six men. It wasn't just because he was manager they passed to him, it was because he could still play, and I think he packed it in a bit too early when he hung up his boots for good later on that season. In my view he should have kept playing for another season at least. He was a good player and for years that quality showed through in training as well. But the responsibility of managing and playing was ultimately a bit much.

Even though there was pressure that came with playing for a big club, there were so many people there that it was never overwhelming. From the very start we had enough characters in the dressing room to make it quite lively and defuse any tension. The flipside was that it took me a while to find my way. At Bury there was probably a good team spirit and a much smaller group, so you'd get to know everybody quicker. Everton took a little bit more time. I was very shy at Bury and very shy at Everton so I didn't speak to many people. I always used to keep myself to myself and did what I needed to do. Nobody took me under their wing and it took everybody a while to get to know me.

It was probably harder for me to fit in and bond because I never used to go out a lot. I didn't drink – not for moral or ethical or health reasons – because it didn't do anything for me. Ever since my two sips of lager as a teenager I've never had another drop of alcohol. Because of that I never went to pubs or nightclubs and sat out most team bonding sessions; I was always set apart from a lot of the players. Howard didn't understand why I didn't drink. The first couple of times he tried to get me out to have a drink, but once I told him no, he just left me alone. Later when I was established at the club he would ask me occasionally to have a beer, but I'd just tell him to fuck off and he'd leave me. I was probably an exception though. Generally he didn't like people who didn't drink, who didn't socialise. He probably let me off because he thought I was just a hopeless case.

My Everton debut came against Ipswich in October 1981. Jim Arnold was injured and I had a feeling I might play. No one knew who I was and the press had no inkling I might start. Like Jim I was also carrying an injury and I wasn't sure whether Howard would risk him or me. In the end, around an hour or so before kickoff, Howard sat down next to me and just said, 'By the way, you're playing.' He must have known all along, but given the way I liked to prepare myself it put me into a panic. The first thought that crossed my mind was 'Shit, what do I do now?' I liked preparing for games over several days, not a few minutes. In the end I told myself there were two ways of doing this; either cool down and go and do it, or mess it up and maybe never get the chance again. I was really scared but really excited at the same time. I told myself I had to go for it, the same as I did when I got my chance at Bury. If you don't face up to these things you just never know what might have been. Not that I had much chance to turn back: once you see you're playing you can't say, 'Well, I don't feel like it,' can you?

The Goodison crowd were great. It wasn't like my debut at Bury a year earlier when they booed me. Evertonians were never like that. They always gave players a chance before deciding whether they were rubbish or all right. Luckily I fell into the latter category but for a few years the mood seemed to be, 'We'll live with you, you might get better.'

Once I was out on the pitch, I suppose you'd liken it to the first day at a job. You're very nervous but really, really want to do it, and are excited too. I think it's that you don't want to let yourself down and don't want to let anybody else down. I suppose it's similar to an ambulanceman taking his first case and actually getting through it. At the back of my mind was the thought that it could all go badly wrong, that I could throw three goals and that would be it. But if you don't go through the experience you don't know how far you can go.

We got off to a good start, which helped. Mickey Thomas floated in a decent free kick and Mick Ferguson's glancing header put us in front. We played some good stuff, and although Ipswich equalised shortly before half-time, Gary Stevens put us back in front almost straight away. In the end we won 2-1 and I did all right. I had to make one stop from Eric Gates but it was a quiet afternoon. Ipswich were a good team at the time, so it was a decent result for us.

Once it was 5pm I knew I could cope with the pressures at the top. It was just one of those steps. Colin and Howard were full of congratulations, telling me how well I'd done. But I can't have done that well because I wasn't playing the next week. Jim Arnold was in good form, so I could have no complaints about that.

—✕—

WHEN I JOINED EVERTON at first I was just trying to bed down in the reserves. I thought, 'I'll give myself till Christmas to see if I'm still there. If I am, I won't be best pleased.' Looking back it was a sign of how naive I was. But as it turned out, six days before Christmas 1981 I returned to the first team. A few days earlier the team had lost 3-2 at home to Ipswich in the League Cup and Howard rang the changes afterwards. Mick Walsh, Alan Biley, Mick Ferguson and Eamonn O'Keefe were all dropped and scarcely played for the club again. Jim Arnold was left out too. For all his affability, Howard could be ruthless like that. But I didn't care as I'd got my hands on the number one jersey.

My return to the first team came at home to Aston Villa, who were reigning champions and ended the season winning the European Cup. We won, I kept a clean sheet and my place for the next game. In fact I was ever-present for the rest of the season. Looking through my old scrapbook I can see there were plenty of nice things written about me, comparisons with the likes of Peter Shilton and Ray Clemence, and a few man of the match awards. When I was named man of the match against Tottenham, they game me a bowl of fruit and a bottle of Moët et Chandon, which I gave to my mum.

You would think that your life would be turned upside down regularly playing First Division football. But it wasn't like that for me. Maybe it's because I think of myself differently to other people. I never saw myself as the big star, I was just making my name. I wasn't earning a massive amount of money, so financially I wasn't very different to most of the people who were paying to watch me. Earning £150,000 a week puts you on a different planet, but £300 was just normal wages. Because of the money I don't think modern players can relate to ordinary people now, and vice versa. They are surrounded by their own security and entourages, they go to the most expensive shops and spend most of their time doing things that aren't normal to most people. The only time they come into contact with the public is when they're on the pitch and that's very different. I, by contrast, lived in an ordinary house in an ordinary neighbourhood. I didn't go out much, except to walk my dogs, and didn't drive a fast car. In fact I didn't drive at all for a long time.

The culture was also different from how it is now. There was no Sky, or people with mobile phones taking videos of you at every moment. I never got mobbed. Because I was quite quiet my profile was low and people left me alone. I liked it that way.

At the same time I existed in my own little bubble. It was nothing to do with growing fame or wealth, it was just the way I was – entirely focused on my next match. Liverpool was still devastated by the Toxteth riots, mass unemployment and a heroin epidemic that affected 5,000 young people in the city. But the social and economic problems never occurred to me. Probably somewhere in my head they might have done, but my memories of the time are of Evertonians following us everywhere. They were brilliant and passionate and loyal, and I think their willingness to follow us through good times and bad, near and far, was bound up in who Scousers are as a people. Every time we turned up for an away game there seemed to be millions of Scousers everywhere. Wherever we went, whenever we went, even pre-season there were loads of them too. Everywhere there was tons of Scousers. Somebody somewhere had money, or just by hook or by crook they got there and into the stadium. A Scouser with no money still gets places, doesn't he? They're just quite inventive in their methods.

By the start of 1982 I was the only one of Howard's 'magnificent seven' regularly getting a place in the starting line-up. Alan Biley was loaned out to Stoke and then sold at the end of the campaign to Portsmouth, where the goals flowed again. Mickey Thomas was kicked out and sold to Brighton after he was supposed to have refused to play for the reserves. I couldn't see that to be honest; Mickey's not one to have bust-ups. Like me, he just wants to play football and if he's not he's a nuisance. I think Howard was just looking for someone different. Neither Jim Arnold, Alan Ainscow, Mick Ferguson or Mike Walsh could get a game, and all except Jim would be gone within a year or so. I was finding my feet but, to be fair, so was Howard. He used 27 players that season; a huge number at a time when there was only one substitute allowed.

Howard never told me I was his number one. There was no stage when I felt that the shirt was my own. Even in later years when I was voted the best player in England and people said I was the best goalkeeper in the world, he never took me aside and said, 'You're my number one every week.' He wouldn't say that, it just wasn't his style. He'd say, 'You're in the team this week,' as if to tell me that next week I might not be. Everything was always black and white with Howard, it was very simple – at least with me. It was either my fault or it wasn't, but he was always good enough to admit when it was his. Early on he told the press that I was the best goalkeeper in the First Division 'outside the big three' (i.e. Ray Clemence, Peter Shilton and Joe Corrigan) and he would always be complimentary when talking to journalists. But we never chatted about things ourselves. I suppose it was good management and it kept me on my toes. I used to go in and train as hard as I could, or play as hard as I could on Saturday, and whatever happened after that was out of my control.

Despite me coming in as an unknown and taking his place, Jim Arnold was really good to me. I got on very well with him and we always had a good training session; we both enjoyed all the training. He was never bitter and twisted about it, and was always supportive. Maybe because he was a bit older – somebody who had been around and been there and done that – and had been all through non-league, he perhaps saw a bit of himself in me. He did what he could to help me and would always put his hand up for me.

Another keeper who was also there in my first days with Everton was

Martin Hodge. He had a horrendously bad knee injury and I watched him every afternoon with Colin. Just Colin and him, trying his bollocks off to get fit and save his career. You could see why he eventually made it into the England squad, because he worked so phenomenally hard. I used to wonder whether I could have done what he did every afternoon. It was hard, hard work, but he got back and had a great career with Sheffield Wednesday. I admired him so much for how he persevered, and also Colin too for giving him so much time and focus.

People look at this as a difficult period in the club's history and maybe it was. Home crowds were often below 20,000, while Liverpool were riding high, winning League Championships and European Cups. But we had a good young team too, one that was learning quickly and gaining experience that would serve us well a few years down the line. By the end of the season several players who would later be considered among the greatest in the club's history had broken through.

Graeme Sharp had come down from Dunfermline under Gordon Lee, reputedly turning down Aston Villa (who would win the European Cup in 1982) and Alex Ferguson's Aberdeen (who won the Cup Winners' Cup a year later). Sharpy was a good centre forward and a great personality. That's why he's ended up with an executive job at Everton, because he can communicate well with people. He always knew what he wanted and came down from Scotland to prove himself. He was good at holding the ball up, used to jump early, was a good goalscorer and wasn't afraid to be physical, but he also had a very good touch. I don't think by everybody's standards he was the best trainer in the world but he did all right. I thought he was our best centre forward during my time at Goodison by a mile. When things didn't work out with Mick Ferguson, Howard gave him his chance, which he grabbed. A total of 15 goals in 27 starts during the 1981/82 season was some return from someone who had never played in the First Division before. I think Sharpy was more mobile than Mick and held the ball up well. He became a focal part of the team.

Gary Stevens was nearly five years younger than I was but broke into the team the same season as me. He was from Barrow-in-Furness, right up the northwest coast, and had worked his way up from apprentice terms to the first team. Like me he was pretty quiet. He was a tremendous athlete – he still is – and quick as lightning, and could run up and down the right side of the defence all day long. It was nice to have somebody who had been through the system and was close to Mick Heaton and other members of the coaching staff. Like the others he was finding his way into the team. He was a really sensible, level-headed kid.

Kevin Ratcliffe that first season was mostly playing out of position at left back. There was talk of a move to Ipswich, but I don't think Howard ever had any intention of selling him. On and off the pitch he was a leader: as quick as lightning, but also very sharp – a proper piss-taker with a dry sense of humour. He'd progressed through the Everton ranks under Colin Harvey and you could see how that had rubbed off on him. He had certain standards and, whether he was in the first team or the reserves, liked to let people know that they had to be met. He was great to play with because you knew he was quick enough to recover everything. If a winger beat him and he was playing full back he'd recover 99 times out of 100. He was quick, but he was also ruthless in his tackling, and he perfected the art of not getting booked too often. He was the sort of player able to go down the back of someone's Achilles, go straight through them, and make it look as though it was an accident. He was one of the dirtiest players I've ever known in my life, but didn't mind taking it either. He never got particularly rough with anybody; the same as Sharpy, who didn't lose his temper that much either. Again, it was probably Colin's influence that saw them channel that aggression the right way. From the outset I knew Rats was a good player, someone who had captaincy written all over him.

From Stoke City we signed 21-year-old forward Adrian Heath for a club record fee of £850,000. Howard had banked a bit of money from wheeler-dealing and there was talk of him trying to buy Bryan Robson from

West Bromwich Albion, but I think the £1.5million Manchester United ended up paying was a bit beyond him. So he went for 'Inchy' instead. He was another one of those players – we had a few of them at the time – that was full of energy. He was a terrific little player, super-confident and a brave little bugger too. He didn't mind getting hurt and with his pace it meant we could put pressure on defenders at the other end.

Inchy was also just about the biggest moaner in the world. He was an absolutely massive whinger and moaned at everything all the time. Nothing was ever good enough for him. It was a constant stream of 'Do this, do that, fucking pass that properly, come on, come on'. It was just Adrian's way of letting his frustration out, but it also made other people do better as well. You need that in your team. Because he was a nark he brought other people together and made them improve too. It was the same when Andy Gray came in. He was an even bigger moaner than Adrian, although I would have found that hard to believe at the time.

And who could forget John Bailey? Bails is the best full back I've played with, bar none. I thought he was the best full back that ever played. He had great skill with the ball; he was quick, he had tenacity. Some people say he wasn't the best tackler but I thought he did all right. He banged forward all day; he was as fit as anything. Howard would controversially replace him during the 1984/85 season with Pat Van Den Hauwe. Going forward he was much better than Pat, but as a defensive player Pat had the edge – and could play centre back as well. If John played today he'd be a millionaire because he was a model full back. I suppose you could compare him to Leighton Baines, but his quality on the ball was better than Leighton's.

Our captain was Mick Lyons, a real bleed-blue Evertonian. He'd been at the club since the 1960s when he joined on schoolboy terms and had watched its glory years under Harry Catterick as a fan. He'd been playing for more than a decade as centre half and occasional centre forward. Some fans cruelly dubbed him a jinx because Everton had never beaten Liverpool when he was in the team and he was considered to be synonymous with the club's trophyless years. That was harsh. Lyonsy was brilliant, a really good captain and player, full of energy, full of love for the club. Like Colin Harvey, he embodied the club's motto – Nil Satis Nisi Optimum ('Nothing but the best is good enough'). I liked that and tried to stay true to it myself. But you looked at someone like Mick who was never the player Colin was and never would be. Yet he had this terrific desire and will to win that made him a tremendous asset to the team. He was also one of the most mischievous players I came across in a dressing room and was always up to something. He was a proper naughty schoolkid most of the time; nothing malicious, just joking around.

For me, Mick Lyons epitomised what an Everton player should be, giving everything he had in every single game. He had so much energy and could do so much for the team. He was brave as a lion and if he got hurt he never wanted to go off. He was a good communicator and set a great example for everybody else. He was also incredibly nice, particularly to me who was quiet and shy. Perhaps this was his one shortcoming as a player, as I sometimes felt it showed through on the pitch. I think he would have been better again if he had more nastiness about him. If he'd had some of the edge of Mick Walsh, he'd have been a top, top player.

Then there were others who were good players, like Mark Higgins and Kevin Richardson, who maybe didn't get the recognition they deserved. Steve McMahon was with us then and possessed a ridiculous will to win. I think of him now as a slightly slower version of Roy Keane; he was full of aggression, but you loved having that sort of player on your side. He left to join Liverpool via Aston Villa a few years later and there was a bit of an edge when he played against some of the other lads. The crowd didn't like him either, but you're always going to get that when you have a midfielder playing on the edge of what you can and cannot do. He certainly never bothered me. Eamonn O'Keefe was another one that people forget. He left before the glory years, but was another decent player. He held the ball up, scored goals and had massive amounts of energy.

If you look at the team it was full of good players, it just wasn't gelling in the way that Howard wanted it to. We ended the 1981/82 season with a flourish, winning five of the last six games and drawing the other and finishing eighth, which, for a team in transition, was okay. But Liverpool were miles ahead of us, winning the title and finishing 23 points in front. So the pressure was on.

The other lads went off on an end-of-season holiday to Magaluf, or somewhere like that, but I wasn't interested. Why would I be? I didn't drink, so I wasn't going to go and watch them get pissed every single night. Most clubs did that at the end of the season as a way of letting the players' hair down but it wasn't for me. Once the season ended I was pissed off because there was no more football. What was I supposed to do? I probably went on holiday with Eryl a couple of times, but nowhere more than a week, ever. A week was a killer; two weeks was a nightmare. Now it's different but then I just wanted to be back in work. I know it sounds stupid but all I wanted to do was play football; I just wasn't interested in anything else whatsoever.

I hated the summer and hated pre-season; hated it. The games were shit because everyone is feeling their way, whereas I'd be completely fit as I kept my training up all through the summer. If it was up to me I'd rather have gone right through the year and played footy every week all the time. I just couldn't see the point in having a break.

During the summer of 1982 Howard did some astute dealing. He didn't have masses of money, but he was always good at shifting out players that he no longer needed and using the money to bring in fresh blood. A lot of his early signings were transferred out. Perhaps most surprisingly he let Mick Lyons leave for Sheffield Wednesday. Mick had been out injured for a lot of the second half of the season and Billy Wright did well in his place.

He brought back an old favourite, Andy King, who had been a Goodison star in the late-1970s. Andy was a much, much better player than anybody gave him credit for. He was one of the best finishers I've ever come across. He was just magnificent in training; he could bend it, smash it, he had real quality. Lots of people thinks he's a bit of an idiot because he used to mess about, but when he put his mind to it he was brilliant. But second time around I think it was wrong time, wrong place. I think Howard wanted someone who would take on more defensive responsibilities. He worked hard enough but to me he was another free spirit, he lacked the sense of responsibility Howard sought.

Kingy was a great player and maybe in a different era he would have won caps for England. But I don't think people always understand creative people. Sometimes they are just a bit bonkers, but people recognise the talent. Like the artist Tracey Emin, who called her bed art and everybody said she was a genius. Maybe Kingy was the Tracey Emin of his time – but people didn't see past the person who always wanted to have a joke and a laugh and talk about horse racing.

Less successful was David Johnson, who had been a brilliant young prodigy in the early 1970s under Harry Catterick, but was sold to Ipswich Town in a disastrous swap deal that brought Rod Belfitt to Goodison. Johnson had eventually wound up at Liverpool, where he won countless domestic and European trophies as well as England caps. Everton fans couldn't forgive his record with Liverpool. He was the only Everton player I remember being booed by our fans and he got absolutely slaughtered. He was the nicest man in the world and I used to feel sorry for him. He'd come and join me for the warm-up and the Gwladys Street would scream, 'Fuck off, Johnson, you're shit!' Dave Watson was a Red, Kevin Sheedy was a Red, so were Alan Harper, Peter Beardsley and Gary Ablett; but Johnson – who had started out at Goodison – they could never forgive.

Probably Howard's best signing that summer was Kevin Sheedy. Sheedy was quiet and for the first few games I didn't know what he was all about. I think he was different from all the other players inasmuch as he didn't tackle anybody, he always looked tired; always looked as if he'd run 300 yards, even if he'd barely moved. After a while, though, you'd look at him and see he couldn't half ping a ball; he couldn't half pass. And, to be fair, every time he played Liverpool he got stuck in. He wasn't anybody's pushover. He was the most mild-mannered man you could ever meet, but he had a real streak in him too. And that's what's got him to where he was. All of those great 1980s players had a streak in them where the mentality was: 'If you want to be nasty with me, I can be nasty back'. Nobody in those Everton teams let anybody take any liberties with them, not even Sheedy. Even though he's quite an unassuming little fellow, he wouldn't have anybody kick him. Once you got him on a free kick or corner, that was a problem for the opposition.

We lost our first game of the 1982/83 season at Graham Taylor's Watford. They had just been promoted and there was an expectation that they were the sort of team we should be beating. But there were no easy games, and they were a quality side with players like John Barnes, Mo Johnston and Luther Blissett, and would finish their First Division debut campaign as league runners-up. Next were Aston Villa, the European Champions. We played them off the park and hammered them 5-0. The following Saturday, the FA Cup holders Tottenham came to Goodison. More than 30,000 – a big crowd in those days – turned out, expectant after our annihilation of the European Champions. Goals by McMahon, Sheedy and Billy Wright saw us win 3-1.

Evertonians went home happy. Expectations rose. It didn't bother me, though. I didn't care about anything else apart from playing in the team.

# CHAPTER FOUR
# VALIANT

ALL THROUGH MY CAREER I was only ever concerned about things that I could control. My focus was always on me; doing my best to be the best. By training hard, cancelling my imperfections, improving, I felt I could be the best goalkeeper in the world. If I was, I could help Everton and Wales. But if I lost my focus and my standards slipped I would let myself, the club and the supporters down. That's why I was at the centre of my own universe. The focus had to be on me. It might have made me slightly strange or insular, but I had enough to worry about without concerning myself with things outside this sphere.

During my years at Goodison, Everton faced all sorts of challenges.

There was the decline of the city of Liverpool, mass unemployment, poverty, emigration from the city – all of which invariably took their toll on the club, particularly attendances. Within the club there were financial problems. There were supporter protests, unpopular owners, relegation battles. There was the European ban, which saw us lose many of our best players and Howard at his peak. But none of this fazed me. I only concentrated on things I could control.

Everton's woes, whenever they had them, always seemed heightened by the presence of Liverpool on their doorstep. When I joined Everton in 1981, they had gone without a trophy for 11 years. Liverpool, by contrast, had won five League Championships, three European Cups, two UEFA Cups, an FA Cup, a League Cup and a European Super Cup during that period. Before Everton's barren spell ended three years later they added three more League Championships and another European Cup to that list. It made every Evertonian sick and magnified our own shortcomings. By today's standards we were okay. We finished eighth, and seventh twice; we were a young, improving side. But for the fans it was all doom and gloom because Liverpool were doing so well. But I couldn't have cared less about them.

How good were Liverpool? I knew how good they were, but in my mind that was them over there. Anfield might as well have been the moon for all I cared. They were nothing to do with me. I only worried about the things that I could actually control and the only thing I could control was me and doing what I had to do to stay in the team and help it perform better. If Liverpool won the European Cup it was nothing to do with us. The troublesome neighbours weren't my interest or problem.

If anything I probably thought at the time it was good to have a strong Liverpool team. Now I certainly think it's good to have a strong Liverpool side, because that means Everton have got to pull their finger out somewhere along the way. You can see now, Evertonians have only started to get really annoyed with the way their club is run because John Henry and Fenway Sports have come in at Anfield and thrown some money and bought some players. When Liverpool were doing badly under Tom Hicks and George Gillett nobody was bothered with Everton's management, were they? But now because Liverpool are doing better, everyone's saying to Bill Kenwright, 'Get rid of the club, you've got to do this, you've got to do that.' The fans are starting to demand investment and change, although it's probably about time they did anyway.

Looking back at the 1980s I came to realise that the two clubs fed off each other. Merseyside football over a period of three or four years provided the best club football in the world, and so much of it was due to the intense local rivalry. Just as Everton needed a strong Liverpool, Liverpool needed a strong Everton. When Everton got miles better in the mid-1980s, that made Liverpool pull up and overtake them again. It was like two competing brothers: one improved, the other had to get even better. It was brilliant to have the two teams as genuine rivals. If it's a level playing field then it's positive, because it means that both teams are striving to get better, and that can only be good for both of them. You can't have one team that dominates the city, because it's no good for anybody.

I was to learn this very abruptly in November 1982. We had started the season okay, beating the European Champions and FA Cup holders in our first couple of games at Goodison, and had played some decent stuff at times. Sheeds was settling in nicely after joining from Liverpool and there was a sense of progress. At the same time we dropped silly points, drawing at home to Brighton who would finish bottom of the table, and at home to Newport County in the League Cup. But nothing could prepare us for what was to follow at Goodison on Saturday 6 November 1982.

Even 30 years later this remains for many Evertonians the darkest day in the club's history. The facts are this: Liverpool scored five goals without reply. My Wales team-mate, Ian Rush, grabbed four of them. Glenn Keeley, Howard's captain at Blackburn who had been brought in midweek on loan as cover for the injured Mark Higgins, was sent off after 30 minutes when we were already a goal down. After that there was no hope.

Even all these years later I've never watched a video of the game, so I can't say if I was to blame or not. I don't think I played that badly; I certainly don't think I was absolutely shocking. It wasn't that I was bitter or because I hated losing (which I do), I just didn't like watching myself on the telly, whether I'd had a good game or a bad one. If I made a mistake I usually knew why I made it, or I'd sit down and talk to somebody or think about it. If I saw a mistake again on television I thought it was quite a negative thing. I know this seems slightly at odds with my perfectionism, closing off something that could be used to my benefit, but I just hated seeing myself on telly, full stop. Even now, I hardly watch *Match of the Day* and I've not played in the Premier League for more than a decade!

Why did we lose so badly? Afterwards Howard said that people had gone 'overboard' about the game. 'We were beaten by a very good side and we only had ten men for most of that time,' he said. 'Any side is going to have it all to do against a side like Liverpool.' There was a lot of truth in that: Liverpool were a brilliant side, one of the greatest of all time. But it was a mistake to put Glenn Keeley in there. I know he was an experienced defender and had played for Howard before, but it's hard for anybody to go into a game like that if they've never played in a match of such magnitude. And Glenn had a nightmare. It was one of those games where he should never have been stuck in.

What nobody outside the club knew was that I was carrying a nasty injury going into that fateful match. Maybe if I wasn't so stubborn and desperate to play a part in every moment of every match I would have sat it out. I had started getting ulcerated toes not long after I joined Everton. Corns would grow on the inside of the toes and spread out, burst and bleed. Lots of times they ulcerated down to the bone. During games my feet would swell up, but I'd struggle on. My feet would be puffed up afterwards and turn a violet colour. It was pretty unpleasant and went on for years. It's one of the reasons that I used to be photographed wearing flip-flops before big matches – even at Wembley when I was in my suit. It wasn't because I was scruffy, it was because my feet needed air. Before the Liverpool match it was particularly bad; so bad, in fact, that I thought I'd broken my toe. My toes were absolutely crippling me.

This might sound like an excuse long after the event and the truth is that I don't know how it affected my performance. What I do know is that when I went to the physio after the game he sent me to hospital, where my feet were put up and my toes literally cut apart and kept that way. I was there for three days. When I got back and went into training I learned I was no longer first-choice goalkeeper.

Howard was never a shouter. He wasn't best pleased with what had happened out there, but it was never his style to rant and rave or throw tea cups about. Colin would have a go now and again, but not on that day. I think because it was such a horror show there was also a degree of shock. But if I'm honest I probably missed the worst of the aftermath as I was in hospital. Howard could act decisively and ruthlessly, and often did. After the defeat he dropped the right back Brian Borrows (who never played for the club again), Bails and Sheeds. Glenn Keeley was banned anyway and didn't play for Everton again either.

Although I was technically injured for a few days, he also dropped me. Maybe the injury was a convenient excuse. Maybe he thought it was too much for me, although I didn't think so myself. He never explained why. In fact he didn't speak to me for some time (although in fairness I didn't speak to him much either). That's just the way Howard was, and the way I was too.

The Liverpool catastrophe marked the beginning of a six-month spell on the sidelines for me. I suppose you could say looking back that it was a battle to save my Everton career, although I never thought of it that way at the time.

⊐⊏

IT WAS STRANGE BEING OUT OF THE FIRST TEAM. With the exception of my first few months at Goodison I had always played every weekend, sometimes three or four times. Now that intensity and regularity was gone. In the Football League there was only one substitute allowed back then, but being goalkeeper I always had to hang around in case some catastrophe befell Jim Arnold on the day. Of course it never did, but with reserve games often scheduled for the Saturday as well, it meant that I wasn't always even getting to play for the second XI week in week out.

Obviously I wasn't happy playing for the reserves, but it was different then. For a start the matches were played at Goodison, and they were decent games too, played at a good tempo. It's not like the reserves now where they play at three miles an hour and pass the ball a million times. They were proper games. Again, it was an end to your week; you trained all week and played on a Saturday, which was great. The reserves don't play many on a Saturday now, they play midweek. You want an end to the week and Saturday is the best day for football, so it was good.

If there wasn't a reserve match my Saturday routine in those days involved going to Bellefield and doing a two-and-a-half-hour weight circuit. I'd really push myself hard, then have some lunch and head over to Goodison to watch the match as the thirteenth man. Sometimes they'd just send me home and I'd listen to the match on the radio or watch it later on Match of the Day. I was supposed to be resting on a Saturday morning like the lads who were playing, but that wasn't my way. Howard knew what I was up to as well, but he let me get on with it. Perhaps he saw that if I didn't push and extend myself the boredom would get to me.

Time, or rather too much of it, was always an issue through my playing career. But the empty hours became more challenging when I was away from the first team. I wasn't interested in golf or anything like that. After training I used to just go home and have a rest. I watched TV, or read a book – I read all sorts of books, as many as I could – or drank tea, or walked the dogs, but there was no real release. I was just bored stiff without football. Absolutely fucking bored stiff. That's why summer was a killer for me, because I just wanted to play football. It was a nightmare.

As you can see, as a player you have an inordinate amount of time to reflect, and when things aren't going well it can get in the way of training and preparation if you're not careful. But in professional sport, I soon learned, it's got to be all or nothing. If it's not then you don't get to where you want; you fall short. You need a balance but you also need to have an impenetrable focus, which for me was striving to be the best I could be.

Over the years I saw plenty of talented players not living up to their potential or dropping out of the game because they lacked this focus and desire. The routine, all too often, would be to go out after the match, get absolutely out of it on the booze, come in on Monday morning still with a hangover and not train well; train a little bit better Tuesday; have a day off Wednesday, which would leave Thursday, where we always had a really hard day's training. Fridays were a doddle and then it was back into the game. This way of living left no room for improvement and if you were out of the team through injury or lack of form there was no focus for the week, so things could spiral out of control.

That was never the way for me to go. Because I worked straight away from school I was imbued with the belief that if somebody paid you to do something you did it as best as you could. In the real world, if you stop working nobody is going to pay you tomorrow. Even if the situation you're in is not great, you work your bollocks off. This was always my basic philosophy: if you work hard you get better, and if you get better you become more valuable to your club. As a footballer you're essentially a commodity and your value – and earning power and chances of medals – goes up and down. I realised that the more valuable I became to the club the more they'd want to keep me, or the more somebody else would want me.

I didn't worry about my long-term future at the club because it was out of my hands. The decision to leave me out of the team was someone else's – principally Howard's – and not mine. I couldn't alter that. But I could make his decision more difficult for him by being a better player.

During those months in the wilderness I didn't accept my fate. I refused to. I did everything I could to get back in that first team. I trained as if my life depended upon it. I told myself I would not be one of those players who thought, 'I think I'll do all right today, I'll just have a jolly little train, fuck about; go home, fuck about, and come in tomorrow and fuck about some more.' You can't do that with sport. At home I rested and planned how I would be better the next day. I obsessed. I wanted to improve. By improving I knew I could play for Everton again.

Two months after the Liverpool debacle Howard called me into his office and told me that Port Vale wanted me on loan. I have no idea how the move came about, but it was obvious that he wanted me out of Bellefield for a while. I never doubted going there for a single minute, because I just wanted to play. I'd rather play in somebody else's first team than the Everton reserves.

Sometimes you can look at a move like that and see it as the first step to get rid of you. Perhaps that's what was in Howard's mind at the time. In my mind I think he was looking to see what reaction he got. Or maybe he was looking at the move as a way of protecting me from the impact a run out of the team would have. Or perhaps he wanted to see what I would be like when I came back.

Port Vale was good for me. My mind was open to everything and I wanted to play again. Although they were in the old Fourth Division they had a good team and would end the season promoted in third place, with a record points haul of 88. John McGrath, an old-fashioned former centre half, was the manager and he was assisted by John Rudge, who later took charge of Vale and led them up to the old Second Division. There were lots of characters in the dressing room, a good mix of old pros and some talented, hungry youngsters as well.

It was a good time to be there and as a team they were just great lads, absolutely great. At the back there was Phil Sproson, whose father and uncle had both played for Vale, and who would himself go on to make more than

400 appearances. There was Jimmy Greenhoff, who had played for Leeds and Manchester United. Up front the pairing was Bob Howard and Ernie Moss, a proper old-school pair of forwards who would graft and graft and graft. Bob was fearless, fearsome and absolutely massive. There'd be no light pre-match meal for him. He'd have a whole chicken to himself. He probably needed it too, he was absolutely huge. The regular goalkeeper Barry Siddall, who was out injured at the time, was an absolute head case. He used to ride a motorbike to training and would wear his crash helmet on the training pitch and bomb around with it on.

I don't think I played particularly well while I was at Port Vale, but it was good for me. John McGrath used to get everyone shouting and jumping up and down in the changing room before the game. It was as funny as anything and they were good times. The match I most remember is returning to Gigg Lane and putting on a good performance in front of my old supporters in a 1-0 victory over Bury. I must have done something right though, because John McGrath tried to sign me on a permanent basis. Everton said no and I suppose Howard must have always thought I was worth keeping, worth a bit of patience. Would I have gone? I'm not sure. I had no knowledge of the bid until after I'd returned to Goodison so I was never faced with the dilemma at the time. With hindsight my career and life might have been very different if I had moved. And so might Everton's history too.

Instead I went back to Goodison after two months and nine games and resumed my place as the thirteenth man each Saturday. There was no welcome back from Howard; that wouldn't have been his style. There had been some steady progress in my absence and the team was lingering around the top eight and reached the quarter-finals of the FA Cup. They were slightly unlucky to lose to the eventual winners Manchester United, but after that the season was effectively over with two months and a dozen games to play. There was no chance of winning the league title and the hysteria about fighting for a Champions League place was never an issue in those days because only the Champions went into the European Champions Cup.

Four games from the end of the season Jim Arnold picked up an injury and I was recalled for the visit of West Ham. Sharpie scored twice and we won 2-0. The following Monday we beat Coventry 1-0 at Goodison in front of under 13,000, but it was another match and another clean sheet. We hammered Luton 5-1 at Kenilworth Road and ended the season with a draw at home to Ipswich. A season that had been struck by some great lows had ended on an upbeat note.

My time in the Potteries was, looking back, a time of catharsis. Without me Port Vale finished in third place, which, in the pre-playoff days, meant automatic promotion. It was a good time for me to get my head straight and try to get back into doing what I wanted to do, which was being the best I could at the highest possible level. I suppose from Howard Kendall's perspective sending me to the Potteries was his way of saying 'sink or swim'. Luckily I started swimming a bit.

# CHAPTER FIVE

# SUPERNOVA

AT THE START OF THE 1983/84 SEASON Jim Arnold returned as Everton's first-choice goalkeeper. Howard Kendall had been quite good over the summer and made sure that everyone got a chance of playing during pre-season matches. But come the opening day against Stoke City Jim was there in the green jersey, with me watching on from the stands.

I can't say I was unduly concerned. As I've already said, I was never one to let things outside my control bother me. I suppose it's one of my many contradictions: I was obsessive to the point of excluding everything else in my life but football, about improving myself as a player and testing myself to the limits. But when it came to team selection my attitude was always 'what shall be shall be'. The only way I could influence anything was by doing as well as I possibly could in training and for the reserves.

Howard's summer transfer business was under scrutiny by Everton's fans, some of whom weren't happy about the club's perceived lack of ambition. The players some of those on the terraces were so quick to criticise would prove their doubters wrong by writing their names into Everton lore. The manager had gone back to Liverpool to sign Alan Harper, who'd been part of the reserve team with Kevin Sheedy. Alan brought huge versatility to Everton at a time when there was only one substitute position. Because he could cover anywhere, for me, he was worth five players. He wasn't just versatile, but could play too and was a very good passer.

We'd lost Steve McMahon to Aston Villa, but Howard had used the money wisely, buying Trevor Steven from Burnley. Trevor brought speed, energy and natural wit to the squad; he could dribble, he could cross. He was good at everything, was Trev. He was a class act and you could see it right away. Straight away he made an impact in training, because he trains like he plays. He's one of the old school where training was the same as the games. He was the only player I've ever seen that was as good in training as he was in the game.

At Bellefield we could see that they were good players. I think you've always got to give new players time, and you can usually see very quickly from their attitude and how they do on the training ground whether they're going to cut it or not. Trevor came in and settled in straight away; it was like he'd always been there, because he could play. Alan could play centre half, right back, mid-field, he could play left back at a push. If you've only got a squad of 16 players and someone who can do four or five jobs you recognise how invaluable they are. For what Alan cost, how many positions he could play, and how many games he actually went on to play for us, he was unbelievable.

Impatient for success and big names, however, the fans weren't exactly pleased with these new signings, or the start to the season. Just 22,658 watched the curtain-raiser against Stoke and saw a Sharpy goal get us a 1-0 victory. Afterwards Philip Carter felt the need to deliver a vote of confidence in the manager. But it was our only win in the first five matches and pressure was building on Howard. We won at Tottenham, but then only drew at home to Birmingham.

A week later, on 1 October, we faced Notts County and I was back. Quite why, I have no idea. I don't think Jim was playing badly at all. Howard just made decisions, sometimes on instinct, sometimes just because he felt the need to shift things around so as to get the winning formula. Things just had a habit of happening without any reason or logic that was apparent at the time.

Looking back, I think if you did well in the reserves that certainly helped. At some clubs the managers were oblivious to what happened in the old Central League but Colin Harvey was still managing the reserve team and Howard was, of course, very close to him. So if things weren't going right he would look at people in certain positions and see the need to change. Fortunately for me at the time, goalkeeper was the one he saw the need to change. For me it was the end of a weird situation in the reserves; I wanted the first team to win and wanted Jim to play well, but also wanted to play myself. But I knew all along that I would never get in the first XI unless the team or Jim were playing badly.

I wish I could say my return to the starting XI transformed the team, but things didn't really pick up. A month after my return we lost 3-0 in the derby match, exactly a year after the Goodison massacre.

A few days later Howard made another new signing to address the lack of goals. We'd managed just seven in the league all season. Andy Gray had once been the most expensive player in Britain and had simultaneously been the PFA Player of the Year and Young Player of the Year. That was in the 1970s, however, and he'd been troubled with injuries for years. Many saw his £150,000 arrival from Wolves as the final throw of the dice, but we could see straight away that he had a spark.

Vocally he made a great deal of difference and his bravery was ridiculous. He wouldn't stand for any shit, which helped make everybody else play well. When you get good players they demand a certain amount of quality out of the players around them. If you haven't got it they can slaughter you. You have to be quite strong; you have to provide quality to people when you're passing or crossing or shooting or saving; and you have to demand it too. That outlook always brings up the standard of everything else at a football club. I think Andy brought up the standard of play around him, because he wasn't going to settle for anything less. He wanted the ball exactly where he needed it delivered, and if not he laid into you.

Above all, I think it took a bit of pressure off Sharpy. He'd come in as a bit of a novice and done well at first. But carrying that centre forward burden can be difficult for a young player. He needed someone to feed off every now and then. But when the two played together they could be a pair of battering rams too.

When Andy first came in he said he wanted to win things and people laughed at him. I suppose you couldn't blame them because we were 17th at the time and had hardly scored all season. Could I have envisaged the impact he'd make? Probably not, because I was just worrying about what I was doing. There's times at a club when you have so many people coming in and out of a door, nobody can see forward. Andy came in. He was loud, he was positive, he started to drain some of the negativity away.

At the same time Peter Reid had come into the team and was starting to make an impression. Howard had bought him nearly a year earlier, around the time I went to Port Vale. He'd been tipped for great things at Bolton Wanderers, but had been ravaged by a succession of injuries. Howard had got him on the cheap as everyone thought he was finished, and his doubters might have had a point. He played a handful of games for Everton, got injured and was then out for six months. He played a handful more games early in the 1983/84 season, having missed the start, and was then injured yet again. By the time he came back into the team around November I think

I'd only played alongside him four or five times. But as far as I was concerned whatever baggage he had stopped at the door. You can only judge someone when you've seen them. Reidy was a good player and a lively lad as well; another character in a dressing room that was becoming a louder and louder place to be. And a more ruthless place too. The banter and stick that went around was absolutely horrendous at times, particularly from him. He was a good laugh, but there was a side to his comedy that was very dark. But then if you want to survive on the pitch, you have to do the same off it.

Although training was good, and so was the atmosphere in the dressing room, on the pitch things weren't so great. We were the sort of team that could lose 2-0 at home to Norwich and then go to Old Trafford and win in front of 40,000 people, which was a big crowd at the time. But because we were struggling for goals and struggling at home, and because we were in Liverpool's shadow, Howard was coming under serious pressure from those fans that were still coming to Goodison. Returning home from training one afternoon he found his garage daubed with the spray-painted words 'Kendall Out', with the same slogan sprayed on a wall further down his road. Leaflets were also distributed outside the stadium demanding: 'Kendall and Carter Out. Bring back attractive winning football to Everton.'

To be honest I didn't feel under any pressure myself. Looking back it probably wasn't right, but I didn't worry about anyone else other than myself. I was selfish because I thought you needed to be selfish to be successful. Being so preoccupied with what I did was an important part of what made me succeed on the pitch. As a goalkeeper you can't make things happen in front of you; it's just impossible. Once you start trying to do that you're likely to mess up big time – and the one thing you don't want to do in a struggling team is to mess up for them. 'Let people do their jobs in front of me and then if I have to I'll do my job' was my view. I couldn't atone for a lack of goals, or a stray pass in midfield; but I could stop goals from being conceded and bring solidity and confidence to the defence. Those were the things that I worried about. I was oblivious and impervious to the woes of others.

Howard chopped and changed his team, trying to bring the winning formula back to Goodison. Things reached their nadir over Christmas 1983. On Boxing Day we drew 0-0 with Sunderland at home in a dreadful game and 24 hours later we went to Molineux to play Wolves. They were bottom of the table, skint and without a win all season. They turned us over 3-0 and their fans taunted Andy with shouts of 'Andy, Andy, what's the score?'

Howard was now in serious trouble. For the most part he had kept his head amid our struggles. He believed in what he was doing, in the pattern of play he was trying to create. He stuck to his beliefs and footballing principles. He didn't rant and nor did Colin; their observations were sensible. Don't forget, they'd both been top-class footballers and knew how to treat people.

But over Christmas, Howard briefly showed the strain. I think he realised that he might lose his job if we lost the next game at home to Coventry. I think he was so desperate at that stage that he just wanted people to tell him what he wanted to hear.

A couple of days before we played Coventry he pulled me aside in training, which he didn't normally do.

'Can you guarantee me a clean sheet against Coventry?' he asked.

'No,' I said, 'I can't.'

And the answer was true. I couldn't, I really couldn't. I couldn't guarantee that even if – as we were not long after – the best team in the world. When you're a goalkeeper, anything can go wrong and there's nothing you can do about it. The possibilities were endless. A team-mate could slip and leave you exposed, or the ball could take a deflection or a bobble, or the wind could carry the ball. Anything is possible in football. Ask David Seaman. When England played San Marino – the worst team in the world – in 1993, Stuart Pearce slipped him a bad back-pass and they scored after just 8.3 seconds. So for freak occasions like that, you can never promise nor guarantee a thing.

It was a stupid question to ask, but probably born of the stresses of the job. Yet Howard wasn't happy with my answer one little bit. So he called Jim Arnold over.

'Can you guarantee me a clean sheet?' he asked.

Jim could have answered, 'Not a fucking problem, boss,' and walked back into that team. But that wasn't Jim, he wasn't like that. He was selfless and honest and he looked out for me. So he gave the same answer as I did and said that he too couldn't guarantee a clean sheet.

Maybe Howard just wanted to see what I'd say, what Jim would say, to try and gauge our confidence and how we were feeling. Or maybe he was desperate, although he never gave the impression of being so. In any case he stomped off and when the team sheet went out on Friday – perhaps because he had no other choice – I was still on it. Jim, by contrast, never played for Everton again.

We played Coventry on the last day of 1983 and drew 0-0. Just 13,659 turned up, but their boos were loud at full-time. But we hadn't lost and Howard wasn't likely to start the new year looking for another job. What's more, I'd kept a clean sheet and played pretty well.

Because I was a bit insulated from the rest of the team and just focused on myself and improving, I went in at full-time with a big grin on my face. Howard saw this and came up to me.

'What the fuck's wrong with you? Why are you smiling?'

I said nothing and just stood there with a big smile. I think if it was anyone else he would have gone mad, but he knew when to leave me alone. He knew that I'd done my job well, done everything that was asked of me and enough to keep my place in the team. He knew that's why I was happy, so he left me alone.

⊐⊏

A WEEK AFTER THE COVENTRY GAME we travelled to Stoke City's

Victoria Ground for an FA Cup third round tie. Just over 16,000 people turned out for it, but I'm sure half of them must have been Evertonians. It was a proper footballing day: a bit cold and crisp, the pitch was a lovely playing surface and the atmosphere was great. All we could hear were our own supporters. Howard's team talk that day has since entered club lore. Before kickoff he instructed that the changing-room windows be opened.

'Just listen to that?' he said. 'Are you going to let that lot down?'

We were aware of football's importance to our fans; that it changed lives and destinies, that people named their kids after Everton players, that some people lived for the club. But in terms of utilising that as a motivating tool Howard rarely used the fan base; or rather, he picked his moments carefully. This was one of them. It was a brilliant piece of psychology. We just sat there listening to the shouts of 'Everton! Everton! Everton!' We got caught in a swell of positivity and by five to three we couldn't wait to get on the pitch. To be exposed to all that hope and expectation, there was simply no way we were going to lose. And we didn't. Goals by Andy Gray and Alan Irvine saw us through to the fourth round.

I suppose you look at turning points and everyone points to Stoke, or the Oxford United match a few days later. For me the critical moment between being a struggling side and a winning one came later that season, but the Oxford match is worth mentioning. We were playing a League Cup quarter-final at the Manor Ground and trailing 1-0 when, late on, Oxford defender Kevin Brock made a stinking back-pass that Inchy latched onto and did well to finish off. It brought us a draw, and six days later we turned them over 4-1 at Goodison. Less than a month after Howard had been on the verge of losing his job we were in the semi-finals of a major cup competition.

But the turning point couldn't have been that great, because we were taken to an FA Cup fourth round second replay against Third Division Gillingham. They were hard games and close games. Gillingham might have been two divisions below us but they had some good players, like Steve Bruce and Tony Cascarino. We went more than 200 minutes without scoring (or conceding) a goal against them. The second replay was decided on the toss of a coin and we were sent back down to Kent, where you could say that we were set up to lose. Priestfield was a hard place to go. It was a small stadium and because of its proximity to the coast was always windy. That night it was windy, raining and the pitch was heavily sanded. There was a big crowd for a ground like that. It was a Monday, so a bit different from our usual routine. In short it had all the makings of a giant-killing. But for once I enjoyed myself there; a brace by Sheeds and a goal by Adrian Heath eased us into the fifth round.

The games were now coming thick and fast. On Wednesday the following week we faced Aston Villa in the League Cup semi-final first leg at Goodison. We rode our luck a little bit and the referee missed Kevin Richardson handling a goal-bound shot. Goals by the two Kevins – Richardson and Sheedy – brought us a 2-0 win. The following week we lost the second leg 1-0 at Villa, but it didn't matter. We were Wembley bound. Less than two months had passed since those wretched matches at Wolves and against Coventry, when Howard's days as Everton manager had seemed numbered. In all we'd played 15 games in seven weeks and lost just that one against Villa. I, of course, loved the routine of matches on Saturday and again on a Tuesday or Wednesday. Playing was what I loved. Winning helped too. From being a team on the brink, we were on a brilliant league run, in the final of the League Cup and also found ourselves in the quarter-finals of the FA Cup, against Notts County after beating Second Division Shrewsbury in the fifth round.

That game is famous for an absurdly brave header by Andy Gray just after half-time. We were drawing 1-1 on a muddy pitch, with the wind and rain lashing around, when we got a free kick. Sheeds lifted it in and the ball evaded the challenge of Sharpy, falling to the back post where Andy slid in, nose almost touching the ground, to head home our winner. Andy was always better heading the ball than kicking it, which I think is why he went in head first.

In my mind there was a growing belief that we had become the best team in the league. Being an Everton player was becoming more and more fun, and training was more and more enjoyable. As things went on it'd become better still. The dressing room was lively, people taking the piss, playing pranks, but also talking of ways to improve. Every time we had a debate we'd just become that little bit better. You can tell a good club by the time people get in. If things aren't going well people get in at ten o'clock, five past ten. If things are going well they get in at half-past nine, quarter to ten. It does make a difference. When the car park is full at a club, you always know it's a good club; car parks say an awful lot about how things are going.

All this was down to Howard and the jigsaw he had created. Some players had been tested and hadn't worked out. There were gambles, such as Andy and Reidy, who would pay off in the end. But I think his real quality was the strength he had in his own convictions. He made his decisions and stuck with them. He never came out and criticised; he always backed his team, which was a major thing in building up loyalty and a sense that his team would do anything for him. He was a proper old-school manager, but had some very modern and progressive ideas on the training pitch. I don't know how much of this Philip Carter saw and I think it would have been very easy for him to have sacked Howard when things weren't going right. I don't know the conversations the two of them had, but obviously Howard convinced him enough to say 'carry on'. And thankfully it was the right decision.

The rewards for this patience would be plentiful over the coming years, but they were – I suppose – instantaneous as well. Less than three months after that dire defeat against Wolves – when Howard was so desperate for a sign that things might change he was asking if I could guarantee him a clean sheet – we were walking out at Wembley in the final of the League Cup. It was the first time Everton had played at Wembley for seven years and the club were 14 years without a trophy – an eternity for a club of Everton's stature. For our opponents Liverpool, by contrast, Wembley was a home from home and they hadn't even lost a League Cup tie in more than four years. In the period since Everton last lifted silverware, Liverpool had done so 17 times. They had that winning mentality that we sought to emulate.

Although we would eventually lose it after a replay, for me the 1984 League Cup Final represented a turning point in Everton history. Because we matched Liverpool every single step of the way, it confirmed my conviction that we were the best team in the league. In fact, because Liverpool were the best team in Europe it put us on the same pedestal. The first game at Wembley – a 0-0 draw on a muggy afternoon – hinged on a goal-line clearance by the hand of Alan Hansen, after Adrian Heath had dispossessed Grobbelaar and hooked a shot in. Had it gone in or we'd have scored a penalty Everton's barren streak would have been at an end.

What did I make of Hansen's handball? I think everything ultimately evens itself out in the end. Those sort of decisions can kill you on the day or save you – as might have happened in the semi-final when Kevin Richardson got away with a similar offence. But the good teams always get more decisions; that's partly why they're good teams. Whether it's something in-bred in the referees, or because they're cleverer players, I don't know, but you do get more decisions in your favour if you're at the top. You know, for example, that if you go to Old Trafford there'll always be a little bit more added time on if United need it. Part of it must be the human frailties of referees; they see famous players or large crowds and want to be liked and bow to their wishes. I've seen it myself when Everton have played a lower-league team with a lower-league referee; it put us at a massive advantage. I think the same thing sometimes manifests itself in the top flight too.

Whatever the reason, that day referee Alan Robinson didn't give us a penalty, nor did he send off Alan Hansen, and the match ended goalless. After all the hype and expectation we made the short journey to Manchester for the replay the following Wednesday. The match was massively anticlimactic and Liverpool won 1-0 through a Graeme Souness goal. But

Souness's strike was a sliver between two evenly matched teams and the way we had performed as Liverpool's equals massively boosted our confidence. All this was less than 17 months after the 5-0 annihilation and more recently the dark days of Christmas 1983. The transition from no-hopers to contenders had been incredibly swift but in other ways it didn't surprise me.

A fortnight later we met Southampton in the FA Cup semi-final at Highbury. It was a good ground to have the game on; everyone was packed closely to the pitch. It seemed to me at the time as if there were only Evertonians in the stadium. The ability of Scousers to get anywhere and everywhere in colossal numbers never ceased to amaze me and that day it was as if they had colonised north London. They helped galvanise us on those occasions, for it was often like playing at home. The crowd never discernibly impacted my play, but I think we all sensed the expectation. Subliminally they must have made an impression on me.

I played extremely well against Southampton. Everton held the balance of possession, but Southampton broke through our defence on a number of occasions and I held them at bay. Afterwards *The Times* wrote that my saves were 'brilliant enough to earn [me] a place in any national team, let alone that of Wales', which was nice. It was an open game and there were chances and near misses at both ends, but no goals. The game went to extra time and the crucial moment came when we got a late free kick; Sharpy touched it on and Adrian Heath stole in to grab the winner.

It was absolute bedlam. Highbury was one of the few grounds at the time that didn't have fences and fans poured on to the pitch. I was elated because I knew that with just three minutes to go we were heading back to Wembley, but at the same time I was trying to keep my concentration because you're most vulnerable after a goal. I knew that those last three minutes might well feel like an hour and I had to focus on that. But at the same time I was aware of the noise and the supporters and their joy, which I shared, although I tried to keep my emotions in check. The pitch was eventually cleared, the Highbury terraces rocking and cheering the name of our club, and before we knew it extra time was up and we were Wembley bound once more.

Winning does become a habit, but it also changes the complexion of the dressing room. With confidence players express themselves more. The humour becomes more cutting, and confidence accentuates that. We just took the piss out of each other unrelentingly; and the more we won the worse it became. I never gave much away, but the lads knew that the way of getting at me was by chipping me in training. It used to drive me mad. I'd respond by booting the training balls out of Bellefield, or by not using my hands in shooting practice. There's no more damning indictment of a striker than a goalkeeper who deliberately uses his head to save his shots, is there? In the dark days humour had been a way of protecting and insulating us from our woes. It was our release in lots of ways. But now we were on our way up to the top it assumed a different dynamic. It was darker and funnier and more biting than ever before.

The 1984 FA Cup Final was by far the biggest match I had played in until then. Everybody was desperate for a ticket. My family must have grown to about 300, because all of a sudden these aunties who I'd never even heard of started to emerge. People were stopping me on the street, asking if I had a spare ticket. Then there was the Wembley suit, which was for some reason part of the whole routine. We went and got fitted out at some shop that Howard or Reidy knew and got these suits for the pre-game routine; they weren't Armani, let's put it like that.

The media focus was massive too. There was a players pool that media organisations were meant to pay into and the players shared it out at the end. I wasn't interested in the slightest. I didn't want to talk to the press and the money you got from the pool wasn't worth talking about. All I wanted to do was train and focus on the task in hand. But I invariably got sucked into the whole thing. (I was persuaded by the lads to talk to the *Sun* one year and told that I had to ask for payment at the end, which I did, thinking that's the way it was done. To cut a long story short the paper published details of my request and made me look an absolute twat. But I was just doing what I was told to do; I didn't want the money for myself at all.)

The media focus in the build-up to the final was largely on Elton John, Watford's pop star owner. That suited me, to be honest. Watford had a good team and had ended the previous season runners-up. In John Barnes they had a player of world-class potential. But the impression we had of them was that it was just a big day out, whereas we were there to win it. Losing to Liverpool had only increased our desire to win. Having fallen at the last fence in the League Cup there was no way we were going to pass on another chance of glory. I never thought that we were going to lose, not ever. It's rare that teams get a second chance of success so soon after defeat and we weren't going to pass up on this.

We travelled down to our hotel in Beaconsfield after training on the Friday. Howard had invited the comedian Freddie Starr, who was a massive Evertonian, with us, and we woke up to him giving an impromptu slapstick performance on the lawns of the hotel. It added to the relaxed mood among us; relaxed and determined, which is not a bad combination.

Watford had some early chances, but once Graeme Sharp put us in front on 38 minutes our superiority was never in doubt. I don't remember being called into action much. There were a couple of testing crosses I had to claim but that was it. Andy Gray put the game beyond Watford six minutes after half-time, heading home a Trevor Steven cross. His goal was considered controversial because he clattered Watford keeper Steve Sherwood while rising for the ball, but it was just a collision of the kind you get in every game; there was no foul, and the referee was right to allow it.

Afterwards I was overcome by a confusion of embarrassment and excitement. I was thrilled to win my first trophy in senior football, and Everton's first in a generation. I didn't mind getting the medal but I didn't want to traipse all the way up to the Royal Box to get it from the Duchess of Kent. I just wanted to get the medal and go. I found it all incredibly embarrassing and this feeling never changed throughout my career. I never watched it afterwards on television; it just wasn't me. Even the lap of honour I found very awkward. I was very happy, but for me if you go to work and you do what you're supposed to do, nobody jumps around for you, do they? It might be nice but we'd just done what we were supposed to do, which was win.

Afterwards I went to the party at the Royal Lancaster Hotel. It was one of the few times I went to the post-match banquet, but my parents were there and keen to go, so that was great for them. Personally, I'd sooner have gone home to watch the telly. The next day we had the victory parade around Liverpool, which again I was not very easy with. I just found the attention embarrassing and always would; it was something I never grew out of.

But, happily for Evertonians, I was to be posed with plenty more awkward moments over the next few years.

# CHAPTER SIX
# D R A G O N

IT WASN'T UNTIL I HAD STARTED playing for Bury that the thought I might play international football entered my head. I was naive and un-assuming; these things just didn't occur to me at all. I know this might sound like false modesty but that's just the way I thought. I never played for any of the schoolboys, Under-21s, anything like that. I didn't even know they existed.

It was about 12 games into my Bury career when the reality that I might one day represent my country was put before me. We were still living in Ramsbottom and my Dad had come up to stay with us for a few days. I'd been out at training or something like that and when I got back home my dad and Eryl were having a furious row. The cause of the consternation was over who I was going to give my first Wales cap to. I was incredulous.

'What are you fighting over that for? I've barely even made the Bury team, never mind the Welsh side,' I protested.

But it was clear that some people were already thinking ahead.

(My dad got the cap in the end and it went in his grave with him after he died. I think the worms have it now.)

I don't think Wales was ever foremost in my mind when I was growing up. I never thought until I was 20 that I would get the chance to play professionally, so the idea of playing internationally never crossed my mind. Until I got to a league club I was never going to play for my country, so it was pointless thinking in such terms. My outlook was always to take one thing at a time: get a league club, see if you're any good at that; if you're not you can go back to hod-carrying; if you are then hopefully somebody will pick you up and give you a chance.

I followed Wales as much as I followed all professional football when I was growing up in the 1960s and 70s. But this was long before football's 24/7 TV era, so the reality was that it was limited to a few snatched highlights of Brian Flynn and Leighton James and the Home International game. Wales often played at Wrexham's Racecourse Ground in those days, which wasn't far from Llandudno, but I didn't go to any games.

Coming from Llandudno I wasn't ever brought up with strong nationalistic sentiments. It just wasn't that kind of place; it was a sleepy seaside resort with lots of Scousers and Irish there. With my English mother and Scouse uncle I was probably a typical son of the town. Maybe had I been brought up in a Welsh-speaking village I would have had a different outlook. There was just one Welsh school in Llandudno and although I was taught the language I found it a difficult subject to get my head around. It's a shame because I would have loved to have been able to sing the Welsh national anthem in Welsh. But despite all this I love my country and there's no prouder Welshman than me.

Towards the end of that season with Bury I was put on standby for a European Championship qualifier in Turkey. That effectively meant I was third-choice goalkeeper. Knowing what I now know about the FAW (Welsh FA) there's no way that they would spend the additional airfare transporting someone who was almost certainly not going to play. I think the standby routine was a case of me playing on the Saturday, then calling the Wales manager that evening to find out if I was needed. And that was it! But at the time I was just chuffed to bits to have come to the notice of Mike England.

Indeed the call-up wasn't long in coming and I joined up with Wales not long after I signed for Everton. There was nothing glamorous about any of this. The FAW sent a letter to the club and I was called into the office and told the news. It was before the days of instant communication so I suppose, looking back, it was quite old-fashioned.

How did international football differ from the club game? Well, when I was at Bury they gave me a kit to train in. When I was at Everton they gave me a kit to train in. When I was at Wales they threw the kit in the room and you had to scrounge your own. You had to be there early on a Sunday, which was the first day of an international get-together, to make sure you got some kit, or you could have a yellow shirt, green shorts, purple socks. They were proper porn-star shorts in those days that got smaller and smaller with washing.

If you think international football is glamorous, you should come and spend a few days with the Wales team. We went everywhere economy class, and we went everywhere at seven o'clock in the morning. We never travelled at a decent hour, presumably because it cost too much. The logistics were farcical. One time they couldn't fit us all on one plane, so half the squad went and half the squad had to wait for a flight the next day. On another occasion, on the way back from Scotland, the bus driver got lost because it was foggy, couldn't find the airport and had to drive us all the way back to Manchester. He got the sack on the way back down, but the lads just took the piss out of him. The poor man was crying while he was driving the bus.

Our manager in those days was Mike England, who had played for many years as a centre back for Wales and Tottenham in the 1960s. He was a brilliant manager who loved his country and loved his players, and we loved him too. His passion for Wales and football was infectious and it was impossible not to be caught up in his enthusiasm.

Before every game, Mike would come around and speak to us all for a couple of minutes each. He'd tell me I was the best goalkeeper in the world and I'd leave the dressing room feeling like a giant. His instructions were always good, but he was absent-minded and eccentric too. When we played France in 1982 I remember him telling Peter Nicholas how to man-mark Michel Platini, who with Maradona was probably the greatest player in the world at the time. But Mike being Mike couldn't remember his name and kept referring to him as their 'number ten'. 'You mean Michel Platini, boss,' said Peter. 'That's the one,' said Mike, as if he was some obscure Second Division player. Whatever he said though was obviously spot on, because we beat the French on their home turf. His catchphrase was 'DK'. He'd go around and tell you that you were 'DK – different class'; I don't know how many times we told him that class began with a 'C' but it never seemed to register. Another time we were training to play Northern Ireland on a rugby pitch and were doing set-piece routines in front of the rugby posts, which are nearly two feet higher than football goals. I wasn't getting anything and Mike was absolutely slaughtering me.

'But they're rugby posts, boss,' I yelled.

'Yeah, but that's no excuse,' he retorted. That's just the way Mike was.

Mike absolutely loved Ian Rush. Whereas he gave us a couple of minutes each, his pre-match pep-talk with Rushy was always 15 minutes long. But we used his obsession to all our benefit. If there was ever anything we wanted, we'd put Rushy forward to ask for it. If I asked in training if we could have a five-a-side Mike would say no. But if we got Rushy to ask five minutes later it would be: 'Great idea, Rushy, let's have a five-a-side.'

Some of the time he was under great pressure and would snap. We played out in Iceland and got beaten 1-0 and Mike came in and went absolutely berserk. It was quite out of character.

'I suppose all you fuckers will be going out tonight fucking drinking and all that,' he ranted.

The room went silent.

Then one of the lads piped up, 'Yeah, but Mike, you organised a disco.'

The rage immediately subsided: 'Oh, all right then, fair play.'

However serious it was with Everton it never was with Wales. I suppose it was an antidote to the intensity of the First Division. Silly things happened, like us not having enough players for a match. When we played Iceland in 1984, Jeff Hopkins was out of the squad and had come to watch the match as a supporter. He came into the dressing room to wish us good luck beforehand. Mike clocked him straight away.

'Have you got your boots?' he asked.

'Yeah, they're in my car.'

'Well, go and get them then. You're on the bench.'

Jeremy Charles went off after 50 minutes and Jeff then had to come on. He'd probably had a pie and a pint before he knew he was playing but he did really well and we won 2-1. It wasn't enough for Mike though, who – seemingly forgetting the strange circumstances of his call-up – then tore into him in the dressing room, asking him why he wasn't doing this and that. We had to tell Mike to give him a break! How can you be short of substitutes for an international match? It was frightening.

But being with Wales was great and having someone like Mike made it all worthwhile. International football was frankly amateurish. It was so bad it was good, but in an odd way that brought the lads together. It was always an honour to represent your country, but the reality was that many aspects of international football were rubbish: the early starts, the terrible travel arrangements, awful hotels, the long distances.

You never made any money out of playing for Wales. We got £100 when I first started plus £100 for a win and £50 for the draw. We used to get pin money in those days off Adidas, but it was never much. Alun Evans, the FAW secretary, did all the expenses, and was very meticulous. By the time he took your room service bill off your match fee and your phone calls and your additional tickets for friends and family (we got four complimentaries each), you didn't have any money. Even when we got £300 a win, I never made anything. I don't think I earned a penny out of Wales. In fact, I probably owed them money in the end.

The committeemen, by contrast, always enjoyed the good life. Their routine went something like this: meet at a hotel in Wales, have a meal, get bladdered, stagger to bed, get up, fly across Europe, get to the hotel, get smashed with the other committeemen, receive their presents, go to bed. On the day of the match they'd have a long lunch, get bladdered again, and maybe watch some football and fly home. They were useless. Utterly useless. I remember some of these old farts falling asleep at breakfast. The president at the time was an old boy from North Wales, Alfred Ellis, who was a nice man. He'd stand there in his vest sometimes singing the national anthem. It was a bizarre setup; a complete contrast to Everton, which was super-professional by comparison.

Mike England was paid peanuts to do the job – just £22,000 as full-time manager, which later dropped to £10,000 when he went part-time. I got more doing the bins than that. The FAW showed him no respect and he had to fight for everything. He fought for better hotels, better travel, better conditions for the players. But it was always going to be a losing battle against the FAW blazers. It always was a losing battle for whatever manager was in charge.

There was one old boy who would hand the caps out. He had terrible eyesight and when we went up to collect the caps we all told him we were George Berry. He'd say, 'Well done, George, well done, here's your cap,' again and again. It didn't occur to him that he'd handed out six of these things to people purporting to be George Berry, who at the time was the only black Welsh footballer and had a massive afro. This was the calibre of person running Welsh football.

The main man was Alun Evans, who the players knew as 'Snowy' because of his awful dandruff. We used to send bottles of Head and Shoulders on a silver salver up to his hotel room to try and wind him up. Every small FA has an Alun Evans-type figure and they probably need such a person in order to survive. He was wily, cunning and Machiavellian and has probably been unfairly maligned over the years. He had to strike a very delicate balance between keeping the players happy, the committee happy and making enough money for the FAW to survive. He would bamboozle the committee into thinking he was wonderful with everything, but this would inevitably bring him into conflict with whoever the manager at the time was. He was abrasive, stubborn and unyielding, and he and Mike would have some terrible rows.

The flipside was that he was also a maverick and constantly thought on his feet. He was a mini Arthur Daley, but it gave him the capacity to help us. Sometimes we'd be held at some sort of obscure border – particularly in the early 1990s after the fall of Communism – and we'd need $50 each to exit the country. Alun would be there with a roll of notes sorting it all out. Of course this also got him into hot water on some occasions and he was later linked with allegations of financial impropriety, but I think he only ever acted in what he believed were the best interests of the Welsh game. I remember coming back from a game in Saudi Arabia and Alun had the £25,000 match fee in cash in a plastic bag. He later got in trouble for this, but actually he was just holding on to it so that he could get the best exchange rate possible for the FAW. That's just the way he worked.

International football not only meant that you got to see the world, but parts of the planet that few other people got to visit, particularly during the 1980s. Communism was still in full swing and half of Europe was cloaked behind the Iron Curtain. I'd hardly been anywhere at that stage, but my first ever trip with Wales was to the USSR. This wasn't just Russia but Tblisi, the capital of modern Georgia. It was frightening and fantastic at the same time. It involved flying to Moscow and then hanging around in the airport for six hours to make sure we were tired. There was then another long flight to Georgia. The Soviet Union seemed to be suffused with this ever-present smell of cigarettes and garlic. There were soldiers everywhere; that's all we ever seemed to see. But we were lucky at the hotel and had a choice of rooms: we could either have one that had a plug in the bath, or one with curtains on the windows. That's how bleak it was.

But it could have been worse, we could have lived there. Our impressions were formed watching from the bus window. Everybody seemed to be going through the motions of life. The streets were busy with people working – there were old ladies brushing the pavements and things like that – but they weren't really doing anything. Nobody smiled. It was as if they were being watched. I said at the time that they must go home and shut the curtains and laugh like mad; I'm sure it was the only way you could keep sane in a place like that.

Dai Davies was still first-choice goalkeeper, so in some ways I was just along for the ride. There was lots of hanging around. We didn't take ourselves too seriously, but for the Soviets there was a sense that it was more than just a game. It was 'win at all costs' for them. We travelled all that distance to win the game but it wasn't going to affect our life if we didn't. We had the feeling that if we'd have beaten them it would have affected their lives. At the time there were lots of rumours and innuendo about Soviet athletes and some of the things they had to go through to get victory, as well as what happened if they didn't. Football is just a game and when it gets to that level of seriousness it's just wrong.

Luckily for them they read the script correctly and ran out easy 3-0 victors. The stadium was meant to be full to its 80,000 capacity, but all we saw were row upon row of soldiers. After the game Joey Jones said that he didn't know what a Russian looked like because he'd only seen the back of their shirt. It was that kind of game. How they never went on to win the World Cup during that era is beyond me, because technically they had one of the best teams on the planet, but they never seemed to travel well. Perhaps that's not surprising given some of the travel conditions. The next day at the airport our two pilots came staggering around the corner bollocksed out of their heads and told us the flight had been delayed. We never found out if it was fog or because they were just pissed.

I made my Wales debut versus Northern Ireland in May 1982 at the Racecourse Ground for a Home International match. The same night Tottenham were playing Queens Park Rangers in the FA Cup Final replay, which had a huge bearing on the crowd. Just 2,315 turned up. It was more like Bury than international football, but I couldn't give a monkey's. I just wanted to play. My dad was there and I was playing against my hero, Pat Jennings. We won 3-0 with goals by Rushy, Alan Curtis and Peter Nicholas. It couldn't have gone better and I couldn't have been happier.

But when we travelled to play France a few days later, Dai Davies was back in the team. I sought Mike out and asked him why I wasn't playing.

'You've had your turn, haven't you?' he said.

'Fair enough,' I said. There was never any arguing with Mike.

My return to the team wasn't long in coming though. When European Championship qualifying started the following September against Norway, I was Wales's number one and besides one game, after I'd been dropped by Everton after the 5-0 defeat to Liverpool, that's pretty much how it remained.

The core of the Wales team in those days was the Swansea lads who had come in and played so well in the First Division. In some games there were six of them playing – Chris Marustik, Nigel Stevenson, Alan Curtis, Ian Walsh, Robbie James and Leighton James – but over time the team evolved so that it had a genuinely top-class core.

Manchester United's centre forward Mark Hughes broke into the team around the same time as me. Sparky is probably the most schizophrenic footballer I've ever encountered. Off the pitch he was quiet and charming, but on it he became something else, a bit of a madman – albeit with controlled aggression. He was a terrible trainer as well, but came into his own when it was shooting practice and would be constantly trying all these outrageous overhead kicks and volleys. He was technically excellent and you could see even at that young age that he was going to do very well both at home and abroad.

Like me, Ian Rush was an unassuming character. If you met him in the early 1980s you would never have imagined he was one of the most famous footballers in Europe. Rushy just let his playing do the talking. He was a truly magnificent footballer, one of the best I've ever played alongside. The tactics very often were just to defend and defend and defend. We always knew that we'd get at least one chance, and if that chance fell to Rushy then it usually counted. We knew we weren't the best side in the world, but players like him could make a massive difference.

Kevin Ratcliffe, my Everton team-mate, preceded me in the Wales team by a year or so and in 1984 not only did he become my captain at Goodison, but for my country too. He was a great captain, more so perhaps for Wales where we relied on his voice to stand up for us against the in-effectual blazers who were meant to be running the show. What did Rats bring to the Welsh setup? Organisation. A voice. And he made sure everybody was looked after. He was still quite young, but he was very mature. In his performances he led by example and wasn't afraid to have a go at people. Nor would he stand for any messing about and if he thought things were right or wrong off the pitch, he'd go and say something. A lot of the time we'd have grumblings about this, that and the other, and he'd go and sort it out. But also he anticipated a lot of things. He did a lot of work that we didn't see: like he'd say, we're staying here, doing this and doing that, and he'd go and have a word with different managers, saying, 'That's not happening, I'm not having this.' He was really proactive, like a union rep, making sure everything was all right for us. And you knew if you had a problem he'd say, 'That's sorted; that's not happening now.' He was a leader on and off the pitch. Don't get me wrong, he was still one of the world's worst wind-up merchants, but he had that aura about him when he was captain. You could walk in an airport and look at the team, you'd know which one was the captain.

Qualifying for major tournaments was tough. Wales have only managed it twice – at the 1958 World Cup and the 1976 Euros – and it was harder in the 1980s than it is now. When the European Championships are hosted in France in 2016 there will be 24 finalists, but for most of my career there were just eight. Only 24 and not 32 countries qualified for the World Cup. We had some good results against some top countries but it was never quite enough and we always seemed to slip up in what were meant to be easy matches. We beat Romania 5-0 but could only draw with Norway, who at the time were supposed to be international whipping boys. We drew 4-4 in Yugoslavia but were beaten by Bulgaria. Such slip-ups were costly. In the 1983 Home Internationals we lost in Cardiff to Scotland, but a fortnight later nearly beat Brazil at the same venue, giving up a 1-0 half-time lead to draw 1-1.

We took virtue in being underdogs. When we played England in the 1984 Home internationals we beat them 1-0 at the Racecourse Ground, which was a big result. There was no anti-English sentiment, we just saw them as a better team and that we had nothing to lose. The crowd got right behind us and we defended like mad. That was essentially the game plan whenever we played one of the big countries – defend like mad and hope Rushy got us a goal. When Barry Horne came into the team the tactics evolved a little bit – we defended like mad, got Barry to smash their best player and hoped Rushy got us a goal.

⌶

TO QUALIFY FOR THE 1986 WORLD CUP IN MEXICO we had a tough but not insurmountable group of Iceland, Spain and Scotland. In European qualifying the seven group winners went straight to Mexico along with the four best runners-up. The rest of the runners-up went into playoffs, two facing each other, with the third playing the best country in Oceania. It gave us a decent chance of making the World Cup for the first time in a generation. In the press there was a lot about the financial predicament of the FAW. The Home International Championship had just been scrapped, leaving a huge hole in its finances, and there were loses of £100,000 expected. Alun Evans was telling journalists that if we didn't qualify Welsh football would be in 'serious difficulties'. There were question marks over Mike England's job and suggestions that the players might lose their small match fee. There was also speculation of the FAW being unable to meet its obligations to FIFA and UEFA, which would have meant being kicked out of international football.

We opened qualifying in September 1984 against Iceland in Reykjavik. A victory was assumed to be a foregone conclusion. We'd started World Cup qualifying there four years earlier and run away 4-0 winners. At the time Iceland were considered international whipping boys, and we were told that not winning wasn't an option. But they had some good players, eight of whom played professionally on continental Europe. Perhaps a more telling reflection of their standing was when they drew 2-2 with us in Swansea at the end of 1982 World Cup qualifying.

Either way, we got off to a nightmare start on a damp and cold September night. We played badly and were unable to exert a hold on the game. Iceland had some good early chances and went in front on 51 minutes when their centre back, Magnus Bergs, rose to head home a corner and score the only goal of the game. I was probably at fault for the goal and afterwards Mike England went apoplectic, telling the press that we deserved what we'd got. 'This was absolutely disgraceful, a professional disgrace,' he told journalists. 'It was an embarrassment for Wales.' As I mentioned, it didn't stop us from going to the disco he'd arranged for us afterwards. That's just the way Wales was though; it was amateurish, but that ethos probably kept us together and in a strange way made us better.

Nobody gave us a chance when we went to Seville to face Spain in our second qualifying match a month later. Spain were a good side, albeit a very different proposition to the great Spanish team you see today, and had the notorious hard man Andoni Goikoetxea at the heart of their defence. The previous summer they reached the final of the European Championships in France. We didn't play badly against Spain, but they were just too good for us and ran out 3-0 winners.

Rushy had been missing from those first two qualifiers, but returned when we met Iceland in Cardiff in November. Even at that early stage of his career, Ian was considered a world-class player and he would have made a difference to any team that he played in, not just one of Wales's size and paucity of resources. His presence gave us all a lift and we beat Iceland 2-1, after goals either side of half-time from Mickey Thomas and Mark Hughes.

The full impact of Rushy's return would not be felt for almost another five months when we faced Scotland at Hampden on 27 March 1985. The old Scottish stadium was one of the largest in Europe at the time and possessed one of its most ferocious atmospheres. Spain had been defeated 3-1 there a month after they'd beaten us. But with Scotland you never knew what you were getting, and like us they could win big games, but then lose what they'd consider easier ones. I'm sure they considered us easier opponents.

At the same time there was always more pressure on Scotland – as there was England – than there ever was on Wales. Nobody cared about us, whereas the newspapers would be full of stories about England and Scotland. We'd sit on the bus and read them aloud and laugh ourselves silly at some of the stories. But in Wales there was no *Daily Record* and the national press left us alone. It certainly made our lives easier.

It was our hundredth game against the Scots and for some players there were was history underlying the fixture. Ahead of the 1978 World Cup we had faced Scotland in a do-or-die qualifier in October 1977 at Anfield. The outcome of that match hinged on an incident in the second half when Scotland's Joe Jordan handled the ball when challenging for a header with David Jones. Unbelievably the French referee awarded a penalty to Scotland, which they scored. A late Dalglish goal killed off our hopes. Joey Jones and Mickey Thomas carried particularly vivid memories of that night and what followed at Hampden gave some kind of catharsis.

Rushy was the difference on a night of high passion and excitement. Scotland seemed on a knife edge and as we unsettled their play we grew in confidence. Mark Hughes had a chance when Rushy robbed Dalglish and sent him through, and Rushy was involved in a few goalmouth scrambles. At the other end I was forced to cut out a difficult cross from Jim Bett as Dalglish seemed set to pounce. The crucial moment came when Hughes challenged Alex McLeish in the air and, as the ball dropped on the edge of the Scotland area, Rush struck a superb volley that flew past Jim Leighton into the roof of the Scotland net, almost before the goalkeeper could move. It was a goal worthy of winning any game.

From being dead and buried, we suddenly found ourselves on the same number of points as Scotland and Spain, although the latter had played a game less. Our next qualifier came against the Spaniards in Wrexham at the end of April 1985. Me and Rats were flying high with Everton and a week earlier we had defeated Bayern Munich in an epic encounter at Goodison.

We weren't the only Everton players picked for our country that night. Although he was brought up in South London, Pat Van Den Hauwe was born in Belgium and had spent his first few years there. It meant that he was eligible to not just play for the country of his birth, but – because he held a UK passport – all four of the home nations. Had he chosen Belgium, Pat might have ended up going to a couple of World Cups, but at the time assuming Belgian nationality carried the burden of national service, which he wasn't too keen on. Bobby Robson also talked to him about playing for England, but Pat was also getting a barrage from me and Rats to get him to join up with Wales. To be fair, we probably harassed him a bit, but I think when he heard that the social scene was better with the Welsh side that swung it for him.

Pat's debut came against Spain on 30 April 1985, as Joey Jones was suspended. The Everton core of the team came in on a high as we were about to be crowned league champions and were in the final of two major cup competitions. Me and Rats had played in virtually every second of 27 league, cup and international matches since 22 December and not lost one of them; Pat had played in most of them too.

Did Everton's run give our country momentum going into that game? Playing for Wales was always like going on a little holiday; it was a break from the tension and strain of club football. You'd go to a hotel, have a rest and a change of surroundings, and unless you were coming back from Eastern Europe you went back into training on the Friday slightly refreshed. Even though Howard Kendall hated us going on international duty I always felt the benefit of it. In this case, coming as it did so close to the end of the season, I actually think playing for Wales helped Everton.

Against Spain Mike England had told us to play cautiously and with patience and advised us that our chances would come. We were playing in Wrexham, which suited the northwest-based players better, although I preferred Ninian Park. Wrexham always seemed to be vast, whereas Cardiff was tight, compact and nosier. Even a draw would put great pressure on Scotland and give us a fighting chance in our last qualifying match against them. We bade our time and got a lucky break just before half-time, when there was a mix-up between the Spain goalkeeper and one of his defenders. The ball fell to Rushy on the goal-line and he stabbed it in. Seven minutes after the break we put the game beyond Spain when they failed to properly clear a free kick, and Mark Hughes scissor-kicked a volley into the goal. We were in no mood to surrender that advantage and scrapped and grafted. In the closing stages Hughes sent Rushy through and he scored a third goal. It rounded off an incredible night.

It meant that we went into the final group game against Scotland on 10 September 1985 with our destiny in our own hands. If we won we'd top the group and send Spain into a playoff. If we only drew, Scotland's superior goal difference would consign us to third place and we'd be going nowhere.

A win for Scotland would probably send them straight to Mexico, so there was a lot at stake.

For once we were marked out as favourites for the match, even though history favoured the Scots. They had won 60 of the countries' 100 encounters to our 18, and 10 matches in Cardiff to our 6. Scottish fans were travelling down in huge numbers and several thousand Welsh tickets had apparently ended up in the hands of their supporters. But the pressure was on them and in the build-up to the game the Scotland manager, Jock Stein, had been tetchy with journalists, which suggested he was a man under pressure. We didn't let any of that bother us. In fact we just laughed at all the bad headlines the Scots were getting.

Mike England didn't approach the game any differently from how he'd have treated a country like Iceland. He just came around the dressing room and gave us all 30 seconds each – until he got to Rushy and gave his standard 15-minute pep talk! He was never hugely into tactics or game plans; his approach was always more focused on building up passion and team spirit. His assistant Doug Livermore was always very thorough on tactics though. It was a nice contrast.

In the warm-up I was posed with an unusual situation. I'd always train with five or six balls, but one after another they went into the huddle of Scotland fans behind me and did not return, so I was left without a single ball to warm up with. I gestured to the crowd, but the Scottish fans just laughed. So I left my penalty area and sought out Jock Stein and asked him to have a word. He came straight back with me and gestured to the crowd for them to return the balls. One after another they were chucked back – they just had so much respect for him, and so, after that gesture, did I. He was very fair and just wanted the game played in the right spirit.

We went out to a cacophony of noise and Welsh expectation and after withstanding some early pressure took the lead on 13 minutes. Peter Nicholas challenged on the left side of the Scotland area and the ball fell kindly for him. He drilled it across the area and Mark Hughes turned and shot cleanly past Jim Leighton. It was a brilliant goal and the battle lines were drawn for what became a particularly intense and physical battle. The Dutch referee let a lot go. Scotland really came at us but we battled and imposed ourselves on the game, fighting every inch of the way.

Everyone was pumped up for the game. I think some of the emotion became too much for a few people. For some reason Alun Evans and Mike England had a massive set-to outside the dressing room at half-time and punches were nearly thrown. Alun was quite abrasive and if he said something stupid Mike was the sort of person who'd go for him. But it was also that kind of occasion.

Nine minutes from full-time came the crucial moment of the game. Scotland had been pummelling long balls to David Speedie and Graeme Sharp all night. On this occasion Sharp headed the ball across to Speedie who, in trying to control it, shot it straight at Dave Phillips's arm. Dave was standing over him and I'm not sure what he could have done to get out the way, but the referee still awarded a penalty. I thought it was an absolutely scandalous decision and as Davey Cooper lined up to take it I told the referee in no uncertain terms what I thought of him.

I was never one to study penalty-takers before matches; I actually think it's quite a negative thing and am fairly superstitious like that. I go on instinct, and my instinct this time was correct. When Cooper shot I dived low and to my left and got my hand to it, but there was a slight dip in the pitch and it slipped in under me. I felt sick in my stomach; cheated.

The last nine minutes of the game were chaotic as we sought the goal that would have brought us redemption and a place in Mexico, but we were done for. In fact it was Scotland who could probably have won the game, but the draw was enough for them, while we were finished.

There were chaotic scenes at the end as the Scotland players celebrated and some of their fans ran on to the pitch. We trudged off, but greater dramas were unfolding.

In the chaos at the full-time whistle, Jock Stein had collapsed on the touchline with a heart attack. He was filmed by the TV cameras being carried off the pitch and down the tunnel into the Ninian Park dressing room. We were initially oblivious to all this, just concerned with our own woes. We got back in our dressing room: tired, deflated, pissed off. But that mood quickly ended.

I can't even remember how we heard, so great was the shock that greeted it. But somehow, within minutes of the final whistle, we learned that Jock Stein had died in the adjoining dressing room. He was a few weeks short of his 63rd birthday. After that there was no bitterness or anger. Just numbness and a horrible, unyielding silence.

# CHAPTER SEVEN

# LEGEND

PEOPLE ALWAYS TALK ABOUT TURNING POINTS that transform a club that is struggling into one that can succeed. For most Everton fans in that era Stoke and Oxford are the games that spring to mind. They were important in giving an Everton side that couldn't buy a win some momentum and may well also have saved Howard's job, too. But the one that counted for me was the League Cup Final. I know we lost the game in a replay, but for more than 200 minutes – notably in the first match at Wembley – we matched the greatest team in Europe kick for kick, chance for chance. We were very unlucky not to win. Afterwards, despite defeat, self-belief grew. We knew if we could match Liverpool we could match anybody. And a few weeks later we'd gone out and won some silverware – Everton's first in almost a generation.

We went on our summer break looking forward to the 1984/85 season. You always look forward as a footballer. You go into the season hoping you'll do well, hoping the team goes well. Sometimes you get a good feeling, sometimes you think it might be a struggle. With Howard it was always good; it was always the same. We did the same things pre-season, so there were no nasty shocks when you went back; you knew what you were getting into. We knew we had a good team. I didn't ever expect us to do as well as we did, to be fair. Football has a habit of kicking you in the bollocks and when you think you're going to do well, you never quite get to where you think you will. As a footballer the desire to do well is always within you, but you keep a lid on it because you can't guarantee anything.

Over the summer I had agreed another contract with the club. I got more than the five quid raise that I'd asked for when I initially got into the first team, but it wasn't the best money. Far from it. I don't think I was ever anywhere near the top earners, but it never bothered me too much. I wanted the security of knowing where I was going to be for the next four years. If I was able to make that commitment to the club it was one less thing for me to worry about. In any case, money was a by-product of what I was doing and what I was intent on doing, which was being the best goalkeeper I could possibly be.

The season opened with a return to Wembley for the Charity Shield match against Liverpool, who were league champions. We placed a lot of importance on it. It was partly a revenge match and partly another chance to use them as a yardstick. We put in a commanding performance in a game that was settled when Sharpy broke into the Liverpool area and took the ball around my opposite number Bruce Grobbelaar. When his shot was blocked on the line by Alan Hansen it rebounded back off Bruce and into the net.

We were delighted to open the season in that manner, but a week later we got a rude awakening. Tottenham came to Goodison and battered us 4-1.

The following Monday we went to West Brom and lost again – 2-1. Why did a team that had lost just a few times in the last six months of the previous season, which had won a cup and just beaten the best team in Europe, fold twice in 48 hours? I don't know, except we never seemed to start seasons well. We didn't play well as a team. There were no individual mistakes or one person that cost us the game. We all shared a part in our failures, just as we did our successes. For a fan it must seem the worst thing in the world to lose two games like that. But football doesn't give you time to dwell too much on stuff. It always makes you think about the next match. There's always tomorrow.

Results did pick up soon enough, but some of our performances were shaky. In the European Cup Winners' Cup first round we played University College Dublin – a student team, basically. Everyone expected a walkover, but they held us to a goalless draw in Ireland and in the last few minutes of the second leg at Goodison had a shot that clipped my bar. We were winning 1-0 at the time, but had it gone in they would have gone through on away goals.

With every game we played the belief in the squad grew. Confidence is the thing. Once you've built momentum then things just happen for you. There were times when we were battered, just didn't get going, but there was an inevitability about the result. We'd scramble a goal, or get a penalty – or I'd save a penalty and then we'd go up the other end and score. A winning streak brought the aura of invincibility. People can sense it. They start believing and everything goes their way.

The games were all hardcore, though. I don't think we ever had an easy, easy game. There was a crazy topsy-turvy game against Watford, who were bottom, at Vicarage Road that we led 3-1, 4-2 and 5-3. But Watford fought all the way and brought it back to 5-4. Lots of games were like that.

Two of the most memorable games in the autumn of 1984 were against Liverpool and Manchester United. Liverpool had had a bad start to the season but even though we – as a team – knew we were as good as them, for the fans there was still a hoodoo. They were our nemesis. But this was to end in spectacular fashion. When Gary Stevens hit a long punt upfield, Sharpy was on the end of it; he flicked the ball past Alan Hansen, then volleyed into the top corner of Grobbelaar's net from 30 yards. It was a fantastic goal, and the win it earned us reinforced how far we'd come.

We came off the pitch at Anfield thinking things couldn't get any better. But when we played United at Goodison a week later they did. United were top of the league and title favourites. We beat them 5-0 with a performance that was flawless. We couldn't have played any better and it would have been hard to pick a fault. When you come off the pitch you normally say, 'I could have done that, maybe done that.' But that day it was impossible to pick up on anything. There were lots of games like that by the season's end. We scored a variety of goals; lots of different people scored goals; we defended well, we attacked well; we just had a whole thing going. We put pressure on people and made them make mistakes.

There was always an added edge when we played Liverpool or United, particularly in the first part of my career when there were more British players than foreigners. I used to love playing against them, not only because it was Liverpool, but because they always had the best players. It was always going to be a different challenge because the noise and intensity of the crowd meant you had to concentrate especially hard and there was a good chance your team-mates wouldn't hear you. In most derby matches you're wasting your time shouting because the noise from the crowd is absolutely deafening. You also had to be very controlled in that environment. I was always aware of what was at stake, but it was no good trying to force things to happen, do things that you wouldn't normally do; you had to control the aggression, control your thinking and try and detach yourself from everything that was going on around you to focus on what you were doing. It was quite difficult at times with everyone screaming. As a player in a derby you've got to detach yourself from the emotion that people are showing on the terraces and focus on the reality of what's happening on the pitch.

For me there was an added edge. Every time we played Liverpool the 5-0 always came back to my mind. That's all I ever thought back to every time I played them: 'You cost me so many months of my career; you beat us 5-0 and you basically fucked my career up for a bit.' I never needed much motivation for any match, but that gave me an extra edge.

After those wins against Liverpool and United people were now going to games expecting us to win. We went top during the first week in November and practically stayed there until the season's end. As a goalkeeper, it was quite difficult sometimes because you've got to concentrate on what you're doing without getting caught up in it all. It was for the same reason that I didn't watch *Match of the Day* because they just go on and on about what might happen. I didn't want to hear it. All I wanted to know was what was thought on the training ground and in the dressing room. That was enough to focus on. I never thought about the last game, only about the next one.

Howard had only made one signing during the summer, which was Paul Bracewell from Sunderland. Paul brought calmness and an ability to tidy things up to the side. He made his living for the first couple of seasons passing back to me (this was in the days when a keeper could pick up a back-pass) and getting a round of applause from the Goodison faithful for it! He was a great foil for Reidy; they hunted in pairs and they closed down well. Brace had a good brain on him too. I don't think he was particularly the quickest player in the world but he had a touch of class. Off the field he fitted in well, which was important to our success. He had a good sense of humour; his favourite saying was something like, 'When you've got a couple of days come and look round my house; I'll show you my west wing and I'll show you my east wing.' He was one of those kind of lads; full of fun, but with the desire to win everything all the time.

All of that team had a real will to win and didn't like standards dropping. You'd soon know on the pitch if you weren't pulling your weight because they'd tell you. That sort of boldness stems from a good team spirit and a good understanding of the people you've got playing alongside you. If they're your mate as well as your team-mate you won't have any qualms about giving them a bollocking if they've messed up.

A couple of months into the season Howard made another new signing, bringing the left back Pat Van Den Hauwe from Birmingham City. Pat came in for John Bailey, who I thought was very unlucky to lose his place. I knew John inside out and he was a much better all-round player than most people gave him credit for. He was a fine attacker. He was honest. He could tackle. I wouldn't say he was a cleverer player than Pat but he at least looked like someone who naturally played on the left side and could get a good cross in, whereas Pat was more a pure and simple defender.

Much has been said and written about Pat, who has attracted his own mythology. But for me, the 'psycho' sobriquet has been overstated. Pat was always a bit of a pussycat as far as I was concerned. There were two Pats; there was the Pat that trained every day and the Pat that had had a drink. I always found him to be nice as pie; never a threat to anybody. He could be a nuisance sometimes, but I never found him threatening. To me Pat's aggression masked a lack of confidence. He wanted to be liked and built up an image that I don't think anywhere near reflects who he is. He's got a reputation of being a hard man but I just didn't see that in him.

Pat was openly aggressive in his game, I'll give you that, but I never found him to be stupidly aggressive. He'd front people up, but it's easy to front people up on the field because somebody always breaks it up. It's like in school when the teacher's round the corner, where kids stand up to each other, start pushing each other, then the teacher comes and they all run off. Pat didn't like anybody taking liberties, and he would kick people. If someone wanted to fight him he'd stand up for himself, but all of our team did. But I don't think he ever sought out trouble.

As well as the busy league campaign we were also playing in Europe. After the trip to Dublin, which was at once a visit into the known – because it was just over the Irish Sea – and unknown – because we knew nothing about UCD – we went to Czechoslovakia to face Inter Bratislava. This was of course behind the Iron Curtain and to step into a Communist country was to step back 20 years in time. The journeys were always ridiculously long, because of a lack of direct flights or – if you were on a charter – airports at which you could land. Then there was loads of bureaucracy at the borders, and all you wanted to do was get to your hotel and get some rest and start preparing. As for the opponents, it's not like now, where you can turn on the telly and watch a million games on Sky. If you wanted to know how they played you had to go and watch them. You had to really do your homework. That said, we just played our way; we didn't change for anyone.

Inter Bratislava weren't the best of opponents. We went there, got a 1-0 win, and at Goodison two weeks later turned them over 3-0. We always had our away matches first that season, which was a big help. After that match there was a five-month gap before our next European tie.

Although we were flying high in the league, we didn't think about where this might lead us. We were enjoying our football, enjoying the buzz in the dressing room and on the training ground. Nobody missed training, everybody was in earlier each day, and nobody wanted to miss a game. But we tried to keep title thoughts at the back of our minds. When it got to Christmas and we were still near the top, we began to think that we had a chance. When you're doing well things tend to fall into place. You get the breaks, the lucky penalties, the fluky goals. But you make your own luck as well.

Sometimes for me, as a goalkeeper, it was harder, because everyone else switches off when you're winning by four or five goals. Sometimes I had to keep myself in the game and keep people in front of me on their toes. When you're dominating a game it becomes harder because you do more shouting than anything physical. You've got to concentrate because a save you might have to make in the last minute might be the one that wins you the game. And even if victory is in the bag, it's no good for me winning 5-0 if I let go and concede and it's my fault. That would spoil the day for me. I had to constantly think about trying to keep myself focused; that there might be one more shot I had to save.

That happened when we played Tottenham at White Hart Lane on 3 April 1985. We were riding high at the top of the league, but Spurs weren't far behind. It was a genuine six-pointer and had they won it might have changed the complexion of the title race. The momentum that had been with us for months could have switched their way. We went into a 2-0 lead with goals from Andy Gray and Trevor Steven but, playing in front of their biggest crowd of the season, under floodlights, there was still plenty of fight left in Spurs. With 17 minutes to go Graham Roberts buried a 30-yard shot past me and suddenly we had a game on our hands.

The moment everyone remembers came three minutes from the end. Glenn Hoddle crossed the ball into the area and from point-blank range Mark Falco headed towards my top corner. I stretched for it and tipped it over the crossbar. What more can I say? It was straight at me and I'd saved plenty like that on the training ground. I always knew I was going to get it.

For many people that was the moment we won the league title. Maybe they're right, because we held on to win 2-1 and Spurs eventually finished the season 13 points behind us. But at the time you never think of the significance of what you've done, or say to yourself, 'That was a great save.' My team-mates certainly didn't congratulate me. Ratcliffe yelled at me: 'Why didn't you catch it? Why are you fucking giving a corner away?'

In the next day's Daily Mail, Jeff Powell described it as 'the most astonishing save since Gordon Banks left Pele dumbfounded in Mexico'. He added: 'Southall twisted through the night air like a marlin on the hook to divert the ball over the crossbar.' I suppose it's a nice way of saying, 'It was right at him'.

The good thing about journalists writing nice things about you and deciding that you're a 'good' player is that they start seeing things in different ways. If you mishandle the ball you suddenly 'did well' to parry, instead of being slated for spilling a shot. If you flap at a cross you're suddenly 'unlucky' coming out for a ball, instead of getting lost in no-man's land. You can see even now when they like a goalkeeper; no matter what the goal he's conceded, he was 'unlucky' when trying to save it. On the other hand, if the press don't like somebody he's considered too slow or over the hill or not trying hard enough. They all have their own agendas, don't they? When the media decided that they liked me, it meant I could do anything I wanted.

Soon after the Spurs match I was named the Football Writers' Player of the Year. It's the older of the two player of the year awards and in winning it I was the first Everton player, the second Welshman (after Ian Rush) and only the fourth goalkeeper (after Bert Trautmann, Gordon Banks and Pat Jennings) to ever do so. No goalkeeper or Welsh player has won it since. It was nice to get the recognition but part of me felt a little uneasy to get all the plaudits when the players in front of me had also done so much.

I went down to an awards ceremony at London's Savoy Hotel with Howard Kendall, but I was hardly able to speak, having contracted laryngitis after all the shouting I'd been doing on the pitch. These dinners were never my thing anyway so I told Howard to do the speech for me. Unfortunately he fell off his chair and off the stage, and ended up splitting his pants. He had to get them sewn up backstage, before saying a few words after I'd collected the award from the former FIFA president, Sir Stanley Rous.

Obviously all the attention was on me, which I was embarrassed about. But by then I'd developed a nice line that the journalists liked and which simultaneously played down my own role and talked up my team-mates: 'I've watched some great games this season.'

THE GREATEST GAME OF THE 1984/85 SEASON, indeed possibly the greatest game in the history of Everton Football Club, came at Goodison in the semi-final of the European Cup Winners' Cup on 24 April 1985. We had strolled through the quarter-finals against Fortuna Sittard in March, winning 5-0 on aggregate, but our semi-final opponents, Bayern Munich, offered something else. They were one of the great club sides in European football; a club that had won the European Cup in three successive years in the mid-1970s. They had famous players like Lothar Matthäus, Dieter Hoeness and Klaus Augenthaler in their line-up. By contrast, hardly anybody outside England knew who we were.

We didn't let this faze us. We never let anything bother us, ever. We just played our game. Reputations counted for nothing. When we travelled to Bavaria for the first leg Kevin Sheedy and Andy Gray had picked up injuries. We didn't have a large squad, but we had a close one and we trusted the players we had in reserve implicitly. So when Alan Harper and Kevin Richardson came in for Kevin and Andy we knew they would do a job. And they did just that. We played with maturity and commitment, like winners, although I didn't think I played that well myself. I was beaten on one occasion by Michael Rummenigge, the younger brother of Karl-Heinz, but Richardson was there to clear the ball off the line and to safety. We drew 0-0 and we knew we'd get them at Goodison.

We knew the immensity of the occasion, that this was our final. If we beat Bayern we would beat anyone. On the day of the match we had a short training session in the morning, something to eat, and then went for a rest in the afternoon. It was a typical match-day routine. But when we got to Goodison we knew that this was very different. There were people everywhere, singing and dancing and chanting our names. The team coach took 45 minutes to drive around the ground to the players' entrance. It was unheard of. The place was mental.

I always loved playing under the Goodison floodlights, but this was different; this was truly something else. The crowd never normally affected me in any way, but on this night – the only time in my life – they worked as twelfth man. We could see how much it meant to everyone there and we wanted to win it for them. But the crowd also intimidated our opponents, jostled and battered them and in the second half almost seemed to suck the ball into the Gwladys Street net. You can beat 11 men, but you'll never beat

50,000 of them. I'd never seen anything like it before and never will again in my lifetime.

But for all the hype and hope it was Bayern that took the lead, seven minutes before half-time. Ludwig Kögl was played in around the back of the defence and was one-on-one with me. I stood up and blocked his shot, but the ball fell to Dieter Hoeness who swept it home. At half-time Howard told me to kick the ball long, to put the pressure on them. We bombarded them; the players with the ball and the crowd with the noise. Normally there's a separation between the crowd and the pitch, even at a stadium like Goodison where the supporters are close to the players. But here we were one. We stood together and they simply couldn't live with us. The intensity of the occasion overwhelmed Bayern. Sharpy equalised three minutes after the break and Andy Gray put us ahead on 73 minutes. A late solo effort by Trevor Steven finished them off and almost brought the lid off Goodison. Andy and Reidy had given the Bayern players a good kicking and they left the pitch bloodied and shell-shocked.

It was an unbelievable night and something that will probably never happen again. It was a perfect storm; an inherent understanding between the players and the crowd. For me it was better than winning the league, better than winning the cup, better than anything that happened before or since.

After that night what happened was, in a strange way, anticlimactic. We still had ten games to play in all competitions and we carried on doing what we'd been doing all season: winning.

Another game people often recall from this final sequence is when we played Sheffield Wednesday. I always remember Wednesday games because Hodgey usually played, so I'd have a chat with him, and the crowd were brilliant; a really great place to play. I love playing at Hillsborough; I think it's a proper old-fashioned football place. I always think there's a strong link between Sheffield Wednesday and Everton too and at the time Mike Lyons was there as well. Anyway, whenever we went there we either did well or got absolutely battered. There was never really an between really. On this occasion we got battered. We had one chance and Andy Gray scored it; I must have made a dozen saves, including one from Imre Varadi, which I scrambled around the post. It was a good save, but people mostly remember it because it was on the opening credits for Match of the Day. That win and a victory over Queens Park Rangers the following week brought us the club's eighth League Championship.

By then all thoughts were on Rotterdam and the European Cup Winners' Cup Final against Rapid Vienna. Howard put a shadow side out against Nottingham Forest the previous Saturday, but there was no way I was giving up my place and I played. And then it was off to the Netherlands.

We travelled to Rotterdam knowing that we wouldn't get anything less than a win. It would have been impossible after Bayern Munich. There was no way Rapid Vienna were going to get anything from the match; no chance whatsoever. The De Kuip Stadium was packed full of Scousers. Their ability to get places in huge numbers, even when the city was on its knees economically and unemployment raged, never ceased to amaze me. I'm sure there were always a few scallywags among them, but there was never any sign of trouble. Evertonians wherever they went were always loud, passionate and good-natured. English fans at the time had a reputation as troublemakers, but Evertonians were just never like that. On the day of the final they were playing games of football in Rotterdam's squares with Rapid fans and the local police.

The thing people ask me about most regarding the final was my goal-keeper shirt. It was red, a colour many Everton fans consider sacrilegious. But there was an odd logic to me wearing it. Because Rapid played in green and white stripes I couldn't wear my usual green, nor white. Black was out because that's what the referees played in, and so was blue for obvious reasons. Yellow was also out because that was only allowed in international matches. Which didn't leave an awful lot more choice. Later at Everton I wore orange and pink and I think now you can wear whatever you want. But back then it was a bit more straightforward: primary colours, which pretty much left red.

Because it was when they lifted their first – and so far only – European trophy, Rotterdam was a night that will be forever engrained in Everton history. I think the most surprising thing was that it took us so long to get in front. Andy Gray put us ahead on 57 minutes after Sharpy latched on to a bad back-pass to set him up. Trevor doubled the lead 15 minutes later after a scramble from a corner. Annoyingly the Austrians pulled one back through Hans Krankl with six minutes to go, but within a minute Sheedy had restored the lead. Don't get me wrong, it was a good night, but after Bayern Munich it was an anticlimax.

We had just 64 hours after lifting the trophy to pick ourselves up and get ready for our next match, the FA Cup Final against Manchester United. We flew back into Liverpool late that night. It was quite businesslike and there was no wild partying. The next day I travelled to London with Howard to collect my Footballer of the Year award at the Savoy. Then it was to Beaconsfield to prepare for the FA Cup Final.

A year earlier there was almost too much build-up before the final with Watford. It had been incessant for weeks. But because it had been game after game after game this time there wasn't the same sort of intensity. We literally got to the hotel on the Friday, did our pre-match routine as normal and then the next day we were at Wembley.

If the Cup Winners' Cup Final win had been anticlimactic, I suppose you could say what happened against Manchester United was disastrous. We'd put together an epic FA Cup run that year, full of memorable encounters and imbued with an ethic that we would never be beaten.

In the quarter-final against Ipswich at Goodison, Kevin Sheedy scored twice from the same free kick: his first effort to the right of Paul Cooper's net was disallowed as the referee hadn't blown for it to be taken; Sheeds kept his calm, and placed his retaken effort to Cooper's left. His left foot was like a wand. I don't think many players in football history could have done that. But with five minutes to go we were 2-1 down. I'd let a Kevin Wilson shot slip under me and Romeo Zondervan put them in front. We just bombarded

Ipswich and when we did that no one could live with us. Derek Mountfield grabbed a late equaliser and we took the replay 1-0 four days later at Portman Road.

Sheeds and Mountfield were our heroes again in the semi-final against Luton at Villa Park. They took a first-half lead through Ricky Hill, and again we just battered them in response. Derek scored 14 goals that season, which was phenomenal for a defender and these days would be enough to make you the club's top scorer. Derek was a good defender and a much better player than some people give him credit for. His goals defined him in many minds, but he was part of one of the most successful defences in the club's history too. He was deeply committed to his wife, Julie, and we used to slaughter him for it. She used to come to Bellefield and they'd get cushions out with 'Derek' and 'Julie' written on them and have a little picnic in his car, which was like Knightrider's. Then when he got inside the training ground itself he'd give her a call to let her know he'd got there safely. He was like that, Derek. I used to room with him and be party to his soppy phone conversations. He'd say, 'We've just had tea, and I had steak and fifteen chips and sixteen peas,' and I'd be sat on the other bed shaking my head. He was certainly under the thumb at home, but a really good footballer when he put his domestic bliss behind him.

Derek was a key man on many occasions. In the Luton semi-final we pushed him up and he caused mayhem in and around the opposition box. Four minutes from the end we got a free kick and Sheedy's effort bobbled into Les Sealey's net. Luton were shattered and there was only going to be one winner from then on. In extra time we got another free kick: Sheedy crossed, Derek headed home and we were heading back to Wembley.

The final probably came a day too early for us. We had plenty of chances to win the match and hit the woodwork twice. But the energy and verve that had carried us through the previous six months wasn't quite there in the same quantities. United took us to extra time and we seemed to be heading for a replay when Norman Whiteside cut inside Pat Van Den Hauwe and curled a left-footed shot past me. I thought it was my fault, but no one blamed me and I haven't looked at it since. Norman later told me he'd practised that technique again and again. It was enough to win the match for United and it ended the most extraordinary season in Everton's history on a flat note.

Little did we know then that things were about to take an even more dramatic turn for the worse.

## CHAPTER EIGHT
# EXILE

THAT EVERTON TEAM WAS SET TO DOMINATE English and European football for years and years. You just couldn't see anybody else that was going to trouble us. Obviously there were good teams but there was no one else we feared anywhere. There was simply no point. We'd already overtaken the best team in the world in Liverpool, hadn't we? They'd dominated European football for years and now we thought we could do the same thing.

As if to emphasise our new-found dominance over Liverpool we met them the Thursday after the FA Cup Final at Goodison. It was a bit of a homecoming for us, but many of the lads had already switched off for the summer. Howard played a load of fringe players, like Bails, Ian Atkins, Rob Wakenshaw and Paul Wilkinson, but we still won 1-0.

The following Wednesday all eyes were on Liverpool again, when they played Juventus in the European Cup Final. It was Liverpool's fifth final, Juventus's first. Liverpool had never lost at that stage of the competition before. They had that sort of winning mentality that we now also believed we had. But what happened that day was one of the most notorious episodes in football history. I watched at home on my television with rising disbelief and anger.

There was trouble before kickoff between Liverpool and Juventus fans. People had been drinking all day and wanted to fight. Bottles were thrown between the two sections and then Liverpool supporters charged at the Italians. This caused a huge crush and a wall collapsed. Thirty-nine Juventus supporters were killed. It was horrendous, utterly horrendous. If that wasn't bad enough, as body bags were still being pulled out of the stadium, they went ahead and played the match. Can you imagine? I still shake my head when I think about it now, nearly 30 years later. Thirty-nine people had died and UEFA still made the two teams play the match. It defies belief. What they should have done, of course, was to call the whole thing off and, if they needed to play, do so behind closed doors 24 hours later. But this wasn't the only catastrophic error of judgement UEFA made, was it?

History has blamed the fans because they're an easy target. I think sometimes it's very easy as an Everton fan to look at Liverpool Football Club and blame them for Heysel. I don't blame them for Heysel whatsoever. I blame other people for Heysel. I've seen how UEFA sweep stuff under the carpet at first hand. Anybody who caused any grief they'd just get rid of them, because that's their way of doing things. And look at what happened after Heysel, a tragedy that started with them.

Maybe Liverpool fans bore some of the responsibility, but too little attention has been focused on the true causes and UEFA's responsibility. Why was the game played at the Heysel Stadium, which was completely unfit – it was utterly substandard – for such a match? Why was drinking allowed to take place all through the day leading up to the game? Drinking makes people want to fight at the slightest hint of grief, and unlike the Dutch police – who were great prior to the Everton game a fortnight earlier – the Belgian police had shown themselves to be incapable of defusing tense situations. I think the final, disgraceful decision to play the game after all those people died showed just how incompetent and detached from reality UEFA were. If they were capable of making such an appalling decision, then you do have to wonder how many bad decisions they might have made when planning that match?

Obviously people died and the tragedy has always got to be remembered in the context of those lives lost. But from a footballing perspective what followed next was one of the most disgraceful, disgusting episodes in the game's history.

UEFA, in conjunction with the British Government, placed an indefinite ban on English clubs playing in European competition. Why would they do a thing like that? Why would they punish Everton, whose supporters had behaved impeccably in Rotterdam? Or Norwich, qualified for Europe for the first time as League Cup winners? Or any of the thousands and thousands of fans who had travelled to support their teams all over Europe without the slightest hint of trouble? Think about that for a moment. Then think about English clubs' record in Europe over the previous ten years. Seven times they had won the European Cup, three times the UEFA Cup and we'd also just won the Cup Winners' Cup. Now, I'm not one for conspiracy theories, but it couldn't be that UEFA wanted to break up that dominance, could it?

English supporters had a reputation at the time, but every nation has a hardcore fringe of idiots, a group of 1 or 2 per cent bent on making trouble. I've been all over the world and seen it. Italy, Turkey, Holland, all over South America there have been major incidents, but never have clubs been banned from international competition before. But then those countries have never dominated competition in the way that English clubs did back then.

The British Government was also culpable, putting pressure on the FA and bowing to UEFA's every demand. They wanted to toe the line and didn't want to have the British shown in a bad light. But that didn't make it right. It was a complete disgrace and all sorts of people who had no part in this horrible tragedy were punished. As a player, to not have the right to compete with the best clubs in Europe was a devastating, bitter blow. You look back and you see careers destroyed by that European ban. I'm sure it must have been awful for a fan as well. It was also to have appalling consequences for Everton at a time when we were considered the best club side in the world.

工

HOWARD WAS A GREAT MANAGER and, although it was sometimes hard to take when confronted by it, one of the things that made him great was his ruthlessness. He was quick to judge a player and if he didn't fit his plans was swift to move them on. He kept the squad fresh, which kept us players on our toes. But that didn't mean we had to like or agree with his decisions.

Shortly before preparations for the 1985/86 season started he pulled one of his surprises. Andy Gray had been our talisman since his arrival during what many saw as the dark days of November 1983. He was vociferous, confident and aggressive and helped forge great self-belief among a young squad. He could also play a bit as well. But when Howard brought in Leicester City's striker Gary Lineker for a club record fee in summer 1985, one of the first things he did was to sell Andy to Aston Villa.

Andy was devastated and many supporters were outraged. They deluged the local newspapers with letters protesting at his treatment. Personally I would have bought Gary and kept Andy, but I wasn't paid to make those decisions. Howard said that it would have 'destroyed' Andy to have played in the reserves or from the bench, which may have been the reality. Adrian Heath had missed the second half of the 1984/85 season through injury and was now back to fitness and we had the England under-21 centre forward Paul Wilkinson, who we'd signed from Grimsby, as well as Sharpy, of course. There were also questions about Andy's long-term fitness. But the irony was that Gary Lineker hardly ever trained; he hardly knew what training was. On a Friday he just sat in the bath.

There was never any sentiment with Howard. Once you were done you were done and as soon as he thought he could get Gary, Andy was finished. Maybe he thought we'd change the way we played as well. It's hard to know what was in his mind, but I'd have rather kept them both to give us a different combination of pace and aggression. With fresh legs and competition Andy probably would have lasted and done better. But the proof's in the pudding, and Gary scored 40 goals while Andy never reached the same heights he managed at Goodison again.

Gary gave us a different dimension and we could play more directly with him in the side. He was a bit like Rushy at Liverpool; if we were under pressure you could just boot the ball over the top and he'd get on the end of it and score a goal. He was a great finisher, every bit as good as Rushy. The difference was that Ian was a brilliant defender too – Liverpool and Wales's first line of cover – but Gary never really defended. As goalscorers I thought they were both top class, but Rushy had more to his game overall.

Among the players there was never any resentment that Gary's arrival had led to the departure of Andy; he was a nice fellow and he settled in quickly. You knew where he'd be on a Friday morning: never on the training ground, just sat in the bath relaxing. Then he'd go out the next day and score. There wasn't much to his game and you could spend months and months trying to analyse what he did. Essentially he just had an almost subliminal knack of being in the right place at the right time; a great understanding and awareness of what was going to happen. He didn't score many from outside the box. But inside the box, he could finish anything. It didn't matter whether it came off his arse, his face or his knee, he'd score a goal. He'd be quite happy doing nothing else, but when you look at his goalscoring record it's difficult to fault that outlook.

For Everton every season during this era began with the Charity Shield match at Wembley. For us this season it offered the chance of revenge over Manchester United, and we took it with Adrian Heath and Trevor Steven scoring the goals in a 2-0 win. Everyone remembers my role in that match for a T-shirt I wore afterwards emblazoned with the slogan 'I Love My Wife'. Why did I wear it? A consequence of being a famous footballer is that you're a source of tabloid stories and that summer I had my own dalliance with the red tops. Somebody had gone to them with a kiss-and-tell story and I saw the T-shirt as a way of getting back into Eryl's good books. Did it work? Eventually, about a year later, I think she might have forgiven me. What nobody remembers is that I wasn't the only one wearing a T-shirt declaring love for Eryl: when we played Sheffield Wednesday my old team-mate Martin Hodge wore a T-shirt saying 'I Love Neville Southall's Wife Too'! In the decades that have followed we've had T-shirts hidden under kits that reveal everything from support of sacked dockworkers to declarations of faith in God; and I started it all!

Gary Lineker's goals defined Everton during the 1985/86 season. I don't think that we necessarily moved on as a football team, but his pace and finishing offered us different options. However, we didn't start particularly well and although we beat Manchester United in the Charity Shield we lost our first league game 3-1 to Gary's old club, Leicester City. There was a 3-0 defeat to Queens Park Rangers on their Astroturf too.

Compared to the artificial pitches now, their 1980s ancestor, Astroturf, was obscene. It was literally carpet on top of concrete; we'd go out and burn ourselves to bits. At first I went out in tracksuit bottoms, but I hated the lack of freedom and felt that all the padding I needed slowed me down. So I gave up and just plastered myself in Vaseline and slid out as if it was normal grass.

It didn't hurt so much – my main fear was banging my head if I landed badly – and because no other goalkeepers did it through fear of burning themselves it got the opposition thinking I was fearless and a bit bonkers. Creating that illusion was always a good thing.

I got myself into trouble when I was sent off against Chelsea at Stamford Bridge in October. It was a strange match because in the warm-up I was absolutely flying and felt brilliant. I don't think I've ever felt like it before. But then everything went wrong. In the 19th minute I brought David Speedie down in the box and ended up getting booked for arguing with the referee, Vic Callow. I was furious because I felt Speedie had cheated me. But then I thought I'd had the last laugh when Nigel Spackman missed the penalty. I hadn't. In the second half I came racing out of the area and caught the ball ten yards outside the box. Callow got out his notebook again and I was off. I tore off my shirt as I stomped off the field and Rats took over in goal. Howard told the press afterwards that I'd 'let the lads down' and that they were all disappointed in me; but maybe I did them a favour – Rats kept a clean sheet, whereas I'd let in two. Certainly he's lived out on that ever since!

The lack of European football meant that sponsors and the football authorities moved in different ways to try and find a replacement. One of the first satellite channels, Screen Sport, came up with the idea of a 'Super Cup' involving the biggest teams in the First Division. Everyone hated it: the fans, the clubs, the players, the managers. Everyone except me. Admittedly it wasn't European football, which I longed for, but my view was that if you never try it you'll never know if it will work or not. I also wanted to play as often as was possible.

Howard used the competition to blood some youngsters and because I was insistent that I was playing no matter what, I also got a few chances to captain Everton. Thus while everyone remembers the competition for empty terraces and it being a poor substitute for European football – which in fairness it was – I remember it as a great opportunity to take new responsibilities, and learning to also focus my game on helping others. In the autumn of 1985 we played group games against Manchester United and Norwich City and would progress to a spring semi-final, which we won over two legs against Tottenham.

The First Division was where the real competition lay, however, and that season was one of the most open and competitive campaigns in years. Obviously there was Liverpool and Everton fighting it out at the top, but West Ham had the best season in their history and might have won the title. Manchester United, Sheffield Wednesday, Chelsea and Nottingham Forest were all good teams; George Graham's Arsenal were also an exciting and talented young side who would go on to do great things a few years later – although we smashed them 6-1 when we met at Goodison in November.

In December 1985 I signed my second new contract in the space of 18 months. It was a six-year deal, apparently the longest the club had ever handed out. I didn't want to play anywhere else and didn't see the point in signing for just two or three years. So I asked for a deal that would take me well past my 30th birthday so that I wouldn't have to worry about re-negotiating in the medium term. There were no incremental wage increases or anything like that. I suppose I could have earned more money by re-negotiating every couple of years, but I didn't care about anything like that; I just wanted to play.

We were troubled by injuries throughout the campaign, which may or may not have had a bearing on the outcome of the league title. Peter Reid and Derek Mountfield were both missing from September for five and six months respectively. Pat Van Den Hauwe switched to centre back and Adrian Heath dropped into midfield, but we missed Derek's goals and Reidy's experience and tenacity, as indeed we did Andy Gray's. But we rallied and adapted and played really well. When we beat Liverpool 2-0 at Anfield in February we went three points clear at the top. It was only our third league win there in 16 years; both previous times we'd gone on to lift the title, so the omens were certainly good.

⊐⊏

TEN GAMES OUT from the end of the season I suffered my own injury nightmare. We'd just played Luton at Kenilworth Road – another artifical surface – and in the last ten minutes had uncharacteristically thrown away a 1-0 lead to lose 2-1. We were still top but it had given Liverpool a little bit of momentum in the title race. I came away from the plastic and concrete pitch with the usual collection of grazes and bruises but was okay. The irony was that after surviving that, a complete bog of a pitch would do for me.

During midweek I travelled with Wales to play Ireland at Lansdowne Road. Ireland's footballers shared their stadium with the country's rugby players and you can imagine what the pitch was like, coming not long after the Five Nations rugby championships (as it then was) in one of the wettest cities in Europe. It was a mudbath and Mike England criticised it before-hand, calling it 'diabolical'. We were winning 1-0 through a first-half Rush goal when, in the 66th minute, I went up for a routine high ball with John Aldridge. As I came down my foot landed in a pothole and I ended up in a heap on the floor. I was unable to get up and the physio and the doctor and all the other players were standing over me thinking I'd broken my leg. There was no break, but I'd dislocated my ankle and torn all the ligaments. It's funny: it was the worst injury of my career and I felt no pain at all. I was in shock, but it never hurt in the slightest. After they'd carried me off I asked the doctor if I could take a shower – that's how little it hurt.

Instead they sent me to hospital, my foot pointing in the wrong direction. They put me in bed and examined me. A nurse asked me to take all my gear off. I told her I wasn't able to do so, but she wouldn't help so I ended up taking my own boots off. A doctor then came in and announced that he was going to pop the ankle back in the socket. I told him to 'fuck off' – there was no way I was going to be conscious when they did that! So they gave me anaesthetic and when I woke up a few hours later, my leg was dangling from a support and there were ten people stood there looking at me. It was a teaching hospital and all the student doctors and nurses had come in to look at me.

I was in hospital for two days before I returned to Liverpool. The prognosis was not good and I was warned that I could be out until Christmas. Given how much I hated the close season, the prospect of nine months on the sidelines was not good at all.

At Bellefield the club doctor told me that I may as well not bother coming in, that I should take a holiday. I knew then what I was facing: I hated pre-seasons, I didn't like going on holiday, I hated the emptiness of it all. I knew it was going to be a long, hard, boring time on the sidelines.

I didn't care what the doctor said, there was no way I was not coming in. I didn't go on holiday or take any break. Eryl would drive me in to Bellefield and I'd start my fitness regime. My leg was all plastered up, but I'd have a ride on one of the bikes with one leg, do some sit-ups and just try and keep myself ticking over. There was no point in being unfit when I got back. At home I still did the gardening, anything to stave off the boredom of not playing. I dug up all of my garden with my leg in plaster and carried heavy sacks. The garden looked good, but when the Everton physio John Clinkard saw the state of my swollen leg afterwards the club weren't very happy.

John was brilliant with me, even though I must have driven him absolutely mad. He was a very good physio and had probably saved Adrian Heath's career the previous year when he also had a bad knee ligament injury. A good physio like that can save a club millions of pounds in replacements, and John was one of the best I dealt with. But how John didn't punch me I just don't know. I was a complete nightmare. I used to get to Bellefield at 8.30am, or just afterwards, and go to the gym and have a hard workout. Then I'd go to the inside pitch and do some work on the Astroturf pitch, throwing myself around, changing direction, keeping the reflexes going. In late morning I'd go to John for my 'official' workout. I have no idea whether he knew what I'd been up to, but he wouldn't have approved. He'd tell me that all I could do was two laps of the pitch, or something like that. I used to give him loads of grief: 'Come on, you twat, I just want to run!' But John just took it all on the chin; he was the model of patience.

The physio work was complemented by top-rate care at the hospitals. Everything was private, so I was always jumped to the front of the queue. It was something I was deeply uneasy about. I remember going to hospital to have my plaster off, and I used to walk through all the other people waiting. I used to think, 'All these people have been waiting here for hours and hours and I'm just going straight in.' I must have looked an absolute twat to them; straight in, straight out.

Match days were less of an ordeal than they might have been. I was looked after by Joe Murray, a friend of Howard's, who was what you might describe as something of a colourful character. He had had his brushes with authority, but was a cracking fellow that we all knew from the training ground. He was a tiny guy, a proper Scouser and real gentleman, who had stories about everything coming out of his ears; he really kept my spirits up. When we got to the stadium I'd go into the changing room, speak to the lads and sit on the bench, then go back with Joe. He was just a great old fellow, and he helped ease the boredom of being on the sidelines.

Everton were top when I got my injury but Liverpool were fast closing in, with West Ham not far behind. Liverpool's form after the Anfield derby was amazing and they won ten of their last eleven league matches, drawing one. Everton's form wasn't bad either, but we slipped up a couple of times; against Luton, then Oxford when Lineker missed a hatful of chances and they scored a winner with moments left. Liverpool won the League Championship by two points and a week later beat us again, in the FA Cup Final at Wembley, where they came back from behind to win 3-1. I felt utterly sick at Wembley when I walked around the famous old stadium on crutches while all the lads were preparing to face our great rivals. That's when it struck me just what I was missing.

People sometimes say that we wouldn't have lost out on both trophies if I hadn't been injured at a key stage in the season. I'm never one to dwell on things that are outside my control and this was one of them. My replacement Bobby Mimms did well. He had signed from Rotherham United the previous May and was an England Under-21 international, but this was his first taste of the big time and he acquitted himself well. Bob was a good player, a lovely guy, but could have been a far better goalkeeper had he worked harder on the training ground. He was the complete opposite of me: completely laid-back, not bothered about training in the slightest. He went on to play for Tottenham and Blackburn, where he's now goalkeeping coach, but probably had the best season of his career standing in for me.

During what was left of the season Bob only conceded four league goals, plus the three in the FA Cup Final, so I don't think you can say he was responsible for anything. I look at what he did for the side and thought about what I could have done and I don't think that the outcome of the title race would have been any different. Goalkeeper was definitely not the weak link.

I don't think Bob was ever fazed coming in to replace me. If he had been a different sort of personality it might have been hard, but being so laid-back it didn't bother him. Bob was so relaxed as to be horizontal and I think that helped him. He came in and there was not too much fuss; he made some decent saves and the lads trusted him. That's the highest praise you could give him; to have the trust of players of that calibre was no mean feat. Unfortunately he was unable to stop Liverpool's inexorable march to the league title. I don't think anybody was.

As well as missing out on the league and FA Cup double, Everton had a third significant loss that summer. At the World Cup in Mexico Gary Lineker finished the tournament's top scorer as England reached the quarter-finals, where they were unlucky to go out to Argentina. A bid of £2.2million came in from Barcelona and while Gary said he was 'extremely happy' at Everton – and I have no doubt that he was – he had 'a desire to play European football'.

Gary left for Spain and there was speculation that Howard would follow him. Not for the last time had the chronic injustice of UEFA's European ban come to haunt us.

━┿━

THE SUMMER OF 1986 was spent getting my fitness back. The plaster came off in June and things became a little easier after that. But it was annoying that I was limited in what I could do. I'd go to the police swimming pool in Aigburth on Merseyside, to carry out low-impact training on the bad leg. If you were at that pool that summer you'd have seen me hopping up and down the swimming pool on my injured leg, trying to build up strength.

I was always at Bellefield early, but things got harder when pre-season training started. I'd be working out from about 9am and the training ground would fill up over the next hour. At 10am the place would empty as my team-mates went out to train. That was the worst moment; knowing that I should have been out there with them, but I was powerless to do anything other than work hard and be patient.

Rumours floated around that my injury was career-ending. Eddie Niedzwiecki called me one day to say that he had heard I was finished. I had no idea where these stories came from, but it infuriated me. What was true was that it was an injury uncommon in football, more like the sort of injury that paratroopers get when landing awkwardly – which was ironic given my dad's wartime record. John Clinkard even consulted with the Red Berets' medical men at their base in Aldershot.

Despite losing Gary to Barcelona, Howard hadn't brought in a replacement forward during that summer. He had, however, gone out and broken the club's transfer record again by signing Dave Watson from Norwich City for £900,000. This was another sign of the manager's ruthless streak: Derek Mountfield had had his injury problems the previous year, but hadn't done much wrong besides being injured. Waggy would go on to be one of Everton's greatest servants and he captained the club for many years. He was an incredibly brave and aggressive player and probably better in the air than Derek. But he didn't score as many goals as his predecessor, nor was he as good in possession. In some ways it was replacing like for like: one fantastic centre half with another. It was a nice dilemma for a manager to have.

There were a couple of good young footballers that Howard brought in, like Neil Adams and Kevin Langley. They weren't household names, but were fine players in their own right and played a part in what unfolded over the season. So too did Paul Power, a veteran from Manchester City, who he signed for just £65,000 to some initial incredulity from supporters. Paul was a studious, conscientious type; a bit like a schoolteacher. I don't think he ever understood me or my peculiar sense of humour, but he was great for the team. Despite being the oldest member of the squad he was probably one of the fittest and played in almost every game in a variety of positions across the midfield and defence, deservedly winning the club's player of the year award.

I watched from the sidelines as the club embarked on another average start to the season. A little like the club now under David Moyes, back then we always seemed to start slowly and build up form. Quite why is a mystery to me.

In spite – or maybe because – of all the long hours I stubbornly put in when I was meant to be resting my ankle, I made my return against Watford in late October. I'd played a couple of times for the reserves, where I'd trebled the gate for a Central League fixture, but I was surprised when Howard told me I was back. I was never really tested in those matches and it was the pace and intensity of the First Division that would be the truest test.

I was a couple of months ahead of schedule and all the feelings that went through my head were similar to those I'd encountered almost exactly five years to the day earlier when I'd made my debut for the club: excitement, trepidation, fear. I knew that if there was a relapse my whole career could be in jeopardy.

My ankle hadn't been seriously tested in training or in the reserves and that was my one great worry. The key moment in my comeback against Watford was when there was a one-on-one. The ball had fallen short of the penalty area and I came charging out. It was a fifty-fifty ball with Mark Falco; I won it and he smashed my ankle. My heart stopped for a moment, and then I realised I was okay and would be okay from then on. It was probably the best thing that could have happened to me. We won 3-2 that day and went up to third, but it was hard fought.

All the elation and defining moments that made the 1984/85 season so seminal were absent for me when we reclaimed the League Championship two years later. It was quite a difficult year for me and became an absolute slog to get through the games. There must have been some amazing moments but all I could think about was the end of the season; get through the game then just try and rest as much as I could and get through the next one. The seven months I'd spent out of the team had almost driven me crazy, through boredom and uncertainty. It was the first time I'd ever spent that much time off, and mentally there were times when I wasn't sure I was ever going to get back at all. You never know until you step on the pitch what it's going to be like, and I think you had to play six months after coming back so that you could be fully insured by the club. So even when I was back there remained a doubt in my mind.

After the first ten games there was a sense of happiness that I'd regained my fitness, that everything was going to be all right. But rather than just flying through games, there was an added, unexpected burden. Because your body relaxes and you think you're back to where you were, there's a real danger complacency can set in, which makes it harder to do anything. That year was a massive battle for me, mentally and physically.

I must have been doing something right though. A flick through my old scrapbooks shows that I was Everton's player of the month for February 1987. Early the following month I scored my first goal for the club – a penalty in a shootout in the Full Members Cup – another competition dreamed up to fill the void created by the European ban – against Charlton. We lost anyway, not that the Goodison faithful – all 7,914 of them – cared too much. There were bigger prizes on the horizon.

The title was effectively won over a five-week spell in March and April when we won seven games on the trot. Howard had brought in midfielder Ian Snodin from Leeds United and Wayne Clarke, the youngest brother of a famous footballing family, from Birmingham City. Both did well, with Wayne scoring a brilliant lobbed goal at Arsenal and a hat-trick against Newcastle at Goodison on Easter Monday. Against Arsenal we got battered and I won man of the match; Wayne's goal was enough to bring the victory.

The key match was at Stamford Bridge against Chelsea when Alan Harper showed the world what a good player he was by unleashing a 25-yard thunderbolt to win us all three points and send us top. I made some good saves in that game too and won man of the match again. Kerry Dixon, who I denied a few times, said afterwards that my performance was 'incredible' and that I was the sort of player 'who wins his team championships'. In the *Sunday Express* a few weeks later, the famous sportswriter James Mossop wrote: 'Southall is looking so confident that he could probably keep goal on a high wire.'

By the time we played Liverpool at the end of April we effectively had the title wrapped up. They beat us 3-1, with Kevin Sheedy famously giving the Kop the V-sign as he grabbed our consolation, but it didn't really matter. Nine days later we were champions after a rare Pat Van Den Hauwe goal was enough for us to beat Norwich City away and make us untouchable.

By the time I played at Carrow Road I was on the verge of having had enough. I was just knackered. Normally I dreaded the summer but this time I couldn't wait. It was great to win the league, great to lift the old League Championship trophy – which wasn't brought out two years earlier (they'd used the trophy of sponsors Canon) – but I was relieved for it to be over, and very glad that I'd got through it all okay.

In a way winning the league title the second time was more rewarding and satisfying than it had been in 1985. It was so easy first time around; we just won games for fun. In 1987 it was more of a struggle, or rather a series of battles. Firstly it had been such a battle to overcome the injury and then there was the continued element of uncertainty that it might reoccur. I was constantly tired but I wanted to play all the games I possibly could because I didn't know when it was going to happen again. There were injuries to a lot of other players too. Gary Stevens, Peter Reid, Pat Van Den Hauwe and Sharpy all missed long stretches of the season. Too little credit is given to the likes of Paul Power and Alan Harper who came in and filled a variety of roles really well, and also to Howard who unified all these players in a winning formation.

It was all incredibly fulfilling. But everything was about to change.

# DISSENTER

RUMOURS ABOUT HOWARD KENDALL'S FUTURE as Everton manager had been floating around almost since the day Gary Lineker left for Barcelona. Some speculated that he intended to follow Gary out there when Terry Venables' time as manager at the Nou Camp came to an end. Unbeknown to us in the Everton dressing room, during the spring he held talks in London with the Barcelona president, Joan Gaspart, and its chief executive, Joan Laporta, and agreed a contract, but the deal fell through. This only came out later but all through the second half of the season, while we were going for the league, his name was mentioned in relation to virtually every top managerial job going.

It was inevitable that Howard's name was in the headlines because he was such a good manager. And because I was fighting my own battles anyway, I just concentrated on myself. In any case, it was just newspaper talk; I always took it all with a pinch of salt. I didn't know whether he was putting it in or whether somebody else was putting it in, or whether somebody else was trying to get him out of a job. I believe, however, that the Heysel ban had an effect on his way of thinking from the very day that it was imposed. I think his long-term ambition was probably to manage England, and to go for that job you really needed European experience.

After the end of the 1986/87 season a second Spanish club – Athletic Bilbao – came in for Howard. They were the premier team in the country's Basque region and had a policy of signing only players native to the region. They were very different from Barcelona, but a big club and had won the Spanish League just a few years earlier. This time there was no hitch in negotiations and Howard was gone.

I can't say I was shocked by his actual departure but I felt slightly let down. I could understand why he was going but I was disappointed because we all wanted to play in Europe as well. It surprised me, however, that he chose Bilbao; had it been Barcelona or Real Madrid I would have understood his decision better. I suppose he could have stayed and built an empire at Goodison as Bill Shankly and Bob Paisley had done at Liverpool, but then they had the extra incentive of European football, didn't they? Howard had proved himself twice in England, but he wanted to take it that stage further and get his team to the highest level. He couldn't do it at Everton and so he left.

In his place came Colin Harvey, who appointed Terry Darracott as his assistant. I was delighted that were would be continuity between the two managers, but also because it was a person who inherently understood Everton. Colin was the club on legs. Even during Howard's reign it was Colin who set the tone and knew how everything should be. I didn't want anybody else coming in because I didn't want anyone else to ruin what Howard had built.

I also thought at the time that we were only a couple of players from being a world-class team again.

There was obviously a great deal of continuity between the two reigns. In fact we didn't notice much of a pre-season change at all, because Colin worked on the training pitch as he always had done. Terry Darracott was a brilliant coach and always great to have around. He was a lot like Colin: he had a good sense of humour and was passionate about football. These were good football people.

Colin was a different type of person to Howard; probably a little bit more stern. I always found Colin great, a man in tune with the way I saw the game. Howard knew how to handle me, but Colin understood my obsessiveness and relentless desire to be the best. As I've said before, he embodied Everton's Nil Satis Nisi Optimum motto and so did I. We were like peas in a pod.

His desire to win and bring the best for Everton also saw frustration mount within him. As that first season progressed I could see it rise as he couldn't quite find the right mix and balance. We knew we had decent players; we just couldn't find a way of winning games. It wasn't for the want of trying because I don't think anybody has worked as hard for Everton as Colin. It was painful to see because I don't think anybody's more pro-Everton than him.

We finished the 1987/88 season fourth and had the best defensive season in the club's history, conceding just 27 league goals in 40 matches. Not that I set any stall by that. If you judge your career by clean sheets you're going to struggle. As a team we played well. We reached the semi-finals of the League Cup, knocking out Liverpool along the way. They knocked us out in the fifth round of the FA Cup and won the league by a mile, but we had some small consolation by preventing them from beating Leeds United's 29-match unbeaten start to the season. Not that it mattered. We wanted trophies, not bragging rights over our neighbours.

Looking back, I suppose the injuries and departures that we'd suffered since 1985 were coming back to bite us. We'd obviously lost Gary Lineker, but he'd never really been replaced. Paul Bracewell's Everton career was virtually over because of injury and when you lose someone of that calibre then it's obviously going to have an impact. Kevin Sheedy had his injury problems and so did Rats. Reidy had suffered too and was coming to the end of his Everton career. In fact I'd also had my injury problems that year and missed the opening stages of the season. At the end of the League Championship winning season I'd been told that a pain in my knee was attributable to part of the kneecap growing away from the rest of the joint. Apparently it's quite common, but the club insisted it was operated on and once more I was a frustrated figure on the sidelines.

We'd brought in some decent players in the meantime, but you wouldn't call them world class. Ian Wilson, Colin's first signing, was a good grafter but he didn't catch the eye. Wayne Clarke did a good job for us and scored some vital goals, but he was never going to get you 30 or 40 goals a season. But then you look at the players Liverpool signed in the same period: John Barnes, Peter Beardsley, John Aldridge. They were improving rapidly while we were, at best, standing still.

In the summer of 1988 we lost Gary Stevens to Glasgow Rangers, as another of our stars left in search of European football. Colin, who by that stage had made no major signings, set about rapidly overhauling the Everton squad. From Chelsea we signed the winger Pat Nevin, from Newcastle United the highly rated full back Neil McDonald, midfielder Stuart McCall from Bradford City, and, for a British record fee, West Ham's Tony Cottee. For me it was at once too much and too little. I thought it was too early to break up Howard's team and that a more gradual approach should have been employed. At the same time I didn't think the signings, while all good players, were of the calibre Everton should have been aspiring to. For starters we should have broken the bank a year earlier and bought John Barnes from Watford. We should have looked at re-signing Gary Lineker or, when he became available not long after, buying Ian Rush from Juventus.

When you look at the really top clubs now, like Real Madrid and Barcelona, they've got good players all the way through. They're all of the same calibre. They can all play. We had stop-gap players, like Wilson and Clarke, who weren't everybody's cup of tea but did fine for short periods. But over a period of a few years the stop-gaps started to become more permanently embedded in the team while the players we'd lost – Lineker, Gray, Bracewell, Stevens and, later, Trevor Steven – weren't adequately re-placed. Thus the overall quality of the squad dipped.

We started the 1988/89 season in brilliant fashion. On a sun-drenched August afternoon we took Newcastle United apart at Goodison, winning 4-0 with Cottee grabbing a hat-trick on his debut. The following week we beat Coventry to go top, Cottee scoring the only goal, then we drew with Nottingham Forest, who were a good team. And then, inexplicably, we sank from the top of the table without a trace. In consecutive games we lost to Millwall, Luton Town and Wimbledon. After that we went on an unbeaten league run that lasted until the new year but were still drawing too many games to be considered contenders for anything.

Nothing changed in my outlook towards the game, but the mediocrity started to become habitual. I think on match day you should always go out, concentrate on what you're doing and play with a bit of hope. It was amazing how quickly not challenging at the top became routine, accepted. We were just gliding along. We weren't going to win the league, weren't going to go down; towards the end of the season it became a non-event in lots of ways.

It was never depressing though, not even the in the very dark days that were to come in the mid-1990s. I'd always rather be positive than negative. I was playing for the team that I wanted to play for. My attitude was, 'As soon as the game is finished, whether we had won, lost, or drawn, there's nothing you can do about it. You've either lost it or you've won it. If you've won it, great; if you've lost it, there's bugger all you can do about it.' So I always looked to the next game. It was difficult at times, but you can't suddenly stop playing. It's hard to describe, but when you go to train in the morning it's just fucking brilliant. You train all week and you're never sat around thinking dark thoughts. Training, playing matches, getting paid to do what millions of people can only dream about is a great life, even when success is elusive.

Although we didn't have European competitions there were diversions in cup competitions and friendly matches. It was the year of the Football League's centenary and Everton, with Aston Villa and Derby County, were the sole founder members in the top flight. We played in the Mercantile Credit Football Festival at Wembley in April 1988, in 40-minute matches versus Wolves (which we won on penalties) and Manchester United (which we lost 1-0). There wasn't much enthusiasm for that and only 17,000 turned out at a time when the stadium held 100,000. Later that year Mercantile Credit sponsored the League Centenary Trophy; we lost to Manchester United in that as well. Then there was the Simod Cup, successor of the Full Members Cup, which had been the scene of my penalty-kick glory a few years earlier. We got to the final of that at Wembley, which we lost 4-3 to Nottingham Forest after extra time. It's difficult to say anyone was very enthused by it. Our attendances on the march to Wembley were 3,703 when we played Millwall at Goodison, 2,477 for the quarter-final at Wimbledon's Plough Lane, and just 7,072 for the semi-final at Goodison against Queens Park Rangers.

Everyone else might have been ambivalent but I absolutely loved it. I loved it because the manager – particularly when Howard was there – didn't want to have anything to do with the competition. I'm sure he tried to pick a team to get knocked out and so picked all the kids. These incredibly young teams with players like Peter Billing, John Ebbrell and Eddie Youds would go out and win when they'd been expected to lose. Howard would be a little bit upset because it meant another match we had to play, but I'd be laughing my head off because that's all I wanted to do. I also loved the responsibility of being an elder member of the team and helping young players develop. It was good for them, good grounding. Not that I was ever going to relinquish my place in the team for Mike Stowell or Alec Chamberlain or Jason Kearton, who were our reserve goalkeepers around that time. Why would you ever want to rest a goalie? It's pointless.

There was, of course, a rather more significant cup run during the 1988/89 season. With no league title challenge forthcoming the FA Cup represented our best chance of winning something. That year the draw was fairly kind, although you could take nothing for granted and we never did. We'd already been dumped out of the League Cup by Bradford City so knew the dangers of facing lower-league opposition. In the third round we beat West Bromwich Albion after a replay and it also took a replay for us to beat Plymouth in the fourth round, although we did so resoundingly, winning 4-0. Barnsley we saw off 1-0 in a hard-fought game at Oakwell, which set up a quarter-final at Goodison with Wimbledon.

There was always a bit of an undercurrent when we played Wimbledon. Their game was about aggression and intimidation and gaining every possible advantage they could. We were the big boys, they were the under- dogs, so it was inevitable that they went a little bit further to topple our crown. Vinnie Jones had been sent off in both the previous Goodison encounters, once for violent conduct and once for head-butting Rats. That most recent encounter, a month before the FA Cup match, had ended in a draw, but there were some big tackles throughout the game. Personally I loved playing them. From where they came from to where they got to was incredible. Would you want to watch them every week? No, I personally wouldn't. But they earned their money and played their bollocks off.

Wimbledon were good for football; they were jokers, they mixed things up and could play a bit. If you're going to win League Championships and cups you need to be able to deal with the Wimbledons of this world. As a goalkeeper they bombarded your area and you had to be strong and hold firm, but why not? Goalies aren't challenged nearly enough these days. Wimbledon was a test and I relished playing them. I even liked going to their decrepit stadium at Plough Lane.

When we met them at Goodison in the quarter-final on a March

Sunday afternoon in front of the TV cameras, less than 25,000 people turned out to watch Stuart McCall score the only goal of the game. When the semi-final draw was made that afternoon we could have played Liverpool or Nottingham Forest, but the gods decreed that we faced Norwich City at Villa Park and Liverpool and Forest met at Hillsborough.

It was a good game against Norwich and it said a lot about how our fortunes had changed that they finished well above us in the league that season. I was always confident in semi-finals though, and besides the two-legged League Cup semi against Arsenal the previous year never lost one in my entire career. It was a close match and in the end Pat Nevin's goal was enough for us to win it. We were all delighted, jumping around and quite oblivious to the dramas that had unfolded at the day's other semi-final.

I'd say it took a good hour after the final whistle, when we were on the coach heading back to Liverpool, for it to dawn on us that something had gone horribly wrong at Hillsborough. Prior to kickoff congestion in the streets outside the stadium's Leppings Lane end had led to a police officer ordering the turnstiles to be opened. This led to a surge inside the stadium, where fans stuck in a central pen became trapped then crushed. It took until 3.06pm for the police to open the fences and let the thousands stuck inside onto the pitch, but it was too late. Ninety-four people died and 150 more were seriously injured. Two more fans later succumbed to their injuries. It was the worst tragedy witnessed in British football.

The full enormity of what had happened only struck home when we reached the M62 on the last leg of the journey home and were joined by cars and coachloads of devastated Liverpool supporters. A good day turned into a nightmare.

The FA suspended the football calendar, although we were playing again within a week, and there was a debate over whether or not the FA Cup should be suspended altogether.

Ultimately though, I believe it should have been up to Liverpool. I don't think it should have been up to anybody else. If it helped them get through what they had to get through, then that was fine. If they didn't want to play, the competition should have been abandoned, simple as that. In the end the decision was made to go ahead. Liverpool won their replayed semi-final and for the second time in three years we had an all-Merseyside FA Cup Final.

For Everton it was a difficult situation to go into because you want to win the FA Cup, but you're playing against a team that morally deserved to win it. I think that was the hard bit. Obviously I had won the cup before but we had some lads who had never played so far in the cup. We had to be true to ourselves and our supporters, but also keep in mind that for Liverpool it was more than just a game. Dalglish was obviously a great manager and held everything together. It must have been even more difficult for their lads, given what the club had experienced and that some of them were playing to bring a sense of closure to the dreadful events.

It was a weird situation, heightened by the fact that it was a really good game. Liverpool led early on and we had chances and they had chances. Stuart McCall, who was only on as a substitute, equalised in the dying seconds. In extra time Rushie put Liverpool ahead again, but Stuart hit a brilliant volley from the edge of the area to equalise again. Liverpool had more chances and I made some good saves before Rushie finished us off. It was a proper game, and although we lost it I thoroughly enjoyed it, even though Liverpool's victory probably had some inevitability. If there were 100 million people watching I suppose only a million would have wanted Everton to win. I think an Everton victory would have been very difficult for some people to take, but we gave it everything and they were just slightly better on the day. At the end of the game I'm sure we were all just glad it was over and that we could move on with life.

⌐⌐

MOST PEOPLE ON MERSEYSIDE knew somebody who was affected by the Hillsborough disaster, whether it was somebody who died or someone who was pulled from the carnage in the Leppings Lane end. It profoundly affected the city as a whole and even today the Sun newspaper is boycotted by many of its residents for the way it reported the tragedy. I was probably slightly shielded from how the Hillsborough disaster affected the place because by then I had moved back to Llandudno.

I was by then a father. Eryl had given birth to a baby girl, Samantha, in 1988 and we returned to North Wales so that we could be near family and because I wanted to bring her up where I was brought up. Being back in my home town suited me down to the ground. It was 70 miles from my home to Bellefield and I enjoyed my drive there in the mornings and back in the afternoon. Although I liked Liverpool I'd had enough of the hustle and bustle of the city by then and enjoyed the peace and quiet of North Wales.

Most people were nice, but some still blanked me, including some of the lads from school. I think that sort of thing is all part of the baggage of being successful: people either like you or hate your guts, there's no in between. They'd be happy for you to be a failure but they don't like you being a success. Most people let me be and I never had any trouble, except for the time a kid with an air rifle decided to shoot the lights on my drive. I caught him, resisted the temptation to give him a good hiding and took the gun off him. I never heard about it again.

Back in Llandudno I developed my own routine. I'd be out for training by 7am, do my stuff at Bellefield and be back in time to play with Samantha for a few hours and then rest. In the summer I was up at 5am, going for a run. I didn't need for anything; everything I wanted was in my house and around me. I hardly went out at all. These were good times.

Over the summer of 1989 Colin Harvey continued his rebuilding programme at Everton. Pat Van Den Hauwe, Paul Bracewell and Trevor Steven all left. Adrian Heath and Peter Reid had gone over the course of the previous season. Of the 1985 team there was only me, Rats, Sharpy and Sheedy left.

Again, the lack of European football had hit us hard and, as with Howard and the two Garys, that was Trevor's primary motivation for leaving.

At the time I don't think that the full implications of these departures sank in. I was angry at the time of the ban being handed out, and I'm angry now when I look back at the careers that were ruined and the opportunities that were wasted. But players come and go at all clubs and the full significance of who has been lost from a dressing room sometimes doesn't register at the time.

I don't think the pressures on me to leave were so great. Obviously I wanted to play European football, but my international aspirations were satisfied. When you play for Wales, you're just happy to represent your country. Although you do your best there's no tournaments to worry about and, because it's a smaller country, as a player you'll always be in the mix. With England I think that it's different. It's more competitive, there's a wider pool of talent, you're up against better players and there's a tournament to compete in every couple of years. Lots of the England squad were playing in Scotland and Europe and tasting European football with their clubs. For those who stayed behind there was a danger that they would stagnate or slip behind in the First Division, which is why so many felt compelled to leave.

There was probably more money on offer in Scotland then but it just didn't interest me. Rangers were one of the biggest clubs in the world at the time, but I wasn't enticed by the prospect of playing four or five big games a season – all basically against the same team – and spending the rest of my time going to places like Airdrie or Morton. Granted, there was European football, but that was at most ten games a season and wasn't ever the be all and end all. Money aside, I'd sooner have dropped down to the Second Division than played in the Scottish League. It simply never appealed to me at all.

To move beyond England would have meant seeking to further my education as a footballer. Spain and Italy never interested me, although the latter country probably had the best league in the world at the time. I wouldn't

This is me as a nine year old. As you can see, the kits were just like Everton's vintage of 1968. *(Personal collection)*

As you can see I was small until my late teens. Too small and too scruffy to be signed by a professional club, anyway. *(Personal collection)*

I was nearly 22 when I became a professional footballer for the first time at Bury. I learned many things in my year there.
*(Personal collection)*

# Brothers and rivals

My brother Steve was a really good player as well, and could probably have been a professional had he got the right breaks.
*(Personal collection)*

Brothers and rivals — 21-year-old goalkeeper Neville Southall, Conwy United (left) and centre-back Steve Southall, 23, pictured on the Morfa.

Myself and Rats relaxing after a game around 1984. Of all the people I played with over the years, he was probably the one that understood and knew me best. *(Personal collection)*

The 1984 Milk Cup Final was a landmark for the team. Although we eventually lost to Liverpool after a replay we matched the best team in the world kick for kick. *(PA)*

The 1984 FA Cup Final was a game from which there was only ever going to be one winner. *(Mark Leech/ Welloffside)*

It was a big day for my parents, Fred and Rose, who came down to the final. Because they were there I even went to the banquet afterwards! *(Personal collection)*

Winning the Charity Shield in 1984 reaffirmed our belief that we were the best team in England and – defacto – Europe. *(Getty)*

The string of saves I made against Sheffield Wednesday a week before we secured the 1984/85 title was one of my best performances. I always loved playing at Hillsborough. *(Getty)*

Everyone still goes on about the red shirt I wore when Everton lifted their only European trophy – but I had no choice in the matter! *(Everton FC)*

I was only the fourth goalkeeper to be named Football Writers' Association Player of the Year, but Howard Kendall had to give my acceptance speech as I'd shouted myself hoarse that season. *(Everton FC)*

With Everton's haul of trophies for the 1984/85 season. *(Personal collection)*

Jock Stein helping me get my balls back from the Scotland supporters during the pre-match warm up before Wales's crucial 1986 World Cup qualifier. 2 hours later Wales's ambitions were over and Stein was dead. *(PA)*

Stretchered off after suffering the worst injury of my career, which forced me to miss the run in of the 1985/86 season. *(Getty)*

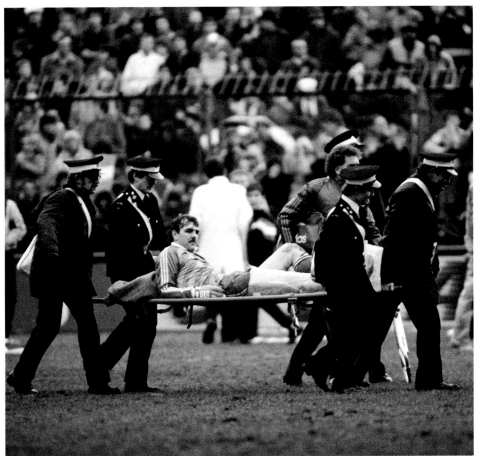

Deep in concentration during Everton's second League Championship-winning season.
It was a great achievement but a hard slog. *(Everton FC)*

The now infamous sit in, although still nobody believes me when I say I was only going to clear my head. *(PA)*

Although I never found fame easy, I always enjoyed meeting and mixing with the fans. Here I am with a young Evertonian called Shaun Wright in 1992. *(Courtesy of Ian Wright)*

Pictured in Mike Walker's first game in charge v Bolton Wanderers. I thought a Welsh goalkeeper managing Everton might have been a good thing – how wrong I was! *(Everton FC)*

Joe Royle brilliantly turned everything around after the mess Walker left behind. The 1995 FA Cup win was one of the most satisfying of my career. *(Mark Leech/ WellOffside)*

Collecting my MBE from Buckingham Palace with Eryl and Samantha. When they wrote to tell me I was getting the award I thought it was a joke to be honest. *(PA)*

No matter how bad things got for Wales under Mike Smith and Bobby Gould I never ever thought of giving up playing for my country – even when they made me wear pink. *(Private collection)*

I loved getting the chance to manage
my country and thought I had a great
chance of getting the job full time.
Sparky was a great choice though.
*(Getty)*

Called upon one last
time – for Bradford City
in 2000. I did my best
but got slaughtered in the
press, despite not training
properly for two years.
*(Getty)*

A portrait by Robert J Wilson for his book 'One, Images of a Goalkeeping Season' – Robert's father, Bob, kept goal for Arsenal in the 1960s and 1970s (Robert J Wilson)

have minded going to West Germany because I liked the way they do things. I know it sounds clichéd, but German efficiency struck a chord with me and my relentless perfectionism. Of the players who spent time abroad I talked to Mark Hughes, who had a spell at Bayern Munich, more than most and he told me about the professionalism of their preparations; taking vitamin injections before games and having individual training plans – things that were mostly unknown in England at the time. As a country, it's spotlessly clean and the people seem to have high respect for everything around them. I wouldn't have minded the chance, but Everton kept me happy.

When I look at other clubs I look at the manager and the way they play football, and I ask myself – would I want to play for him? Would he improve me? Would I learn anything? Brian Clough is someone I would have loved to have played for. I liked the way West Ham played football under successive managers. Ron Atkinson would have been a good manager to play for. I would have loved to have played for Alan Ball. These were people who wanted to play football, to entertain people.

Kenny Dalglish was another manager who had a certain aura and commanded my respect. He was a football man who was massively enthusiastic, who always wanted his players to improve and was clearly very good at his job because he won lots of trophies. If he had ever managed Wales I would have been very happy, but that was unlikely. So too was the chance of either of us crossing Stanley Park. But that wasn't through his want of trying.

In the late 1980s Dalglish started to call me at home from time to time. I didn't know him at all; I never socialised with my own team-mates so I wasn't likely to go out with those of our biggest rivals. It was a bit strange, but I didn't mind. I liked Kenny and still do; he's a great football man and good fellow. They were just general football conversations really, but the underlying agenda was seemingly to find out if I was interested in joining Liverpool.

Clearly he could see the situation at Everton, that things weren't going well and the team were going nowhere at the time. I don't think he was doing anything wrong. But I would never ever have left for Liverpool: Everton was part of me and I knew how it would hurt the fans and the club, which had shown faith in me by giving me such a long contract. I know footballers today sometimes don't value the paper their contracts are written on, but I was a man of my word. There was no way, having asked for a long contract, that I could have turned around and said, 'Oh, by the way, I want to go to Liverpool.'

Later someone told me that Liverpool were prepared to pay £4million for me, which would have doubled the British record fee we had paid for Tony Cottee. It would have been one of the most sensational transfers ever, but I was never going to be interested in defecting to Anfield.

Some of the players Colin had signed underachieved. For a while Tony Cottee just couldn't get a look in; he'd gone from being the most expensive player in Britain to a Central League striker within a year. Pat Nevin was good but unpredictable; you didn't know what you were going to get from one week to the next with Paddy. Neil McDonald was a player who should have played for England. He was very accomplished, good on the ball, versatile, could pass it over five yards or fifty, but it just didn't seem to work out for him. Maybe it was because he didn't get the breaks, or maybe – a little like Bobby Mimms – he just lacked that bit of desire that would have made him a great player.

From Leicester City Colin bought the centre forward, Mike Newell. Mike was a good player; underrated, better than most people gave him credit for, but he suffered by comparison to the likes of Sharpy and Andy Gray. I used to relentlessly take the piss out of him because he seemed to have this one unending eyebrow, like Bert from Sesame Street. He was also the boniest person I've ever met, with ridiculously long fingers. If you went up for a ball with him and collided you always came off worse because there would be some sort of bone sticking out into you.

Colin also signed Norman Whiteside from Manchester United, the player who in the 1985 FA Cup Final was responsible for one of my most painful moments. Norman was still only 24 when he joined us, but considered to be at the veteran stage of his career. How he passed the medical is beyond me. He was still a very good player and scored lots of goals; he had that knack of arriving at the right moment at the right time. He also never gave possession away.

Norman was great fun, but at United had a reputation for being part of the club's drinking culture, which Alex Ferguson was trying to wipe out. The story goes that Colin phoned him up before signing him and asked if he was still drinking. Norman's response was that he didn't drink 'any more than the next person'. I'm sure that the 'next person' he was referring to was Paul McGrath or Bryan Robson!

From Sweden came the club's first foreign player, Stefan Rehn. Stef was great, a lovely lad who went on to have a top career, playing in World Cups and being made Swedish player of the year. Stef was decent in training. To look at him training you'd think he'd be far better in the games. But it didn't work out and Colin, despite signing him, just didn't fancy him. After a couple of starts and a handful of appearances off the bench he brought him on as a sub in an away game at Millwall and took him off again 15 minutes later, and that was the last the Everton supporters ever saw of him. It was a shame. His interpreter was even better. He was a Scouser and used to come to Bellefield wearing these big Doc Martens boots. We used to get him in a circle and everybody used to tackle the living daylights out of him. We had lots of fun at his expense, but he wasn't happy and disappeared after a while.

From Aston Villa came the centre back Martin Keown, who was probably the best of all Colin's signings, but a very funny guy. When I say funny, I mean in a strange way. People say that I'm grumpy, but they don't know Martin, who was born moaning. He was like a little old man. Martin's the only person I've ever deliberately kicked in training because he got on my nerves. I like him, but he's one of those people that can rub you the wrong way for no reason whatsoever; he's just got that way with him. In return, we absolutely slaughtered him. Just before the season started, we told him, 'Martin, you do know that you get your mortgage paid when you're away from home, don't you; and you get gardening fees; you get everything!' Of course, it was all made up but by the time we finished with him he'd gone back to Colin and asked: 'What about these mortgages and all that?'

I think it was harder for Martin than any of the new players because he had been brought in to replace Rats. I think he felt the pressure more than anybody else. It was a difficult time for him, but being the person he was he constantly sought reassurance. He was strong mentally in some ways, but needy in others. He shouted at his keeper, namely me, which didn't go down well and we had a little bit of a row about it. He could be abrasive. But at the same time he was always looking for encouragement. He'd be passing the ball back and asking, 'How do you think I'm doing?' Or at half-time he'd follow you into the toilets asking the same question. He soon learned that if he asked me he was asking the wrong man. My stock response was: 'Fuck off, you idiot!'

We started the season untypically well. Mike Newell was in great form up front and when we beat the league champions Arsenal 3-0 at Goodison in late October we went top.

A fortnight later we played in front of the TV cameras against Aston Villa. There were only a handful of matches shown live each season at this time, and it was on free-to-air TV so quite a big thing. Villa absolutely battered us. We were losing 6-0 with ten minutes left and although we pulled a couple of goals back we never fully recovered from that hammering. Any talk of a title challenge was dead by Christmas.

I used to sit down in the afternoons and try and work out what we were doing wrong. But I just couldn't manage it. We were good players, Colin was there, we had all the right components – and yet it just didn't click. We were doing okay in games, we were a decent team, but just weren't doing what we were supposed to do. I had no idea why. It mystified me and it befuddled Colin. I think he tried everything; tried everything anybody could do to make it change. There wasn't one thing that was abundantly wrong with the setup. It was a number of things that just didn't quite click.

I also had my own career worries at this time. I had a bad back, a problem with one of my discs, so Colin sent me to a private clinic in London. The specialist examined me and gave me his prognosis. It was grim.

'I'll give you an operation, but you might be out for eight months.'

I asked what the alternative was.

'If you do nothing you might be finished in eighteen months.'

I asked him if I'd be all right after surgery and he replied that he wasn't sure. My response, as it tended to be in these situations, was blunt: 'If you're not sure you can fuck off then.'

When I got back to Liverpool, Colin was the first person I sought out.

'Why did you send me down there to tell me that I'm finished?' I demanded.

I was in denial but the problem wouldn't go away. That's why I wore my socks down, because the nerve went right from behind my back all down my legs and I sometimes couldn't feel them. Sometimes I had needles in my legs and I couldn't feel them; my legs were that numb. At the same time anything that I wore on them really affected them. I got a shin-pad deal out of it but my back was causing havoc with my nerves.

In the end they found me a specialist in Rochdale or somewhere out of the way like that. Martin Keown, of all people, came with me because he said he had a bad back too. The specialist gave an examination to both of us for three hours. It was the best examination I've ever had. He said, 'Neville, you've got a bad back. Martin, there's nothing wrong with you.' Martin replied, 'Well, what about my hip then?' The specialist just laughed: 'I'm a back doctor aren't I, not a hip doctor!' That was Martin all over; a bit odd, but just feeling his way and seeking reassurance. Once he was settled in a few years later he became a top player.

As for me, I refused to live with the possibility that my career was in jeopardy. And little by little my ailment got better. I'm no medical expert, but I think it was probably something as simple as things clicking back into place.

We finished the 1989/90 season sixth but with an extra four points would have finished third. Not that that was much good either, as Liverpool were champions yet again and had beaten us twice in the league. The European ban was now at an end, but instead of the usual four UEFA Cup qualifiers there was just one, so even third place wouldn't have seen us compete at the level we all craved so badly.

—⊏⊐—

MY UNHAPPINESS WAS GROWING at the club, but I couldn't quite put a handle on it. I enjoyed training. I liked my team-mates. I believed we had a good team, even if I thought we could be better. I thought Colin was great. I was doing all right in terms of my performances. But I was in a situation where I was unhappy, yet wasn't sure why. Maybe it was a reaction to Howard going and us not winning everything. It was a strange time for me. I lived in a house I wanted to live in, I was at a club that I wanted to be at, playing for fans that I wanted to play for, but still wasn't happy. I just couldn't work it out.

Things came to a head before the start of the 1990/91 season, on the eve of which I asked for a transfer. It was my third transfer request in a year, all of which were rejected. I don't know why I asked to move: I didn't really want to leave Everton and was sure I wouldn't be as happy elsewhere. I liked Colin Harvey and my team-mates but I couldn't see things getting any better at Goodison. In truth, I didn't know what I wanted.

One thing that annoyed me was the attitude of the Everton boardroom. I was the best goalkeeper in the country – some people said in the world – and one of the most decorated players in the club's history. I had put my body on the line for the club for nearly a decade. Yet some of the people in the directors' box treated me as if I was still a binman. They thought I was stupid and wasn't worth listening to. They liked the fact that I played for

Everton but as a person did not respect me.

With Sir Philip Carter I never had a problem, and I maintain that he is the best chairman in the club's history. But when I sought him out for a meeting he wouldn't see me. Requests for a meeting fell on deaf ears.

In the end I tracked him down and told him I was unhappy. I think, in fairness, he just thought that I was being a knob. He asked me what I wanted, but I couldn't say. I didn't need or want any more money, what I wanted was something more intangible: respect, to be valued. I don't know if you can put a price on that or define it. In the end I told him, 'Give me the same car as you have and I'll be happy.' I drove a Volvo Estate and he had a massive Mercedes. I didn't really want a Mercedes, I just wanted a symbol that the club valued my commitment. But he told me no and I ended up with nothing.

On the opening day of the 1990/91 season we played newly promoted Leeds United at Goodison. It was shit. We were shit. By half-time we were 2-0 down and conceded a third not long after. At half-time I needed to get out of the dressing room and get my head together, so I left and went and sat down in the goalmouth. People went on about it and said it was a protest, but it wasn't at all. At worst it was badly timed, coming around the same time as my transfer request. I certainly wasn't protesting against Colin, who didn't even know about it until that evening.

I'd actually done the same before at Wimbledon a year earlier and nobody had said a word about it then. It cleared my head and allowed me to focus on the second half. But coming when it did it propelled me to the back pages.

Colin phoned me that evening at home. He wasn't a happy man.

'What the fuck are you doing? he asked.

I explained my reasons and he seemed to calm down. But the next day he called me back to tell me that he was fining me two weeks' wages and suspending me.

I could be awkward as well, so I phoned my agent and told him that I was suspended for a fortnight. 'If I'm not allowed to come in, tell him I'm going on holiday,' I instructed him. Me, on holiday! I hated holidays. That's how absurd the situation had become.

Colin was soon on the phone again.

'Come in on Monday,' he said. 'We'll talk again.'

On Wednesday, when we faced Coventry City at Highfield Road, I was in the starting line-up, as ever.

But speculation about my future rumbled on. One Sunday afternoon I was at home when the phone rang for me.

'Hello, it's Alex Ferguson here,' said a Scottish voice. The voice I thought was familiar, however, wasn't that of the Manchester United manager but Andy Gray.

'Fuck off, Andy,' I said, and hung up.

But it really was Fergie! He called back a minute later, but I told him if he was interested in signing me he had to speak to my agent. I never heard back from him and a few months later he signed Peter Schmeichel. I probably put him off.

Knowing what I know now it was the right thing for me to stay at Everton. If I'd been that kind of player I could have gone to United or Liverpool and won the title again. But it wouldn't have ever been my club. I don't think I would have felt at home.

Everton, by contrast, were *my* club; we were meant to be. When I walked in every day at Bellefield I felt at home. It was my club and I could do whatever I wanted to do within it. They used to give me a free rein. I was very happy there; it was just the fact we weren't winning things that meant I got more and more frustrated.

I used to talk to Colin about it. I'd say, 'I'm not happy,' and he'd ask why. 'Well, we don't win things, do we?' I'd give him my advice on who he should sign and how we should play and he'd take it all in. He was brilliant, to be fair. He could see my frustration and understand it too. He shared the same inherent bond with the club that I did and the same desire to win. Nobody wanted Everton to do well more than Colin and he tried everything he could to make us successful. But it just wasn't working.

The unhappiness permeated the dressing room. There were definite splits between the old players, who had enjoyed such great success, and the new ones who had come in to replace them. I don't think it got so bad that players weren't passing to each other, but we were a long way from where we had been five years earlier. Team spirit had been the foundation of our success. Because we got on so well we felt so comfortable in each other's company that we could criticise one another too, which in turn forced us all to improve. Now there was tension and infighting.

I was oblivious to some of this discord because I didn't mix with one group of my team-mates or another, and I was not there the night that Colin took us out for a Chinese meal to help clear the mood. This was one of Howard's famous ploys, and it always seemed to work – we never lost after one of our get-togethers. But this time it backfired spectacularly. Kevin Sheedy had a really dry sense of humour and was goading and taking the piss out of Martin Keown. They just rubbed each other up the wrong way, but Martin didn't react at first. Then Sheeds said something about Martin's brother, who was out with us, and it all went off. Punches were thrown and Sheeds ended up with four stitches.

The incident ended up in the papers, but ultimately I thought it was misconstrued. These things happen at football clubs all the time. The atmosphere at the time wasn't great, but it certainly wasn't toxic. What was happening on the pitch was of more pressing concern.

We didn't win any of our first six league matches and were bouncing around the wrong end of the table. On 30 October we went to Sheffield United for a League Cup tie. It was an awful game and we lost 2-1. Within 48 hours Colin was sacked as Everton manager.

# CHAPTER TEN
# NEARLY MAN

IN THE LATE EIGHTIES Wales had a core of players who would have walked into just about any club or international team in Europe. This world-class pedigree ran through the spine of the team – myself, Rats, Mark Hughes and Ian Rush – and should by rights have given Wales a great chance to challenge at a major tournament. In the early 1990s, as Rats slipped from international view and I and the others entered our thirties, Ryan Giggs and Gary Speed joined our number. And yet we remained perennial nearly men. That we ultimately didn't progress to the finals of the World Cup or European Championships was attributable to a mixture of poor executive management, bad luck, and the limitations of drawing from a population of just 3 million in a country where rugby is considered the national sport.

It was always a different proposition playing for my country than it was for Everton, where a bad result could linger over a team and affect form. With Wales you went away and did something different for a few months and when you came back everything had changed. Absence makes the heart grow glad and with Wales things were always fresher. Thus the disappointment of failing to qualify for the World Cup in Mexico never really hung over us.

To qualify for the 1988 European Championships in West Germany we again had a tough yet not insurmountable group of Denmark, Czechoslovakia and Finland. It was a strange group where any team could beat any other. Czechoslovakia, for instance, beat Finland 3-0 at home, yet lost by the same scoreline in Helsinki. We hammered the Finns 4-0, but were unable to get more than a 1-1 draw against the Czechoslovaks four weeks later. And so it went on.

The key game was on 9 September 1987, when we played Denmark at Ninian Park. I was called up to the team, despite only having played two reserve games that season for Everton as I recovered from a knee operation. I don't think Howard would have been too happy seeing me risk my recovery, but I thought my inclusion showed great faith by Mike England. In any case, who could possibly turn their country down?

On a rainswept night both sides attacked early on, and there could have been goals at either end. I saved at the feet of Preben Elkjaer, and then from a long punt forward Mark Hughes was shoved over but there was no penalty. But we didn't need to wait long for the breakthrough. On 19 minutes Dave Philips broke down the Denmark right and struck a long back-post cross, which Andy Jones headed against the crossbar. The ball bounced out, and who else was there but Sparky with a full-length diving header to score the only goal of the game.

The result put us top of our group on goal difference with a game in hand on the Danes. If we won our next match – the return fixture in Copenhagen a month later – we would go through to the finals. If we drew and avoided a heavy defeat in the last match against Czechoslovakia we'd also go through.

But there was one noticeable absentee that night: me. I'd suffered a slight relapse after my knee operation and missed a couple of Everton matches. I was also judged unfit to join up with Wales. I was gutted. Instead of travelling to Denmark to be with my compatriots the very best I could do was sit at home and call the Wales hotel to wish my old friend, Eddie Niedzwiecki, the best of luck. Then I settled down to watch on BBC Wales.

Once more we didn't get the result we so badly needed. Preben Elkjaer was played through in the 50th minute, looking a good yard offside, and he struck the only goal of the game. The Danes also missed a penalty and we went home empty-handed and dejected.

Within minutes of the defeat the FAW were already whispering about Mike England's future, moaning to the press about their financial problems and the cost of not making it to West Germany. We still, of course, had a game to play, but that didn't seem to matter. I think at that stage the relationship between Mike and Alun Evans had broken down. Because he was quite manipulative Alun wasn't the sort of person you wanted to get on the wrong side of; you'd be done for, in fact.

Although we still had a slim chance of qualifying going into the Czechoslovakia match, Mike's future was all that anybody was talking about. I don't think it undermined our preparations because we never let these things bother us, but in some minds the 2-0 defeat we suffered carried some inevitability.

Afterwards it was announced that the manager's contract wouldn't be renewed. He had already taken a £13,000 per year cut on his £23,000 salary in 1986 to go part-time. That summed up the disgraceful way he was treated. I don't think I've come across anybody that's as passionate about Wales as Mike. He was a true players' manager: open and honest and enthusiastic.

But he wasn't a politician. You know when you see films in which actors play themselves? That was Mike. Wherever you put him he would just be the same, and when you had to deal with the stupid old men on the committee it worked against him. He'd try anything to make Wales do well, but he couldn't play the backroom games and that's what did for him.

In his place came Terry Yorath, who had been in the same Wales squads as me when I first broke into the national setup at the start of the decade. Despite our unhappiness at Mike's departure, Terry was a good appointment and the squad were happy with it. Him and Mike were like chalk and cheese, and although Terry also had a great sense of humour he was far more intense. He was very enthusiastic and a little aggressive, and because he had played for a very good Leeds team with massively high standards he set the bar high for all of us. As his assistant he brought the former Tottenham manager Peter Shreeves, who was a great coach and very different again to Terry. He was this cockney geezer who came in dressed in a pink shirt and with a jumper draped over his shoulders. But he was a good coach and he and Terry made a good combination.

Terry, however, would have his work cut out in sating the demands of Wales supporters and those of the FAW. To qualify for the 1990 World Cup in Italy not only would we need to overcome the European Champions Holland, but the mighty West Germany too.

ONE OF THE THINGS I LOVED most about playing for Wales was the mix of players that we had. Although Rats and myself had been denied the chance of playing European football, Sparky and Rushy had left England in search of it. Mark played for Bayern Munich and Barcelona, Rushy for Juventus – clubs that you can't get much bigger than. At the other end of the scale we had Andy Jones, who played for one of my former clubs, Port Vale, and Tony Norman and Alan Davies, who also played in the third tier.

I didn't find going from playing alongside First Division players at the weekend to playing with a mixture of superstars and lower-league journeymen midweek difficult at all. In fact, it was great because you knew they would come in and be honest and give their all. It was far harder for them, because we met up on a Sunday, they only had Monday and Tuesday to adjust their game before we played Wednesday. But they'd come in, give everything and were just chuffed to bits to be there. Who's to say they're not good players? Sometimes with their clubs they had found their level, but they were playing international football so I just treated them the same as anybody else. I don't go along with this idea that because they were in the Third Division they were shit. They had a clearly defined role and did a job for us; they played to the maximum of their ability and let no one down.

There was no better example of this than Alan Knill, a young central defender with Halifax Town and Swansea, who was born in Slough to Welsh parents. When we played our first 1990 World Cup qualifier in Amsterdam's Olympisch Stadium against the newly crowned European champions we were beset by an injury crisis. Pat Van Den Hauwe and Rats were both missing, while we were up against Marco Van Basten and Ruud Gullit – considered not just the best forward partnership of the era, but one of the greatest of all time. Thrown into this battleground was Alan, who was used to playing against third-tier sloggers in front of several thousand fans in some of England's less auspicious arenas. But he did brilliantly on his debut, and for 90 minutes looked as if he wouldn't have been out of place among the Dutch team itself. Van Basten was in Alan's pocket, and for most of the game it seemed as if we might get something. But eight minutes from the end Gullit scored the only goal of the game and the European Champions got the result they expected.

You look at that game and you think that Alan would have gone on to do great things. But he never played for Wales again and I don't think he played beyond the third tier either. What he did on that afternoon was incredible and it shows the hidden potential that lies in many players as well as the limitations of our scouting systems. In most managers' eyes there are preconceived ideas about players and they're given a level – Premier League,

League One, or whatever – by the age of 20 and, generally speaking, not expected to rise above it. They're not given an opportunity but, as we saw with Alan, if given a chance to sink or swim players can grasp that opportunity. If I had been a First Division manager at the time I'd have signed him up on the basis of that performance.

In such a hard group our chances relied on us getting something from the two matches against its fourth team, Finland. But when we played them a month later at Swansea's Vetch Field we only drew 2-2, which ended any realistic hopes we had of going to Italy. We then drew 0-0 with West Germany, which was an obstacle on their way to qualifying but didn't really do anything to strengthen our own chances. When we lost 1-0 in Helsinki that was us finished.

Of course we were frustrated to miss out on another big tournament. We'd have loved to have gone to Italy, as we would West Germany for the European Championships. But even in a qualifying campaign in which people doom you to failure before you've even kicked a ball you can get numerous things out of the experience. During that campaign I played against Andreas Möller, Andreas Brehme, Rudi Völler, Jürgen Klinsmann, Van Basten, Gullit and Frank Rijkaard. I experienced the passion and intensity of the Dutch crowd. I learned how expressive and arrogant the Dutch players were. It was all a massive learning curve.

While we watched at home, West Germany went to the 1990 World Cup and won the tournament. The Berlin Wall had come down at the end of the previous year, and when they re-entered international football it was as a unified Germany. The world champions had an extra 16 million people added to their pool of talent, and guess who had drawn them for the qualifying campaign for the 1992 European Championships? That's right, Wales, again.

You can view these draws as a curse or you can welcome the challenge. I know I always did the latter and I'm sure most of my Wales team-mates did too. We always played better against the big countries and raised our game. We liked the challenge and we took a lot from the learning experience.

Having Germany in our group probably took the pressure off us a bit, too. When we started the qualifying campaign we got a couple of really good results against Belgium, who we beat 3-1 at home and then held to a 1-1 draw in Brussels. We beat Luxembourg as well. It put us in a good place when the first of our two games against Germany came up, at Cardiff Arms Park in June 1991.

We had a good combination going into the game: we had home advantage, a great and passionate crowd, and little expectation that we'd get anything from the game. We were massive underdogs, but that's what Welsh football's all about. We could have turned up on Tuesday night, had steak and chips, got bladdered, and gone on and played the same; because the motivation was there. You don't need anything else. Team talks, whatever, you just don't need them, because you're there with people that want to be there and win. We did a bit of tactical stuff, but not much. Training was relaxed and fun. We knew what we had to do.

When we got to the Arms Park it was full. It was a nice warm night. As a goalie you expect to be busy when you play the world champions. When you play those sort of teams it's always good for a goalie because you like to be challenged. You know they're going to throw a lot at you, but that's good. At the same time it's slightly different from being an outfield player. If I was a midfield player I'd be thinking, 'Shit, I might have to chase a few shadows here; I'll never catch anybody.' But as a goalie you can see what's coming to a certain extent.

We had a good team system, with Rushy always able to get goals, no matter the calibre of the opposition, and Sparky or Dean Saunders who could drop back and help in midfield. We always defended well and knew that if we got a goal in front against a good team it was going to be hard to break us down. What you've got to remember is that the lads, some of whom were in the Second or Third Division, were used to grafting, and their fitness levels were brilliant. Allied to this we had people like Rats in the team who could run all day, but had brains as well. There were lots of good things in that Wales team. But the main thing was the will to win and the desire to put on a performance for all those people who supported us through thick and thin. I think once you get that it pulls all the footballing factors together.

That evening against Germany was one of the days you dream about. Everything came together. Barry Horne was magnificent in midfield, and marked Lothar Matthäus out of the game, to the extent that Germany's captain and talisman was eventually substituted. We had to defend lots and defend well, as you would expect when facing the world champions. But then on 66 minutes we broke away. We hit a long ball over the top, and Rushy wriggled free of his marker and had that magical extra yard of pace. The ball sprang up nicely for him and he hit a fine half-volley into the back of the net for the only goal of the game.

Beating the world champions is nice, of course; but beating Germany carried some extra resonance for me. I really admired their football culture and the arrogance of their players, the way they inherently believe that they're the best. I still think if Wales could have had some of that they'd have done ten times better. Germans are brought up to believe they're good players. By contrast we were brought up to believe you might win, but then you might not. The German way I always find fascinating; everything's got to be right and they've got to be the best. They book the hotel for the World Cup Final as soon as it's announced where it's going to be; that's how confident they are. That's the sort of mentality you need. And to beat a country versed in such thinking was just brilliant.

Three months later we were back at the Arms Park, facing Brazil, and we won 1-0, this time with Dean Saunders getting the goal. It was another unbelievable result, but there was never any sense that we might have cracked it. International football is completely unlike club football and we'd never carry any momentum – good or bad – from one fixture to the next. It just wasn't like that. But I was happy. I played Brazil twice in my career, won one game and drew the other, which is not a bad record.

The Brazil friendly was, of course, a mere interlude ahead of the main business, against Germany in the return fixture in Nuremburg a month later. If we avoided defeat our destiny, going into the final qualifying match against Luxembourg, was in our own hands.

Four thousand Welsh fans – 1,300 more than witnessed my international debut in Wrexham a decade earlier – made the trip to Bavaria. But if they were hoping for a repeat of the Cardiff heroics they were soon to be vastly disappointed. Lothar Matthäus had promised that Germany 'will not fail' prior to kickoff and that proved to be a huge understatement. We held our own for 25 minutes, giving me a Welsh goalkeeping record of 385 minutes without conceding. But I didn't advance that record by much. Three times over eleven minutes Germany breached my goal, and by half-time we were 3-0 down. Hopes of an unlikely comeback were all but extinguished in the 51st minute, when Dean Saunders lost his cool and was sent off for kicking Thomas Doll. Germany scored a fourth and although Paul Bodin pulled one back from the penalty spot, we were finished again.

IT WAS BACK TO THE DRAWING BOARD AGAIN for Terry Yorath. When qualifying for the 1994 World Cup started I was a few months short of my 34th birthday, Rushy was nearly 31 and Sparky 29. Rats' Wales career was over; Pat Van Den Hauwe was long off the scene. We were an ageing team.

Thankfully Terry Yorath was helped by the addition of some excellent young players, who would go on to have top-class careers longer even than my own. For years, Manchester United fans had been promised that there was another 'new George Best' about to step up to restore their team to forgotten glories. I'd played with one of them – Norman Whiteside – at Everton. But in Ryan Giggs, a thrilling teenage winger, they had just that. Best of all, he was Welsh.

Ryan was quiet, but could obviously play. He ultimately suffered a bit

with Wales, I thought, because as soon as he was half-established he was expected to win the game on his own for us, but the opposition doubled up on
him. It was hard for him. I thought he was under more pressure playing for
Wales than he was for Manchester United, purely because people expected a
world-class player to win us the game. But it didn't always work like that. He
suffered because of his own genius, if you like, because opponents were also
content to kick him off the pitch. And if you were Alex Ferguson you clearly
didn't want him going to Moldova to get kicked in the air when he had to
come home and play a league game on the Saturday, so he faced additional
pressure to withdraw from squads at the slightest hint of injury.

Gary Speed came in with a wise head beyond his young years. From
the outset it was obvious he had a very good knowledge of football. For me
he could have played in any position he wanted to. He was brought up to be
dedicated by his manager at Leeds, Howard Wilkinson, which certainly advanced his playing career to the age of 40. I remember mad Mickey Thomas
being at Leeds and coming back with all these nutritional supplements, diets
and summer training plans. That was the ethos he was taught at Elland Road
and Gary took it on board and never lost it. He always had that dedication, a
game plan in his head, and could adapt to any position. I still think his best
position would have been centre half, or sweeper. That's where we used him
a couple of times under Bobby Gould; he had such a good football brain I
thought that's where his long-term future lay.

When Gary first came into the Wales squad in 1991 he looked liked a
model; he just looked liked somebody who was destined to be really good.
It's hard to put your finger on it, but he had that slight aura about him. He
looked good, he looked fit, and when he talked you would listen. It never
surprised me that he went on to be a fantastic captain for most of the clubs
he was at and internationally too.

These two players gave Welsh football hope for the 1990s. By recent
standards we had an open group for qualifying for the 1994 World Cup
in the United States: Romania, the Representation of Czechs and Slovaks

(RCS –Czechoslovakia split into two countries halfway through qualifying), Belgium, Cyprus and the Faroe Islands.

Qualifying, however, got off to a nightmare start. We travelled out to Bucharest in May 1992. It was a couple of years after the fall of the country's dictator, Nicolae Ceausescu, and the post-revolutionary elation had dissipated. The country was in a terrible state, with children begging everywhere. People had nothing. We'd started taking our own chefs to these countries by this stage, and if you left anything on the table – brown sauce or ketchup, whatever – it'd be gone. It was a grim place. But its people had football to give them hope and Romania had a great team, spearheaded by the wonderful Gheorghe Hagi. They completely outclassed us, scoring five first-half goals and everything after that was damage limitation. It was a match in which we were just completely overwhelmed.

Slowly we settled into our groove. We beat the countries we should have done and held our own against the RCS and Belgium (who we defeated in Cardiff but lost against in Brussels). Perhaps we should have beaten the RCS when we played them in Cardiff, but that ended in a 2-2 draw. What all of this meant was that we went into the final round of qualifying matches with our destiny in our own hands. If we beat Romania in Cardiff we would be travelling to the United States for the World Cup finals. It would be the first time in my lifetime we had achieved such a feat, and possibly the last time in my career I would be able to do so. Wales expected and so did I.

With England and Scotland virtually out of contention for qualifying in their respective groups there was a huge amount of attention on us going into the game. Oddly, given my obsession with being prepared, my initial memory looking back is of being stuck in training. What I used to do was drive my car down to the ground early, four o'clockish, do a little warm-up and then I'd stay there. And this particular day I couldn't find my keys, so in the end I got a police escort from the training base to Cardiff Arms Park. They put me in a police car going 100 miles an hour down the dual carriageway; it was fucking brilliant to be honest, absolutely brilliant. So I was half an hour late, which didn't go down very well. Of course, when I got to the Arms Park and I was getting changed, the first thing I found was my keys in my kitbag. Which didn't go down very well, either.

The game was obviously a tight one as indeed all of the big games were for Wales. The plan was always to keep things close at the back and use our pace on the break, and it had served us well in the past. But on 31 minutes I let in a bad goal from Hagi. He was one of the finest strikers of the ball in the world, but I should have had this one; his shot from 25 yards just slipped under my body and suddenly we had to score two goals.

The crowd were terrific and cheered us on and 15 minutes after the interval we were back in the game when Dean Saunders jabbed home an equaliser. Seconds later Dan Petrescu brought down Gary Speed in their penalty area and we had a wonderful chance of going in front. Paul Bodin had never missed any of his three penalties for us and was the regular taker for Swindon Town – then in the Premier League. We never had any doubt he should take the penalty. He struck the ball cleanly, but the ball seemed to alter trajectory in the final milliseconds and it struck the crossbar.

We still had 30 minutes to try and get a winner, but seven minutes from the end Florin Raducioiu struck a shot between my legs and all hope died. Again, I should have saved it.

There were tears at the final whistle. There were no bad refereeing decisions or misfortune this time, we'd only ourselves to blame. But our distress was brought into sharp focus as news filtered through that a fan had died at the end of the game. Some idiot had fired a distress flare across the stadium and it hit a poor fan on his way out of the stadium, killing him. Most Wales supporters had watched in horror as the trail of smoke had been left behind by this deadly flare, and within hours all were aware of the death of a retired postman, named John Hill.

With many of my team-mates I attended his funeral. It was a terrible day and one that brought home yet again that there's no such thing as a football tragedy when human life is at stake.

# CHAPTER ELEVEN
# STRUGGLER

AT EVERTON DURING THIS PERIOD we never got so close to such glory.

I was gutted when Colin Harvey was sacked as manager. I didn't think it was the right thing to do; he should have been given more time. I was devastated for Colin, who lived and breathed the club. There should have been more faith and patience shown in him by the board, as there had been with Howard seven years earlier. Sometimes these situations just need a spark to reignite a winning mentality.

Six days after Colin was fired the club held a press conference at Goodison. I had absolutely no inkling of what was going to follow. Most people expected Joe Royle, the former Everton centre forward and Oldham

Athletic manager, to be appointed as Colin's successor. Ron Atkinson and Arthur Cox were also mentioned. Personally I would have liked to have seen Brian Clough given a chance, although some people said he was finished by then. No one expected it at all when Howard Kendall was named as Everton's new manager. To everyone's surprise, Colin came back as his assistant.

Colin's sacking and then his return in a lesser position was seen as an admission by the board that they had got his appointment as manager in 1987 wrong. I didn't see it that way, though. If anything they should have kept Colin and brought in a more experienced figure that he could have gone to when he needed advice. Terry Darracott was great and all the players liked him, as we did Colin. But perhaps if there was someone in the background they could have approached to sound out every now and then it would have made a difference.

In the dressing room I don't think anybody wanted to get rid of Colin. We hadn't been doing well under him and the inexplicability of our demise inevitably led some people up high or on the terraces to demand change, but I don't think anybody in the dressing room wanted to him to leave, because he was Mr Everton. What happened when he was Everton manager wasn't through a lack of effort or work rate, or desire; it just didn't work for him. It was just one of those things.

Having said that, those who had worked with him before knew and trusted Howard. Footballers don't like change and I certainly didn't. My only thoughts before the appointment was announced were: I hope it's somebody that I can get on with and somebody that won't fuck Everton up too much.

After leaving Bilbao Howard had spent the previous 11 months as Manchester City manager and stabilised their institutionally unsteady ship. But Maine Road, he said, was 'like a love affair' while Everton 'was a marriage'.

He hadn't changed at all, but then people don't over a few years, do they? As a person he was probably slightly less tolerant; or expected better. When he didn't get it he was a bit more sarcastic this time than he was the first time round. But otherwise, he was just the same old Howard. For me it was good because it meant that I could keep doing things my way.

Things steadied very quickly. I don't think there was any magic formula to our stabilising, which shows that we weren't a bad side in the first place. But Howard had a fresh voice and there was a shift in mood. That's all it took and we were soon out of relegation trouble.

The game everyone remembers from the 1990/91 season is the 4-4 draw with Liverpool in an FA Cup fifth round replay. It was under the floodlights at Goodison, which is always special, and the crowd were loud and passionate and voracious as ever. Four times Liverpool went ahead and four times we pulled them back level, with Graeme Sharp and Tony Cottee getting a brace apiece. It was a game that had everything: goals, saves, tackles, a brilliant crowd; it was a proper old-fashioned game of football, one of the best I've ever played in.

Forty-eight hours later Kenny Dalglish announced his resignation as Liverpool manager. At Everton we were all completely shocked. Although we were rivals, there was a huge amount of respect for Kenny at Goodison that I think was shared throughout the game as a whole. But the burden he carried after the Hillsborough disaster must have been huge. Whenever there was a funeral Kenny was there, showing his support to the families of the victims. Nobody can say how big a burden he carried through those times and his departure was probably the right decision for him at the time. I saw it as the end of an era at Anfield, not just in terms of the monopoly on success Liverpool had had – and the trophies did dry up after that – but for another reason.

I think that Merseyside football lost something more intangible the day Kenny left Anfield. Because he was such a great man and such a defining figure, the whole city struggled to come to terms with his departure. He had been a giant through Hillsborough and everyone respected him for that. He brought dignity and class to Merseyside football. As Everton players we measured ourselves against him and what he'd achieved at Anfield. To beat Liverpool with Kenny in charge was a great achievement; he elevated the

Merseyside derby to a different plateau and I don't think that the rivalry between the two clubs has been the same since.

Everton won the second replay at Goodison the following week, through a Dave Watson header. In the quarter-finals we faced Second Division West Ham at Upton Park, but despite being hotly fancied lost 2-1. We were the sort of team that could do that kind of thing: beat the biggest team in the country and then lose to a lesser club.

There was, however, a return to Wembley, for the final of the Zenith Data Systems Cup, where we faced Crystal Palace. This was always something of a grudge match because Martin Keown had some sort of history with them. It was funny because it was supposed to be a competition that no one wanted to play in, but because of this history we battled and scrapped and fought like nobody's business. I loved those sort of games, so long as it was honest battling. What I didn't like was people standing on your toes and spitting at you. If someone's going to smash you, well, fine; at least they're blatantly honest about it and you know it's coming and can prepare yourself. But nothing snide.

Everton had a new doctor that day, who was absolutely hopeless. Mike Newell got concussed during the game and the doctor tried to send him back on; and then Martin got smashed between Geoff Thomas and Eric Young. They absolutely did him a treat and he had something like 10 or 12 stitches inside his mouth. But the doctor missed all that, missed all the blood, so they had to go somewhere else and get it all stitched up. By then we'd lost 4-1 after extra time. I refused to go and collect my medal. I mean, who wants to get a Zenith Data Systems Cup runners-up medal? Howard, however, wasn't best pleased with me.

We finished the season ninth, which after the poor start wasn't bad, but it was still the worst showing in my decade at the club. Over the summer there were more changes. Some of Colin's signings were dispatched, such as Mike Milligan and Stuart McCall, as Howard sought to rebuild again. Sharpy was also forced out the door and sold to Oldham, which I thought was a bad move for him; he was better than that and could have gone to a bigger club. But once Howard wanted to get rid of you that was that. He wouldn't be the only one to face the cold side of our manager.

Howard bought Mark Ward from Manchester City, a player he had previously let go when he was a kid at Everton, then signed from West Ham when at Maine Road. Alan Harper also came back from a spell at City. He was linked with my Wales team-mate Dean Saunders, who ended up joining Liverpool for a British record fee, and that meant Peter Beardsley, their outstanding deep-lying forward, was free to join Everton for £1million.

Peter was a truly great player, probably too brilliant for us at the time and frankly far too advanced for the players that we had. He would play passes that nobody else could see. He loved creating chances for his team-mates, but he often ended up giving the ball away because the others couldn't see what he could see. Beards was not just a great player, but a leader too. What people didn't see was how good he was with the kids and how he would take them out in the afternoon sometimes. He was good like that.

Although like me he didn't drink, he was always one of the most popular members of the team and at the heart of everything off the pitch. On tour I remember one night when we were the last to go to bed at 5am. Everyone else was pissed off their faces, but we were stone-cold sober. He always made sure everybody was happy on the bus, and brought all sorts of cakes for everyone and always had a collection of videos to keep us amused. Peter was an absolutely diamond fellow. But again, wrong time, wrong place, and he was too good for us at times. He just played things that nobody else saw and it stood out.

We started the season amid high expectation. We played pretty well in the opening game at Nottingham Forest, despite losing 2-1, then beat the champions Arsenal 3-1 at Goodison and held Manchester United to a goalless draw at home. We played some lovely football at times, but lacked the finishing touches we needed in front of goal.

Howard knew what he wanted, but just couldn't get it. He wanted people with personalities. If you look at who he bought or relied on in the past – Andy Gray, Sheeds, Rats and Reidy, Trevor – they were all good personalities and good characters, and good mixers. I think he wanted a bit of Andy Gray in every player. It wouldn't matter what happened off the pitch as long as they performed on there. But the likes of Tony Cottee and Pat Nevin were conscientious; good pros, but probably didn't have enough character or charisma for Howard. He'd look at them and think, 'Well, is that it? Is that what you do?'

It was unfair in some ways because they were good players, but that was never enough for Howard. Team spirit was always an integral part of the way his teams had operated. He believed that if you stuck together, then your good team spirit and strong characters would see you through. During the glory years we won some games we shouldn't have won on team spirit alone. The way players interacted in the dressing room gave us great strength, because if you didn't do your thing you'd get absolutely hammered by your team-mates. I don't think he could picture someone like Tony slaughtering Paddy; they were nice people and not nasty or mean enough to be top, top-level players. Tony scored goals and Paddy was a wonderful player, but they didn't have the nasty streak to get where Howard wanted. I think he had a problem where he thought they were good players in their own right but were they going to run through a brick wall for him? Would they be ruthless enough? Were they going to be strong enough characters? I don't think he thought they were. He didn't see them as leadership material.

One player who did have all that nastiness and ruthlessness was Rats, our captain through the glory years. But he found his place in the side under threat from Martin Keown and Dave Watson had replaced him as captain. He'd probably lost a bit of his pace due to injuries, but he was still only just 31, still playing for Wales and still a good player. Howard brought him back for a League Cup fourth round match against Leeds at Goodison in December 1991. We got absolutely battered and Rats was brought off at half-time. After that Howard made it known he didn't want him at the club;

he dumped him in the reserves and Rats, Everton's most successful ever captain, never played for the first team again. His treatment just wasn't right. Looking back it was Howard's way of trying to get him out the door, whereas maybe he could have embraced him a little bit more.

I think it's hard sometimes when you're coming to the end of your time at a club. I'd have liked Rats to have been kept on as coach. He could have played when needed and the dressing room could have retained his experience and winning mentality. Maybe it's the way it's sold to you sometimes; it can put your nose out of joint and create an atmosphere. Perhaps Howard could have put his arm around Rats and said, 'Martin's our first choice now, but you have an important role to play still. We need your experience with the kids and from time to time with the first team.' But it didn't happen like that. We lost him at a time when we shouldn't have lost him. But then Andy Gray had gone like that, too. So did Sharpy. And a month or so later, so did Sheeds, who joined Newcastle on a free transfer.

Howard brought in some new players to try and freshen things up. From Liverpool came Gary Ablett, who was a terrific player. I knew Gary from way back, and his father too. Gary was the mirror image of his dad, a policeman who I got to know while undertaking my rehabilitation at the force's swimming pool in Aigburth in the mid 1980s. He was a cracking fellow with a very dry sense of humour, but a good player too. He was always hard-working and conscientious and could play left back and centre half. He was one of those players who you knew would never let you down.

Howard also signed the striker Mo Johnston from Glasgow Rangers. He was a real character, very funny and generous and full of life – the sort of person that you need in the dressing room. I suppose you could say he was an Andy Gray-type personality, which is what Howard so desperately wanted. But for whatever reason he just didn't rate Mo, and never really gave him a chance.

The departures of Sheeds and Rats left me the sole survivor of the 1985 side, with only Waggy and Ian Snodin who had been there when we last won the league. That had been less than five years earlier, but it seemed a long time ago. We finished the 1991/92 season 12th; yet another low. There were no cup runs as we exited both the League and FA Cups in the fourth round.

I was only 33, young for a goalkeeper, but at this stage I never entertained thoughts of leaving. I was reconciled to the fact that Everton and me were meant to be. I thought, 'There's no point in leaving now, is there? I'll just leave when they get rid of me.' Things were changing around me, football was changing. Maybe that was part of Everton's problem: the club couldn't keep pace with the game's evolution. The game was becoming more commercial, media-driven, and the Premier League was about to start. Sports science and nutrition were becoming important factors at clubs, there were new training techniques. But if things went wrong at Everton we still went out for a Chinese to try and talk things through. Or we'd do Howard's routine of lining up the YTS lads in goal and hammering them with shots until there was blood pouring from their faces.

There was a drinking culture too, and that impacted on the dressing room. Some people involved in the club were drinking too much and although it was no more than in the past, the way football was changing meant that they couldn't keep it up and do their jobs properly. Although I'm teetotal I don't mind anybody in the world drinking as long as they do what they're supposed to do, but that was no longer happening.

Some of this change I liked, some of it I didn't. I never consciously sat down and thought, 'I've got to leave here because it's shit.' I was always enjoying what I did. I loved training, I loved the banter of the dressing room and loved initiating people into Everton Football Club. And for me, because we had a high turnover of people and we had different sorts of people coming through the door, it meant there were more people to take the piss out of.

ON A PRACTICAL LEVEL what Howard needed was a target man to play up front with Beards or Tony. In the summer of 1992 he was linked to players like Duncan Ferguson and even Alan Shearer, but given the club's financial situation and standing at the time we were never realistically going to get them. We ended up signing Paul Rideout and Barry Horne, who both ended up doing great for us after slow starts.

But more than the players on the pitch I think what it boiled down to with Howard was the character of the people and the leadership qualities they had. I can honestly say there was nobody at the club that I personally disliked, ever. Some were better than others but on the whole I got on well with all of them, mainly because I floated between every group. I didn't live in Southport so I wasn't part of that clique, I didn't live in Cheshire so I wasn't part of that clique. I'd see my colleagues in their natural environment where they behaved just as they wanted to behave. But I think when Howard came in, he looked at them and thought, 'They go there and they go there and they go here.' I believe he thought there were factions. They weren't his cup of tea.

The dressing room wasn't an unhappy place, but you could sense this tension coming from the top. Howard tried a few short-term fixes, such as bringing in Kenny Sansom on a free transfer. Kenny was a good player who'd been there and seen it all; he was a great fellow to have around, but it didn't really help. Nor was Howard helped by the fact that there was uncertainty over the long-term future of the club. Everton's patriarchal owner John Moores was nearly 100 years old and not in the best of health. Philip Carter was no longer chairman and there was no direction from the boardroom. There was talk in the press of big debts. In January 1993 Martin Keown was sold to Arsenal, supposedly to keep the banks at bay.

During that season we saw the emergence of a home-grown midfielder who captured the imagination of every Evertonian and gave them hope in their hearts. You could see straight away that Billy Kenny was destined for great things. He could pass over short and long distances and possessed energy and verve and desire. He had all the components to be one of the best players we had ever had. When we played Liverpool in the Goodison derby he put in a stirring performance as we won 2-1.

But unfortunately, for whatever reason, Billy just couldn't handle the pressures of professional football. Other substances got the better of him and he went missing from training. The club protected him as best they could when the rumours started to get out, but there was only so much they could do. He later joined Oldham and Joe Royle did what he could for him, as did Sharpy when he became manager there. But they couldn't get him back and he slipped out of the game. I don't know where he is or what he's doing now. It was such a great waste and tragic for him and his family.

We finished the 1992/93 season 13th, down a place on the previous year. More tellingly, perhaps, we were just four points off relegation, whereas a year previously it had been 11 points.

In some minds we'd completed the transition from good team to a mediocre one to a bad one, but I never saw it like that. Even when we were in real trouble I never saw us as a bad team. I got on well with the lads and individually they could play all right. I didn't think we could win the league because I thought there were better teams than us. But I was enjoying myself at the club and I was playing really well myself, probably the best football of my career if I'm honest.

There was no money available for signings, or what little was in the bank was said to be ring-fenced for a centre forward. Howard did what he could with his limited resources, but it wasn't enough. He signed this Serbian player who had been playing in six-a-side leagues in the US, called Preki. He was never an eleven-a-side player. He wasn't fit and didn't understand foot-ball as we played it. In short, he wasn't good enough for Everton.

Yet on the other hand we had a player like Robert Warzycha who was everything that Preki wasn't but couldn't get a game. Howard had signed him not long after he returned and after having a great start he faded from view. He was a Polish international and super-fit; a great player. He couldn't get over English football. In his homeland they trained three times a day in pre-season, whereas we'd go away on tours and half the team would be up drinking most of the night.

Howard's hunt for a target man went on and on. It was all the press seemed to talk about through 1993. He'd tried to sign Dion Dublin from Cambridge United a year earlier but had been foiled when Manchester United unexpectedly came in for him. As the year was coming to its disappointing conclusion, with Everton ensconced in mid-table, Howard became alerted to his availability.

Dion was an aggressive centre forward; a good player, a good character, a good pro who also had that bit of devilment and leadership quality in him. But I think it was getting to the point where the board no longer trusted Howard's judgement. They couldn't see Dion Dublin being worthwhile for us. When they vetoed his signing Howard handed in his resignation an hour after leading us to a 1-0 win over Southampton. Just 13,667 had come to see it, the lowest league attendance in a decade.

Just as I never had any inkling that he was coming back to Everton three years earlier, so I was in the dark about Howard's decision to leave us. After the Southampton game he never told us his intentions and I didn't know he had quit until I read about it on Teletext later that evening. I was aware of his frustration, but it wasn't as palpable as Colin's had been. Howard was a different fish and would never show his feelings. He got a bit tetchy now and again, but not usually with the players.

Dion went on to have a brilliant career with Coventry, Aston Villa and England, which probably says a lot about whose judgement was best.

Jimmy Gabriel, who was in charge of the reserves, took over as caretaker manager. He had been rough, tough wing half as a player, but he wasn't like that at all as a manager or coach. He was a lovely man, and reminded me of Great Uncle Bulgaria off The Wombles. I don't think he was ever ruthless enough to be the manager, but then I don't think he really wanted that job anyway. Things didn't go too well under his caretakership and we lost six of the seven games he was in charge, failing to score in six of them.

Not for the first or last time, Bobby Robson was heavily linked to the Everton job. Robson had managed England for many years and had gone on to have a successful coaching career in Europe. Bobby would have been brilliant for Everton. He was not just a brilliant manager but a great man too. His knowledge and understanding of football and footballers were way in advance of most people working in England at the time. His enthusiasm was infectious and it would have picked everyone up. He would have transformed Everton. But when he made it clear he wished to remain in Portugal where he was in charge of FC Porto, the Everton board went for somebody very different. Instead of someone who loved football, we got someone who loved his suntan.

⌶

WHEN I FIRST HEARD Mike Walker was going to be Everton manager, I thought it might be okay. He'd nearly won the Premier League with Norwich a year earlier and was a former goalkeeper. He was Welsh as well, from just down the road from me in Colwyn Bay, although he never played for Wales. His son Ian was Tottenham's goalkeeper and a good player. When I first met him he seemed like a nice man. Scarcely could I have imagined that he would oversee one of the most disastrous episodes in Everton's history.

Managing Norwich and managing Everton are two entirely different propositions. At Norwich you don't carry the same insatiable burden of expectation and nor do their players. I talked about Howard struggling with the lack of characters at Everton; well, he would have hated a club like Norwich where it was a bunch of 'yes sir, no sir, right away sir' type players. By contrast the characters that we had at Goodison – even if they weren't enough for Howard – were too much for Mike to handle. I include myself in that equation.

He brought with him David Williams as his assistant manager, which meant Colin left the club. I'd played with Dave for Wales, I'd been coached by him and even managed by him on one occasion. Dave was a whipping boy for the Welsh squad. We used to take the piss out of him all the time, so it was a funny position for me to be in. We used to take the piss out of him about his clothes, about being so quiet, and – how should I put it? – boring, I suppose. I was probably one of the ringleaders, to be fair. He'd been a good player but was very quiet, which made him an easy target. When he got the Wales job for one game, Dave gave his team talk. Now Dave never swore, but this time it was 'Fuck this, fuck that'. We sat around laughing; we just couldn't believe it. It was as if it wasn't the real Dave.

When he came to Everton as coach, he did everything on the training ground. He was very methodical in what he did, but training was just incredibly boring. Everything was circle work. We might do a few doggies, but that was too easy. There was no reward, no fun; it was monotonous, tedious. Walker was never anywhere to be seen until five minutes before the end of a session when he'd pull up in his Jag, make his face seen and then bugger off again.

He changed the pattern of playing, which didn't do us any favours. We just weren't good enough to play the kind of football he wanted us to play, which was a continental-type game, lots of passing from the back. It wasn't suited to Everton at the time and it wasn't suited to English football. We'd pass the ball 50 times without it leaving our half, give the ball away and our opponents would score.

Walker's signings were a mixed bag. The first player he bought was the centre forward Brett Angell, who was absolutely slated by the fans. If Brett put his head outside the door he'd get stick; he was just one of those people. I loved Brett though. In all my years at the club I don't think I came across anyone who was more desperate to do well for Everton. If some of the players that Colin Harvey signed had showed some of his desire and determination I don't think Everton would have found themselves in the position they were in at that time. Brett was a good player in the lower leagues, where his scor-ing record was phenomenal, but the step up to the Premier League was prob-ably too great for him. He had a first touch like a tackle, and we slaughtered him for it. But then we were allowed to, because we were playing with him!

Peter Beagrie was sold to Manchester City and Walker brought in the Sweden international winger Anders Limpar from Arsenal on the same day. Anders was a wonderful talent; a flair player who could do things that no-body else could even conceive of. I would look at him and some of the things he did on the pitch and the training ground and think, 'We've got one of the best players in the world on our hands.' Anders was that good. Quite why he never established himself as one of the greats is beyond me. With the amount of natural ability he possessed he could have done. But to play that way he needed the freedom to excel, and some of the clubs he turned out for didn't give him licence to be Anders.

Off the pitch he was great company. One of the things I was lucky with during my career was that we always had good fellows in the dressing room and I worked with some very nice people. Anders was one of the best and had a terrific sense of humour. He's quite shy in lots of ways, but underneath he's an absolute raging inferno of wickedness. Of course, he was a target of some of my piss-taking too. Once he confessed to me that he wanted to be a fireman.

'How the hell are you going to be a fireman?' I asked, looking at his 5ft 6in frame. 'Are you going to be a Lego fireman? Or are you just going to do bungalows?'

It was a big mistake telling someone like me something like that. Even now when I see Anders, I ask, 'Are you a fireman yet? How's the fire-fighting going?'

The new manager also brought in some young unknowns. Gary Rowett would go on to have a decent career elsewhere, but the previously un-heralded Joe Parkinson made the Goodison grade. He was a solid, depend-able northern lad from Wigan who gave his all and pushed himself to the limits. Straight away I got him on my early-morning head-tennis routine, telling him to be in for 9am, which he did for the first six weeks before getting sick of it. When he first came I thought he was just a good grafter, but he was actually far, far better than that; he was a really good passer, who became invaluable to the way we played. Unfortunately for Joe he became a bit too invaluable to Everton and was played when he was injured, which caused a career-ending injury at the age of 28.

Our results from March 1994 onwards were just atrocious. We lost the derby at Anfield 2-1, then went down 3-0 at Norwich in front of the TV cameras with the Norwich fans singing, 'Walker, Walker, what's the score?' We lost at home to Spurs on Anders' debut, then drew 0-0 at Aston Villa. Over Easter weekend we lost 5-1 at Sheffield Wednesday, then 3-0 at home to Blackburn. Tony Cottee got us a crucial, crucial win at West Ham but that didn't stop the rot. A goalless draw at home to Coventry separated a 2-1 defeat at Queens Park Rangers and a 3-0 loss at Leeds. It meant that we went into the last day of the season, at home to Wimbledon, in the last relegation spot and needing to better the result of Sheffield United, who were above us.

Goodison at the time was a strange place, as the old Park Stand had been demolished to make way for a new all-seater stand. It's funny though, because I can't even really remember that now. I think I was too worried about the predicament we found ourselves in to be concerned about it.

I never ever thought we were going to lose the Wimbledon match. A game of such importance, I never thought we were going to lose, ever. For me, back then, Everton getting relegated was just completely and utterly inconceivable. Even when things got particularly bad, which they soon did.

On four minutes Anders handled in our penalty area after a corner. I've no idea what he was doing there, as he hardly ever came into our half, never mind our box. He wasn't even anywhere near the goal when it happened. Dean Holdsworth took the spot kick, and although I got a hand on it I couldn't stop it. On 20 minutes Dave Watson and David Unsworth went for the same ball, Andy Clarke had a shot, which he mishit, and the ball went in off Gary Ablett's shin as he was back-pedalling, trying to clear it.

It was a catastrophe of errors but even then, when we were 2-0 down, the thought of losing never entered my head. Don't ask me why because I don't know. I never panicked, never worried; I always thought we were going to win; somehow, some way, I always thought we were going to win. I just don't know why; I can't explain it. I've never had that feeling before.

The atmosphere went a bit flat after that, but just before half-time Anders took a tumble in the Wimbledon area and the referee awarded a penalty. Mark Ward and Tony Cottee had been our designated takers that season, but Wardy wasn't playing and I could see that Tony didn't fancy it, so I took the ball. And why not? I was the most experienced player and after my goal in the Full Members Cup shootout seven years earlier I had a 100 per cent penalty record. I'd said before kickoff that if there was a penalty I'd be taking it, but I don't think anybody took my pledge too seriously until we were faced with that situation.

I think seeing me take the ball shamed some of the other players. I'm sure that's what spurred Graham Stuart into action. I reckon he said to himself that it would be too embarrassing for the club for the goalkeeper to take such a crucial penalty. He took the ball off me, and I thought, 'Fair play, if you want to take it, then take it.' If someone has the bollocks to take the ball off you in a situation like that then they deserve their chance. Had he not stepped forward I'd have smashed it as hard as I could at Hans Segers' face; that's the way to score. Graham, by contrast, placed it, but he didn't make any mistake and the score was 2-1.

Half-time came and in the second half we were kicking towards the Gwladys Street goal. Graham Stuart had another good chance that he created himself, but Wimbledon had the best opportunities and Dean Holdsworth might have added another on a few occasions. I, however, had total confidence. There was never any doubt that we'd do it, not at any point.

On 67 minutes Barry Horne picked up a loose ball on the edge of the centre circle and drove forward. About 25 yards from goal, the ball bobbled up nicely for him and he unleashed a fearsome curling shot into the top corner. It was a brilliant goal. Ten minutes from full-time Anders broke down the left and played it into Graham Stuart; he played a wall pass with Cottee and stabbed it in from the edge of the area. It was a toe-poke really, but it brought Everton salvation. In the other game Chelsea beat Sheffield United to send them down. As I said, there was never any doubt at all that we'd be saved and we were.

Lots of mud has been thrown around about our win against Wimbledon that day, with some saying it was a fix and a conspiracy. It's certainly true that the Wimbledon bus was burned out the night before by some scallywag Evertonians. But knowing some of the Wimbledon players I'm not sure they'd have been too unsettled by that or the raucous atmosphere at Goodison. More revelations came. The following March, Wimbledon's goalkeeper, Hans Segers, was arrested on suspicion of match-fixing and subsequently charged. At the trial, he was asked about a payment of £19,000 into a Swiss bank account six days after the Everton match. It was one of a number of payments totalling £160,000 that had been made over a period of two years. Segers denied any wrongdoing, claiming the payments were from legitimate business interests. Hans was eventually acquitted of all charges and is now goalkeeping coach at Fulham.

I spoke to Hans about it a few times and I know what he's like. He's not one of those players that is going to chuck a ball into the net for you. He's just not that sort of person. In any case, it's harder than you'd think just to let goals in. If you look at Stuart's second goal, which is supposed to be the dodgy one, he didn't dive over it; it went past him. It's really, really hard to just let in a goal. If the training is going badly and you say to yourself you can't be bothered saving any more and you dive around, going through the motions, the ball can still hit you. You just can't get out of the way. It's sod's law that if someone shoots and you try and get out of the way, it hits you. I don't see anything dodgy about the Wimbledon game, it was just one of those days.

After the game there was lots of talk of never letting Everton fall into such a perilous position again, about fresh starts. It was a complete and utter disgrace that a club like ours were ever in such a situation. But I didn't hear many people taking the blame for it. Who was to blame for the mess? The players, because we were shit. But then it didn't help that we had Walker in charge either, because he was clueless. I remember someone saying that they only learned after Walker was gone that football was played in two halves of the pitch, because we only ever played in our own half under his management.

⊐⊏

THE CLUB WAS TAKEN OVER A FEW WEEKS LATER by Peter Johnson, the Tranmere Rovers chairman who had built a fortune selling hampers. He spoke of revitalising the club and promised lots of investment. One of the players Walker was said to be interested in was his own son, Ian. He might have turned out to be a good player for Everton; who knows? He wasn't a bad goalkeeper. Like his dad, he liked to look his best, so they might have run out of hairbrushes at Bellefield. But he didn't sign and at the start of the 1994/95 season I was still Everton's number one.

In fact, by the start of the new season, the only new player he'd brought in was the Tottenham midfielder Vinny Samways. Vinny was a good player, but because he basically only played in our half he merely accentuated our problems.

It became clear on the pre-season tour of Scandinavia that Mike Walker wasn't right for a club like Everton. It was a complete shambles. We went over to Sweden pre-season and it was absolutely roasting. We trained in the hottest part of the day, eleven o'clock till one o'clock, in blistering heat (so that he'd get a tan, we thought). We used to just mess around. One day Jimmy Martin the kit man was late getting our gear out and I had my boots on, my gloves and my socks, but I didn't have a top or shorts. I got fed up of waiting so walked out with just my gloves and boots on. There was all these people watching us, but to be fair to Mike he never batted an eyelid. I just wandered round like that, stark bollock naked, until Jimmy came running out with my kit.

Mike only ever did one training session with me. It was the worst I'd ever had. 'There are two poles,' he said. 'That's green, that's grey, so when I shout "green" you go to "grey", when I shout "grey" you go to "green".' I spent about an hour and a half doing that. So much for his goalkeeping expertise.

Another time we were throwing the ball to each other, messing about, and he called Barry 'Horney'. Barry hated to be called that so lashed the ball as hard as he could at him. Can you imagine? Walker was meant to be manager and that's the respect we had for him.

The season started badly and quickly got worse. The problem was less the personnel than the way we played and the way we trained. Tempers were boiling over in the dressing room. Walker would come in and rant and rave about us not being fit – it was always our fitness he questioned, oddly – and we'd just sit there. When Spurs beat us at White Hart Lane he lobbed a teacup at the wall and covered my CD player with tea. I'm not one to lose my temper, but I told him he was a prick. A few days later we got battered 4-0 by Manchester City and he started ranting about our fitness again; this time Waggy stood up to him.

'Listen, you twat. If you don't sign some fucking players you're going to get us relegated.'

'I know what I'm doing,' he answered.

'No, you fucking idiot. Sign some players.'

We sold Tony Cottee, which said it all. The first rule of management is always to sell your top goalscorer, right? There were some new signings, like the Nigerian forward Daniel Amokachi and the former Liverpool left back David Burrows. But none of this was enough. To stay in the Premier League you need to score goals. If you don't score goals you're not going to win games. You never sell your top goalscorer, ever, unless you've got one waiting in the wings that is better, and we didn't.

Both Dave Watson and I were taking a hammering from some fans, just a small minority. When we played Queens Park Rangers at Goodison someone ran down to the front of the Gwladys Street and started screaming abuse at me: 'You're fucking shit, fuck off, Southall.'

This guy really annoyed me so I waved the wanker gesture at him. But then after the game someone complained to the club and before I knew it Mike Walker was in the press saying that he wouldn't hesitate dropping me and playing Jason Kearton in my place if I didn't apologise. The funny thing was he didn't even bother coming to me to tell me all this.

Things quickly took a darker complexion. I received a death threat, which said they were going to blow up my house and kill my wife and daughter. I took it to the chairman rather than Walker, but his attitude was strange. With his posh accent he was almost like Sergeant Wilson in Dad's Army saying, 'Don't worry, Southall, we'll carry on.' I've no idea if he took it to the police or not.

The atmosphere was toxic. After another game I was walking to my car and someone started ranting and raving at me. More of the usual – 'fuck off, you're shit', that kind of thing – so I went and had a word. He quickly backed down.

'I wasn't talking to you,' he stammered. 'I was shouting at Dave Watson!'

In total we went 14 league and cup games without winning – the worst start to a season in the club's history – and were knocked out of the League Cup by Portsmouth. Some people said we'd turned a corner when we beat West Ham in our 15th game and then drew at Norwich. But we hadn't. Just as sure as I had been that we were staying up against Wimbledon, so I was convinced that we were going down that year with Mike Walker in charge. Not because he's a terrible manager, or because Dave Williams was a bad coach, but the way we played was easy to play against. We were too easy to beat. We were going to sink without a trace.

# CHAPTER TWELVE

# VETERAN

LUCKILY, THE CHAIRMAN, Peter Johnson, also recognised where we were heading. Three days after we played Norwich City, he sacked Mike Walker. In eleven months we had won just five times.

There was no accident behind the timing of Mike Walker's dismissal as Everton manager. Between the Norwich City match and our next game, a Goodison derby, there was a 16-day gap to allow for the last round of 1996 European Championship qualifying matches. I flew off to Georgia with Wales while Johnson went about hiring a new manager.

The chairman went to Oldham and hired the man many thought should have succeeded Colin Harvey in 1990, Joe Royle. Joe had been Everton's youngest ever player when he made his debut in 1966 and went on to be one of its greats, his goals helping seal the 1969/70 League Championship. He played for England and later for Manchester City, Bristol City and Norwich before turning to management at Boundary Park. Given the amount of resources at his disposal his achievements were staggering and he not only took the tiny Lancashire club into the top flight but kept them there for several years as well. There was a League Cup Final and a few FA Cup semis too. But by 1994 many thought his chance of managing Everton had passed.

From the outset Joe recognised the two factors that were holding us back: that the way we played was completely unsuitable and that – like Mike Walker had said often enough – we weren't fit enough, but it was because we weren't getting anything out of training.

'The simplest things are the best things,' said Joe on his first day at Bellefield. 'This is what you're doing at the moment, you're making mistakes in your own half. We're not going to do that any more. We're going to get it, we're going to press the other team, we're going to play at a high tempo. As soon as Neville gets the ball, you've got to boot it; you've got to be quick and everyone's got to get out and it's got to be really quick.'

He showed us a video, I think of AC Milan, who were the top team in Italy and Europe at the time. He showed how they played a pressing game: getting it, giving it; closing opponents down when they were in possession; hitting them on the break.

'This is the best team in the world,' said Joe. 'They get more money than you; they work ten times harder than you lot at the moment. If it's good enough for them, it's fucking good enough for you.'

So then we set about ensuring we were fit enough. His assistant Willie Donachie was absolutely brilliant. He was the first holistic coach I'd come across and his routines were superb. We played at a high tempo and trained at a high tempo. We trained Monday morning, Monday afternoon, Tuesday morning, Tuesday afternoon. We did weights and hurdles and stuff like that. I thought it was brilliant. I thought, 'This fellow's come in, enthusiastic, a

proper Evertonian, and he knows what he's doing.' Everybody was grafting and grafting; and Joe just focused everybody on doing what they were
supposed to do.

One of Walker's last acts as Everton manager – although it may well
have been the doing of the chairman – was to bring in the midfielder Iain
Durrant and centre forward Duncan Ferguson from Rangers. Until a few
months earlier Duncan had been the most expensive footballer in Britain,
but it hadn't worked out for him at Ibrox and there had been off-the-field
problems too. He carried a reputation as a troublemaker and a thug, but you
could see right away that he was just misunderstood.

Duncan's one of the nicest people that I know, the sort of person that
would give you the last penny in his pocket. I think he's a terrific fellow,
but an idiot at the same time. Duncan should have been – and I've said this
to him on numerous occasions – the best player in the world. But he just
wasn't motivated enough to do that. If you look at Duncan's record, look at
his great games, Duncan played exceptionally well against all the best teams,
but couldn't get himself going against the Coventrys and Ipswich Towns,
unless someone punched him or something like that. Duncan was a big-game
player and for Everton no game was bigger than the Merseyside derby.

Duncan loved playing against Liverpool because he absolutely hated
them. He'd been a bit lost on the pitch in his first weeks at the club, but when
we faced our neighbours in Joe's first game in charge he went to war. Liverpool
were near the top of the table while we were rock bottom, but you wouldn't
have known it that night. We pressed and harried and chased and attacked
and did all the things Joe had told us to do. From an Andy Hinchcliffe corner
on 56 minutes Duncan rose above the Liverpool defence to plant a header
home. Two minutes from the end Duncan caused havoc in the Liverpool
area and Paul Rideout stabbed the ball home to double our lead. The win
was only our second all season and lifted us off the bottom of the table.

On a personal level it was my 35th Merseyside derby match, meaning
I'd broken the appearance record for the fixture. It wasn't the only record we

broke at that time. We embarked on an unbeaten run that lasted until Boxing Day, during which time we didn't concede a single goal, a seven-match run that was also a club record. I was never one for records though and not that interested in clean sheets; winning games was my thing and we still had a lot of hard work to do to get out of the relegation battle we'd found ourselves in.

A few days after the Liverpool match, Joe made Duncan's signing permanent in a £4.5million deal, the second highest fee ever paid by an English club. I'm sure Joe looked at Duncan in the way that I did and just thought he was going to be a world-beater. Certainly he had all the attributes necessary: strength, power, technical ability; he was fantastic in the air and a decent finisher. Among the fans he became an instant cult figure and, for some, a legend. But he never lived up to his potential, never quite had enough desire to push on and become the player he should have been. Unless it was a big game he just wasn't switched on. He reminded me of a big-time entertainer who can't play small venues and can only get excited about big arenas. That's just him. There was no challenge in playing Coventry or West Brom away for Duncan. It was as if it was too easy for him. But he could motivate himself for Manchester United. I don't think he ever set out to be like that, it's just the way he was.

He could be a bit daft as well. He was into pigeon fancying and some-times that was all that would get him excited if there were no big games coming up. I remember him rushing into the dressing room all excited at full-time after we'd been beaten at one of the London clubs.

'Yes! Yes! Yes!' he said.

'What's up with you?' I asked.

'Me and my dad got first, second and third in the pigeon race today for the first time ever!'

I just shook my head, perplexed.

Duncan's back at Everton now, on the youth coaching staff. Even now, when I see him, I have a go.

'How the hell are you going to tell these kids how to play better when you didn't listen to anyone yourself?' I tell him. 'You should be the best player in the world, you idiot.'

But I probably don't need to tell him that. For nobody is more aware of that lost potential than Duncan Ferguson himself. I'm sure if he had his time again he wouldn't waste it as much.

AS WE ROSE UP THE TABLE, Joe – who was always good for a quip – dubbed us the 'Dogs of War'. In our three-man midfield, comprising Joe Parkinson, John Ebbrell and Barry Horne, we had three lads who grafted their bollocks off for the club. They tackled anything that moved and squeezed the opposition, forcing them to make mistakes. They were a top combination and far better players than any of them were given credit for.

My Wales team-mate Barry Horne in particular came into his own. He had signed two years earlier, but hadn't really won over the fans until that goal against Wimbledon. He was the most intense man I've ever met in my life. He was my room-mate and the sort of person who was so clever that he could watch TV, read the paper and listen to the radio at the same time. His mind never stopped. Normally the night before a match we'd have a cup of tea and a sandwich about 9pm and I'd try to go to sleep by 10pm, but Barry would still be up in the small hours of the morning. I, however, always posed him a few problems. Because of my bad back I'd sleep on the floor and block his way to the toilet. Come the morning the teapot would be filled with Barry's piss.

Barry, like the rest of the Dogs of War, played to his strengths. He wasn't Maradona, but he didn't make a career out of trying to be Maradona. Barry made a career out of being Barry, which was giving you everything he had every single week. He was hard and brave and would do anything for Everton. When we'd played Swindon the previous season, someone kicked him and he had a hole in his calf, as if he'd been shot. Barry stuffed the wound up with cotton wool and kept playing; he was that kind of player.

Without that kind of effort we would have sunk without a trace. But we became hard to beat, we were competitive, we got in peoples' faces and other teams didn't like playing against us. But we played some good football too. Which team wouldn't with a player like Anders Limpar in the squad?

We also had Daniel Amokachi, who had been one of the stars of the previous summer's World Cup. He was a good lad, Daniel. When he first came in he had a bit of a BO problem but we soon changed him, and after that he was just pongy with perfume. He was a clever lad and had earned a law degree in the USA before becoming a professional footballer. He was an exporter/importer and had all sorts of things going on. His obsession was with 'sexy football'; he was always banging on about 'sexy football', and he just couldn't understand why we played like we did because it wasn't 'sexy football'. He'd occasionally wander on and do something brilliant or wander on and do something that was just a waste of time. Like Duncan, he was another one of those players who on his day was fantastic, and on a bad day was just dreadful. There was no in-between with him. But he loved playing the game and this bizarre idea of 'sexy football'.

Daniel's moment of glory in an Everton shirt came in unlikely circumstances. We were still battling relegation – four teams went down in 1994/95, which made our plight particularly perilous – and would continue to do so until the penultimate game of the season, but had made the semi-final of the FA Cup. We had been drawn against Tottenham Hotspur at Elland Road and on a slate-grey Sunday afternoon made the journey down the M62 to Leeds.

Elland Road, at the time, had the largest cantilever stand in Europe, which was where the Spurs fans were. We had the other three sides of the stadium. It was brilliant, just like playing at home. I remember the Everton bus rolling up at Elland Road and us all thinking it was a home game. We couldn't see any Spurs fans anywhere.

Tottenham, who had the PFA Player of the Year Jürgen Klinnsman up front, were many people's favourites to go through and the media spoke of a 'dream final' between Spurs and Manchester United. But Joe used this to our advantage and spoke mockingly of a 'dream final', playing on our status as underdogs.

We took the game to Tottenham and chased and harried them all day. They never got a second on the ball. We took the lead on 35 minutes, when Matt Jackson flicked home a Hinchcliffe corner, and doubled the lead on 55 minutes. Ian Walker, the man who a few months earlier was meant to be replacing me, kicked a free kick straight at Paul Rideout. Although he saved Paul's effort, Graham Stuart knocked home the rebound, leaving Ian in tears. Tottenham got a goal back from a penalty, but there was only going to be one winner – and Daniel ensured it was us.

Daniel was on the bench and when Rideout went down with an injury he started warming up. Les Helm, the physio, was busy treating him and signalled to the bench that he was going to be okay, but Daniel took it as a signal to come on and just wandered onto the pitch before anyone could stop him. He was bonkers. Twelve minutes later Tottenham were piling on the pressure, and I'd just made a decent save from Stuart Nethercott when we broke through Anders. The ball was played out to Graham Stuart on the right-hand side of the penalty area and Daniel headed his cross home at the far post. A few minutes later he repeated the trick on the other side of goal. Anders broke down the left and played in Gary Ablett and Daniel lobbed his cross over Ian Walker.

Joe, who was sensitive to the press coverage, started his press conference with the line: 'Sorry about the dream final, lads, now bollocks to you. And that's with a double "l"!'

For me it meant, at the age of 36, a fifth FA Cup Final. I'd lost the last three, but I was relaxed this time. I wanted to enjoy it because I knew it would be my last FA Cup Final. It was also Samantha's first chance to see me at Wembley and maybe win something, so that was an added incentive. I also knew it might be my last match for Everton. My contract was coming to an end and it wasn't clear whether it would be renewed or whether Joe was going to bring in someone new, someone younger than me. At the time, even though I was playing really well, the writing seemed to be on the wall for me. It was just a feeling I got that Joe was going to try and sign somebody else through the summer; bring one of his own players in. So I was very conscious it could be my last match for the club.

We were playing against Manchester United, the best team in the country, and we had nothing to lose. One of the great things about playing for Joe and Willie is that we always went out to win. They were both naturally positive people and they brought their attitude to life to the football pitch. We never went anywhere to draw a game. I don't ever recall being told to sit and defend a game. We were told to get the ball early, be positive, get the ball forward and play in the opposition's half.

Joe kept the team that had played so well against Tottenham in the semi-final. The only question mark was over the substitutes, with Duncan back from injury, Daniel having shone in the semi, and John Ebbrell, who had played most of the season, contesting just two outfield spots on the bench, alongside the substitute goalkeeper Jason Kearton. In the end he opted for Duncan and Daniel. I think leaving John out was the hardest decision Joe ever had to make as a manager and he has said as much. It was devastating for John, who had done so much for Everton that season.

We played as we had done ever since Joe came in: without fear, as if we had nothing to lose, which, as I've said, we didn't. United were big favourites and had missed out on the Premier League title a week earlier, so the pressure, I suppose, was on them to end the season with a trophy. But we just did our thing. Anders was the key man again when we got our goal in the first half. He seized the ball not far outside our penalty area and sprinted the length of the field before playing it down the right flank to Matt Jackson. Graham Stuart hit his low cross onto the bar, it bounced onto the ground and up again, and Paul Rideout rose to head the ball home.

Anders remained our most dangerous player, but United, inevitably, put us under more and more pressure as the game wore on. I made a good double-save at my near post from Paul Scholes, where I blocked his first shot and got a leg to the follow-up. Gary Pallister had a stooping header, but I dived and caught the ball. I also saved from Nicky Butt at the near post. Even as a veteran, the old reflexes hadn't left me. There was no way anything was going to get past me, no chance.

'The most abiding memory will be of Neville Southall's trio of remarkable saves,' opined the *Observer*, after victory had been secured, 'especially the double act of defiance that enabled him to thwart Scholes. To save Scholes's first shot was impressive enough – but to keep out the follow-up effort with his legs while he was on the ground must have caused even United to think it was destined to be Everton's day.'

In winning the FA Cup I became the most decorated player in Everton's history, but there was no way I was hanging around for the banquet afterwards. Everyone kept going on about it, but my idea of celebrating is getting the chance to do what I want to do. Samantha and Eryl had come down with our next-door neighbours to watch the final, but they'd long gone by the time I was finished up. How did I celebrate, then? I drove home, got back about 10.30pm, and went to bed.

But I'll tell you this, driving home all smug and happy, and seeing all the happy Evertonians heading back north, was one of the most satisfying experiences of my life.

Halfway back home I saw a broken-down car full of Manchester United supporters. I thought, 'Shall I pick them up? Yeah, we beat them and won the cup; I'll pick them up.'

I bet of all the people in the world I was the last person they wanted or expected to drive them to the nearest garage.

⌁

IN THE SUMMER OF 1995, 14 years after my arrival at Goodison, we held my testimonial. My agent Peter McIntosh and his secretary Barbara handled most of the arrangements. We held dinners in London, Liverpool and Ireland and a match against Celtic at Goodison. It was nice coming after the FA Cup win, although it would have been a complete nightmare had we gone down. But this wasn't the end for me. I still had plenty of football left.

I was also awarded the MBE this year and attended Buckingham Palace with Samantha and Eryl for an audience with the Queen. When I first got the letter telling me I'd been honoured, to be honest I thought it was a joke. It said that I wasn't allowed to tell anybody that I'd got it, which was quite difficult at times because it was obviously a nice thing to receive. Going to Buckingham Palace was surreal. I'm the sort of person that if I wear a suit – it doesn't matter if it's Hugo Boss or Jaeger – I still look a twat. It's just one of those things – clothes don't suit me. If I could walk around in my underpants all day I think I'd be a quite happy man, really. I've come to the conclusion it's not the clothes that are all creased, I think it's just my fucking body that's creased.

Anyway, I digress. I was there in my posh gear, albeit still looking like a ratbag. It was a nice day, but as I walked through the Palace I realised that, although it was surreal for me, it was just a working day for Her Majesty. The way it was done was really methodical; I think they had four corners of Buckingham Palace, and in each one there were a different people awaiting their awards. So there might be MBEs in one corner, CBEs in another; Knights in another and they all filtered in to her. And then suddenly, I was before her.

'So what will you do now that you're retired?' she asked.

It was a bit of a killer, really, because I was still very much a professional footballer.

I came out really pleased with myself, but a bit depressed too after that. Looking back I should know that that's just the way things are and it was a really, really good day, to be fair; absolutely brilliant. When I was carrying bricks and playing for my uncle's team, I was just a scruffy little twat really, and I never ever thought I'd end up somewhere like that.

⌶

EVERTON STARTED THE 1995/96 SEASON with a Charity Shield win over Blackburn Rovers and I think that raised expectations even higher than they already were. People were looking at the cup win as a turning point in Everton's history, as it had been in 1984, but this wasn't realistic. History wasn't going to repeat itself. With the exception of Craig Short, and the Russian international Andrei Kanchelskis, this was the same squad that had narrowly avoided relegation for two successive years.

And so it came to pass. We started the season slowly, but weren't helped by injuries to Duncan and Andrei. Kanchelskis was a truly outstanding player: fast, direct and a sublime finisher. He would have held his own in the class of 85, although I feel Trevor was probably a better defender than Andrei. It's great watching Nikica Jelavic at Everton now because he reminds me of Andrei in so many ways: his poise, the way he runs, his ruthlessness in front of goal.

Andrei finally came back into the Everton team in November 1995 and helped turn our season around. He scored twice in the derby match at Anfield and would score a goal every other game in the Premier League. Opponents couldn't deal with his pace and finishing. At times he was unplayable.

The second half of the season was much better, although we were humiliatingly dumped out of the FA Cup by Port Vale in the fourth round – as we had been by Millwall in the League Cup. We finished the season sixth, just missing out on a UEFA Cup spot. In fact we would have played in Europe but for the fact that UEFA had withdrawn one of the English places after Tottenham and Wimbledon had played weakened teams in the Inter Toto Cup. It wasn't, of course, the first time that kind of thing had happened.

Considering I thought I might have left the club the previous summer, I'd had a decent season, playing every minute of all of our 49 league and cup games. It was considered a year of transition and big things were expected of our next campaign. In Andrei we had a world-class player, and in Duncan, who had played in fewer than half the games, someone who might have been able to match him given a clear run in the side.

The summer of 1996 should really have been my last at Goodison. There was lots of speculation about my future that summer and about who Joe might or might not be bringing in. We needed to sign a lot of players because the squad was thin and, although we had some good players, short of quality. He signed Gary Speed from Leeds United and Paul Gerrard from Oldham. Paul had been Joe's goalkeeper at Boundary Park and was an England Under-21 international. He was seen as a long-term successor to me, but Joe was still meant to be in the market for a senior keeper.

He tried to sign Nigel Martyn from Crystal Palace, who I presume would have been his number one while Paul developed. Indeed the deal was basically wrapped up by the Everton director Clifford Finch at Peter Johnson's Park Foods headquarters in Birkenhead. That was until Nigel's agent was alerted to the interest of Leeds and asked Mr Finch if they could go and talk to them. Joe wasn't around, as his wife had been taken ill, so this director apparently told him to go to Leeds and see what they said! Once at Elland Road, a wily operator like Howard Wilkinson was never going to let Nigel leave without becoming a Leeds player. So Nigel joined Leeds and Joe was furious. Not only had he lost out on a new signing, but he was stuck with me!

Nothing, however, was resolved when we started pre-season training and it still looked as if I might leave. One day Joe pulled me into the office.

'Wolves want to speak to you,' he said.

I didn't know what to say: was this a test to see if I was after a move, or his way of telling me that he didn't fancy me any more.

'What do you want me to do?' I asked.

'Go and speak to them,' he told me.

So I left his office, not knowing whether the next time I came back to Bellefield I'd still be an Everton player.

Wolves at the time were managed by Mark McGhee and had had a lot of money invested in them by their millionaire owner Jack Hayward. However, they were still in the First Division, as the second tier was then still confusingly called, and although they had high ambitions would remain rooted there for some time. I met with them and the talks went well: they offered to double the wages I was on at Everton and I watched Wolves play some German side in a pre-season friendly believing I was about to sign for them.

But I wasn't the only one watching a pre-season match. Paul Gerrard was playing against Wrexham in a pre-season friendly for Everton that night. I think it was his debut, but unfortunately for Paul he had a nightmare and let in three goals. It was enough to deter the Everton management from considering him my immediate replacement.

The next day Joe phoned me up and had changed his tune a bit.

'You've done really well since I arrived,' he said. 'We'll match anything Wolves offer you and I'll give you two years.'

So I stayed at Everton and was happy to do so. The news of the new contract was sold to the press as if it was a last big payday for me, but that wasn't the case. I was on about £6,000 per week, which is a lot of money, but I was far from the best-paid player there. Being at a club a long time puts you at a distinct disadvantage because players who move around a lot inflate their wages with every move, while those who stay loyal to a club get paid what they're given. Put it like this, when Claus Thomsen came in four months later from Ipswich, he was meant to be on £10,000 per week.

Money was never an issue for me, though, and I never thought about any of the iniquities until after I'd finished playing. We were given win bonuses of about £300 per game; a nice top-up, but not a massive incentive. Not that I particularly have any strong feelings towards performance-based contracts;

you should only ever sign a contract if you're happy with it, not base it on how a team might do. Although money was starting to creep into football there weren't many commercial deals around. I had a boot deal and a glove deal, which paid a small amount – £3,000 or £4,000 per year. I also signed up to do a couple of books with the *Liverpool Echo* journalist, Ric George. If I'd have moved four times I'd have made much more money, but I would never have been as happy as I was at Everton. They were my club.

At the time I thought I had a decent relationship with Joe, but it's since transpired that he didn't share those sentiments. In his autobiography, which was published in 2005, Joe devoted an entire chapter to me, entitled 'The Southall Factor'. In it he said that my agility was 'waning', I'd put on weight, that he identified me as a 'potential weak link' when he first joined the club. He also rubbished my managerial aspirations, saying that I lacked the 'indefinable quality of being able to treat players as people', whatever that means. I don't think I did too badly for him, all these things considered.

I'm not sure what his problem was with me, because I always thought we got on fine. Maybe, because I was 36 when he came in, he just had preconceived ideas about me and what I could do for him. He just thought it was time I should push on and maybe because I did so well when he came in I surprised him.

Things got worse after we both left Everton. I wrote a diary of the 1996/97 season with Ric George that Joe was furious about it even though he had left as manager by then. He thought I'd slaughtered him, but I hadn't; I just told things the way they were, the same as I'm doing now. There were no hidden agendas and no personality issues. I played with and worked alongside hundreds of people at Everton, with Wales, and all my clubs, and I can say in all honesty that there was not one person that I disliked. I certainly liked Joe. But it seems that he thought there was a certain section of the press out to get him, particularly Ric, and the issue was clearly black and white to him: you were either with him or against him, and he saw me in the latter camp.

After Everton I'd often see him at dinners and matches, and there was always an underlying tension. This was 10 or 15 years after we'd both left the club; two so-called Everton legends and we'd be put together on the top table of some supporters' dinner or other and sit there awkwardly. He was always prickly to criticism, as lots of managers are – think how many journalists Alex Ferguson has banned – but it was getting to a point where I thought it needed sorting out, so in the end I went to clear the air. I apologised if the diary had caused him any offence, and hopefully we've now both moved on.

⌶

PAUL GERRARD, my new understudy, was a perfectly good player. My philosophy, after the way that players like John Forrest and Jim Arnold looked out for me, was always to treat up-and-coming goalkeepers with the respect that I'd once wanted myself. I worked with them, not against them. If they were good enough there was nothing I would be able to do about it. Was Paul good enough? He was certainly better than some of the people who followed me into the Everton goal, like Richard Wright. Was he better than me at the time? I don't think he was – but then I would say that! At the time I didn't think there was ever going to be anybody as good as me. Even now, without wanting to sound big-headed, I still don't think they've found anybody to replace me. It's not Tim Howard's fault or Nigel Martyn's fault or Paul Gerrard's fault; it's Everton's problem. They had me for 17 years; that's a long time to find a good enough replacement, but they clearly didn't look hard enough.

Expectation was higher than ever when the 1996/97 season kicked off but the reality was that we'd added just one senior player to the squad, my Wales team-mate Gary Speed, for whom we'd paid £3.5millon. Gary was an absolute class act; a really good attacking midfielder who could do everything. He could pass over short and long distances. He could defend. He could score goals. He was a brilliant header of the ball. He was composed. He was brave. He had that magical quality, even as a youngster – and I'd played alongside him since he was a teenager – that set him apart as a leader. He was also imbued with a winning ethos, which he probably derived from his manager Howard Wilkinson at Leeds – who was one of the more forward-thinking managers of the era – and growing up watching Everton in the glory years. He was a massive Evertonian and had previously been Kevin Ratcliffe's paperboy while growing up in the North Wales village of Mancot.

The assumption was that Joe had a lot of money to spend, and certainly by comparison to his successors as Everton managers he did. But despite being linked to all sorts of players he never quite seemed to pull off the deals he should have done. Whether that was down to him or the chairman I don't know; Everton didn't have a proper chief executive at the time so that can't have helped. I think part of it was that Joe wanted to buy players that he trusted, like Paul Gerrard. But when it came to other signings – the Alan Shearers and Roberto Baggios we were meant to be after – I just think there was a struggle going on behind the scenes about what sort of money they could offer. Don't forget the Nigel Martyn fiasco. Maybe the money wasn't there for him to be able to sign who he wanted to sign. Personally I don't think Everton had that much money at the time. If he'd have got all the players he wanted he might have lasted as Everton manager. I still believe if he had stayed Everton would be in a better position today.

Despite the lack of transfer action we got off to a flyer. On the opening day of the season we hosted Newcastle United, who had just signed Alan Shearer for a world record fee of £15million. It was my 700th Everton appearance and the start of my 15th season with the club. Duncan, who had been flying in training, outshone Shearer completely, winning us a penalty, which David Unsworth scored, and then setting up Gary Speed for a second. Four days later Duncan scored twice against Manchester United at Old Trafford, but they equalised late on. Afterwards Alex Ferguson described us as 'Wimbledon with one or two good players', which infuriated Joe, but was a clear sign that we had him rattled. We drew against Spurs and then went on one of our losing streaks that took in a 4-0 hammering at Wimbledon and a League Cup humiliation at York. I think the frailties and lack of strength in depth of the squad were plain for all to see.

The England forward Nick Barmby became available and Joe signed him for a club record fee in October 1996. I don't in all honesty think he knew what to do with him or where to play him. But in the short term form picked up. We hammered Southampton 7-1 – our biggest win in all my years at the club – and rose to within sight of the top of the table. Suddenly we were being touted as title outsiders, but I remained sceptical. We weren't good enough, didn't have enough players, and were losing silly games. When we played Sunderland at Goodison in late November they hadn't scored in an away match since the start of the season. We had loads of possession, battered them at times, but they hit us on the break and we ended up losing 3-1. The boos that rang out around Goodison Park at the end said it all.

Very quickly, the wheels fell off. From Boxing Day until 1 February 1997 we lost every single league game that we played, six in total, which was a club record-equalling run. But the nadir came in the FA Cup fourth round, where we met Bradford City at Goodison. Despite our poor form it should have been an easy game: they were a division below us and fighting relegation while we were almost at full strength.

Bradford had a veteran Chris Waddle playing for them and he was behind everything positive. There was a 15-minute window of madness just after half-time. Waddle set up John Dreyer for Bradford's opener. Then Kanchelskis got caught in possession, played a terrible pass across the front of defence and Waddle lobbed me from 40 yards. We pulled a goal back, but then Waddle set up Rob Steiner, who made it 3-1. For the next 30 minutes we laid siege to the Bradford goal and although Gary Speed got a late consolation it wasn't enough. Afterwards, Joe got absolutely hammered by fans calling for his head. I went on the City FM fans phone-in to defend him, as I had done in my column for the Football Echo.

Two days later in training, Joe took me aside and told me he was leaving me out of our next match. I wasn't happy with this one bit: I was very upset and felt that I'd been made a scapegoat. I asked him why he was dropping me and his response was, 'Because I am!' When I pressed him, all he would say was, 'You'll understand one day.' But I didn't understand and I still don't. If he had so much faith in Paul Gerrard, why did he try and sign Mark Schwarzer from Bradford a week later? Yet again he was plagued by Everton's inability to complete transfers and Schwarzer went to Middlesbrough instead.

Although we ended the losing streak, things had got really bad. Joe wasn't talking to the press. I didn't think I was going to play for the club again. Andrei had left to join Fiorentina. And given the way we were playing and slipping down the table, relegation had become a possibility yet again.

From title contenders to relegation candidates in three months, how had this happened? If I was brutally honest I'd say that we had a good system of playing and changed it too quickly. People wanted School of Science, not the Dogs of War, and didn't think we should be playing the way we did. But there was no point in fans looking down at a team of grafters, because we were winning that way and weren't able to play as successfully with the ball on the floor. The other factor was that other teams had started to work us out, which may have had a bearing on the change of tactics as well.

I was miserable on the sidelines and didn't want to be anywhere that I wasn't wanted. I returned in March after Paul got a calf strain, but was dropped as soon as he recovered. I told Joe I wanted to leave, but he wouldn't let me go without signing a replacement. In my previous contract there had been a clause that let me leave on a free transfer if I was dropped. When we'd renewed it the previous summer, however, it was replaced with a 'gentleman's agreement' between me and Joe. My future was basically in his hands.

A week before transfer-deadline day Chelsea came in for me. The offer was almost too good to be true: over an 18-month contract they were going to double my wages (again) and let me train up north, flying me down to London twice a week. It would basically take me up until my 40th birthday.

I didn't want to leave Everton. I loved Everton. But I was desperate to play, and didn't want to be anywhere I was unwanted.

Joe, however, wouldn't sanction the transfer. He told me he'd been trying to bring in a goalkeeper but hadn't been able to. I kept on at him and it ended up in a row. Joe, for the only time, raised his voice with me and ended up slamming the phone down. I didn't get my move.

A day later we were parted, but it was Joe and not me that had left Goodison. In the end it was his struggles in the transfer market that did for him. He lined up a deal to buy Slaven Bilic from West Ham, although Bilic wouldn't join until the end of the season, and the Norway centre forward Tore Andre Flo. He also wanted to buy back Barry Horne, who had joined Birmingham City the previous summer. The problem was the Flo deal; his club Brann Bergen also wanted the defender Claus Eftevaag to join as a makeweight in the deal for £300,000. Joe was happy to go along with this but Peter Johnson wouldn't have it. Joe took this as a challenge to his authority and resigned.

I felt very let down by the whole episode. As I was nearing the end of my career – although part of me believed I could play until I was 50 – a move to a club like Chelsea while I was languishing on the sidelines wouldn't have come along every day. And I craved first-team football. I just wanted to play.

—⊐⊏—

DAVE WATSON WAS APPOINTED CARETAKER MANAGER. There was talk of me being involved, but the club hierarchy were never going to appoint me. They thought I was an idiot, a troublemaker, that I'd do something stupid. I think I would have done just fine: I might have upset a few people, but sometimes that's what a situation demands. As it was Dave did very well. The first thing he did was reinstate me in the team. I was a happy man again. He surrounded himself with people he knew and trusted.

Paul Rideout, who had gone to play in China, was brought back and played really well in central midfield. Dave was never easy on me or anyone else. He was the boss, not our team-mate and captain any more. He was quite quiet and never a shouter or a raver; but that wouldn't be his style anyway. He just got things done. That's the type of person he is.

Dave steadied the ship. We finished 15th, but just two points off relegation and it wouldn't have taken much for us to get sucked in at the bottom. We held Liverpool to a draw at Goodison, which simultaneously secured our safety and ended their title hopes. Duncan, inevitably, got the crucial goal. For me, I was just glad it was all over. As I wrote at the time in my diary of the season, it was the worst season of my career: I was good enough for my country, I was good enough for Chelsea, but not good enough for Everton.

Peter Johnson promised us a 'world class' successor to Joe and Bobby Robson led an enormous list of names linked to the job that ranged from Arrigo Sacchi, the former Milan manager (whose AC Milan team Joe had once shown us so admiringly), to Joe Kinnear. Robson eventually turned us down, as he had done in 1994 and in the 1970s, and an excruciating three-month search went on. Eventually Johnson settled on a name that was close to the hearts of Evertonians and was what I considered an inspired choice: Andy Gray.

I think the prospect of Andy managing Everton would have been really good. He knew enough about football, he knew enough about the players, he knew enough about coaching; he knew what we wanted. He knew the club inside out, he knew some of the players, he knew what he wanted to achieve. He's quite single-minded, that's how he ended up on Sky. He obviously knew where he wanted to go. He was his own man; he would have made some decisions that would have upset a few people but that might not have been a bad thing. In short, I think he knew enough to have done well. Highly publicised talks took place and just as Andy seemed set to take over he had a change of heart and decided not to turn his back on his burgeoning career as a pundit.

By now it was June, pre-season was about to start and Everton had become a laughing stock. I think all the problems emanated from Joe's resignation. I just thought they should have kept him longer. And for the sake of signing somebody for £300,000, in the great scheme of things it's incidental, isn't it? I think that was Peter Johnson's biggest ever mistake.

Johnson had now got to the stage where he desperately needed somebody, anybody, to appease Everton's increasingly belligerent fans. In the end, I think he just thought, 'What do the fans want? The fans want a link with the past, with former glories, and someone they can trust.' So he appointed Howard Kendall, who had been managing Sheffield United. Adrian Heath came in as his assistant. I could see Johnson's point of view: He was a safe pair of hands and knew the club inside out.

Was it the right choice? They say you should never go back, and this was the second time Howard had returned.

He was the same old Howard. It was as if nothing had changed. He came in and said 'hello', but there was no discussion of where I lay in his plans. Nothing long term, nothing short term. Howard just got on and did what he did. We had the same old boozy pre-season tour. Preparations weren't the best, nor were the players we brought in. We went the entire pre-season without practising a single set-piece.

If 1996/97 had been a nightmare, it was nothing compared to the season that followed. We won just one of the first five games of the season and for the League Cup tie against Scunthorpe Howard brought in Paul. I was never happy about losing my place, ever, not even when we were playing nothing competitions like the Zenith Data Systems Cup. We won that game but I was expecting to return for the league match against Barnsley the following Saturday. Paul kept his place and we won again.

We played Coventry in the next round of the League Cup at Highfield Road and I went down as substitute goalkeeper. We were excruciatingly bad, just terrible, and lost 4-1. Gerrard was probably at fault for three of the goals.

At the end of the game there was an altercation between Howard and some of the players, such as Craig Short and Slaven Bilic, after they refused to go out and warm down. I'm not really sure what it was all about: Howard might have sent them out to try and humiliate them in front of the visiting supporters, or it might have been to buy time. To be fair I've done it myself when I've been managing and I was so angry that I sent the players back out for a cool-down so that it would give me a few moments to think what I was going to say.

Whatever the reason for the bust-up it was a public display of the tensions between some of the players and the manager. As I've said, football was changing but Howard hadn't at all. Some of the players, such as Gary Speed and Craig Short, took aspects of the game like diet and psychology very seriously indeed. Gary, who was now our captain, wasn't outspoken but he said what he believed. He had his own training regimen and would ordinarily have been leading any warm-down. But I think he would have seen the contradiction between being ordered to have a warm-down and stopping off for fish and chips on the way back to Merseyside, which would have happened after most away games.

Other players, such as Bilic, had their own outlook on the game, which wouldn't always have gone down well, either. Slaven was a great guy, confident and very funny. Although things didn't work out for him at Everton, he was a great defender and a colossal centre back. But if we were losing at half-time he would say to Howard, 'I'll tell you what's a good idea. I'll go in midfield and we'll turn this around.' He was bonkers like that.

On the Saturday after the Coventry game we faced Liverpool and I was restored to the starting XI. There was no fanfare to my return. In fact it was a bit like my debut against Ipswich all those years earlier. I'd done a two-hour weights workout at Bellefield in the morning, because I hadn't expected to play, before I learned Howard was picking me. We put in a stirring performance, inspired by the dreadlocked teenager Danny Cadamarteri, who scored a brilliant solo goal as we won 2-0.

Was this a turning point? No, absolutely not. We drew the next match

0-0 at Coventry City then lost five on the bounce. The last of these games, a 2-0 defeat against Tottenham, sent us bottom. The atmosphere was poisonous. Afterwards several hundred fans stayed behind to protest at Peter Johnson before being told to leave by the police.

It was my 751st game and the lowest point I'd shared with the club I loved. But it was also my last.

The following week we travelled to Leeds. I'd gone expecting to play, but at the hotel on the morning of the match the goalkeeping coach, Mervyn Day, told me that Howard wanted to speak to me in his room.

'You do know I love you,' he said when I came in. He looked awful, like he had the weight of the world on his shoulders.

To be honest, this wasn't what I wanted to hear. Howard Kendall stood in his dressing gown with his bollocks hanging out and telling you he loves you is not a good sight.

'I've been tossing and turning all night and I've decided to leave you out.'

What could I do? I'd already had a painkilling injection in the expectation that I'd play. But I wasn't the sort who was going to flounce out in protest. There was not much more that I could do, so I left the room and caught Mervyn Day in the corridor. He was incredulous when I told him I was dropped.

The Norwegian goalkeeper, Thomas Myhre, who we had just signed and played instead of me, did really well, and we held a good Leeds team to a goalless draw.

Maybe his display gave Howard confidence to change his tune when we next met on Monday. Here I was told that I couldn't train with the first team, the kids or the reserves, that I was finished. I was basically told to stay away from Bellefield, from the club that I'd given over 16 years of my life to. That was Howard. It was just his way of doing things. It wasn't personal; it's just how he dealt the knockout blow to a player's career. I'd seen it with Rats, with Sharpy, with Sheeds. Now it was my turn.

I went in to go and see him and pleaded my case, not to stay where I wasn't wanted, but to be able to leave.

'Look, I never played Saturday, I just need your help to get a move so I can go and play, because I want to play,' I said.

'You can stay here as goalkeeper coach for £500 a week if you want,' he said. 'It would be good.'

'Fuck off,' I said. 'I just want to play.'

He signalled that the conversation was over.

'Well, you have to go and do it,' he said. 'You go and find a club.'

And that was the end of my Everton career.

# CHAPTER THIRTEEN
# PATRIOT

AFTER LOSING TO ROMANIA IN NOVEMBER 1993 I was unsure whether I wanted to continue playing international football. It was one of my black moments when I couldn't see the light for the shadows. The death of the supporter John Hill also impacted me greatly. It showed me again what really matters, and it's not football but life. Football ultimately means nothing, when you've lost somebody and you'll never get them back.

I sat down after that match and said to Peter Shreeves, 'If I can't do better than that with Wales I may as well pack it in.'

'Stop being a tit and feeling sorry for yourself,' was his blunt reply.

I'm a firm believer that nobody has success all the time; you need to have some bad times to appreciate the good ones, and know how to deal with them. Sometimes bad experiences can also help you focus on things. Everybody can get a bit blasé in what they're doing when you suddenly get a kick up the arse. Sometimes it's extreme and sometimes it's just a nice little kick but it helps you refocus on your priorities. This was one of those times and so, after my chat with Shreevesy, I decided to carry on.

Failure to qualify for the 1994 World Cup immediately threw Terry Yorath's future as Wales manager into question. In fact there was no question as his contract expired six weeks after the Romania game. That that says a lot about the FAW and how they operated and that they were clearly hedging their bets. If we'd have qualified they might have had to give him a rise, but if we didn't it put them in a position of strength at the negotiating table. Either way it would have suited them because they knew Terry was never going to walk away from a team of World Cup qualifiers.

Terry said that in order to do this job properly, a manager 'would need a long-term contract, a good youth structure and to dictate rather than being dictated to'. He added, rather hopefully, 'That's the way it should be in football.' He should have known, of course, that that wasn't the way things were done in Welsh football.

There was some vacillation over a new deal and in the end talks ground to a halt. I'm told the sticking point amounted to something like an extra £30 per week. That's right: I'm not missing off a couple of noughts there. My understanding is that the FAW refused to sanction an extra £30 to continue the progress we'd made under Terry, progress that went against all the odds and despite the poor way they ran the national team.

In the dressing room everybody was very annoyed with the FAW. You've got to realise what the Welsh FA were like. They were butchers, bakers, candlestick makers; they weren't professional people in lots of ways. They all had their own shops, their own businesses, and what right that gave them to choose a manager is beyond me. I always thought they should have had an ex-player on the board, and still do. They're all nice people, but their football knowledge you could write on the heel of my shoe, because they haven't got a clue. I'm not being nasty, it's because they've never worked in football. Even though they're in that environment every game, no one goes into the dressing room, or knows how players think. I was absolutely gutted for Terry.

In Terry's place came John Toshack who, in fairness, was one of the few Welsh managers with some pedigree. He had led Real Madrid to the La Liga title and also managed Real Sociedad with some success. Tosh had the attitude that he wasn't bothered what you said or did because he was going to do whatever he wanted to do anyway. He wanted all the players to stay in the hotel all the time, because that's what the Spanish players did. We used to go out and about and do our own thing. I went to him before the game and said, 'Look, John, I'm not being funny but this is what I do; I like to go to the theatre the night before the game, take my mind off football, just watch it, come back, and I'm happy.' He just replied, 'Do what you fucking want.' I saw my play and did all right in the game for him, even though we lost 3-1 at home to Norway.

But I think John saw the writing on the wall from day one. From the outside he'd thought Wales were in better shape than they were, but from within he recognised the state of the FAW and the people who were in power and seen that it was in a rotten mess. I think he realised he couldn't work with people who didn't have a clue about football. And so he quit after just 48 days in the job.

People called him all sorts of things for walking out like that, but I do think it required a lot of intelligence and bottle to admit, 'This ain't going to work for me this time; I'm not having it.' And even though he got loads of stick, I think in leaving Wales, John Toshack made the right decision.

⌶

FROM BEING SO CLOSE TO QUALIFYING for major tournaments the Welsh national team went into a period of sharp decline from which it has never fully recovered.

With Tosh, Mike Smith was the only manager of his generation associated with Welsh football to ever win a major trophy – the 1986 African Cup of Nations with Egypt. He was a former schoolteacher and had managed Wales in the 1970s, leading us to the European Championship finals. Although he was English he was deeply identified with Welsh football. But after Egypt he had dropped out of management and was seen by many as yesterday's man.

I think the FAW asked him to help with the recruitment process for a new manager, but he ended up getting the job. It was ridiculous. No disrespect to Mike, but it was as if any old twat would do. Let's just wheel someone off the street who can do the job. There was no proper process. It was just embarrassing. And the message they sent out to us in the dressing room was like it or lump it. Just get on with it. It was just a shambles.

And yet I never felt like jacking it in. You're never going to walk away from your country. It became harder because it wasn't as enjoyable, and because things had changed slightly. Training was less fun. Mike brought Dave Williams, who was also coaching me at Everton at the time, in as his assistant, which frankly wasn't so great.

I think, looking back, Dave did what Dave does, and Dave's done it all the way through his career: trying to put on good coaching sessions. Well, at the time we didn't need them. We needed a bit of tactical work and five-a-sides; a bit of shooting. We didn't need anything else. There was no point in reinventing the wheel. The mood became quite tense when what we needed was to relax, enjoy ourselves a bit and inject a bit of fun into it all. The players didn't need discipline or more fitness because they were all good pros. Very good players don't need loads and loads of circle work; they're intelligent enough and if you tell them something they can understand it. People over-complicate football lots of times and that's what happened under Mike Smith.

The other problem we faced – and it was the same at Everton under

Mike Walker – was that we saw the manager as just a figurehead. Mike Smith didn't take any of the training; he did some of the team talks, but not an awful lot. There was huge pressure on Dave, too much in my view. I think Dave would be one of the best youth coaches you could ever get for Welsh football, but he was patently unsuited for the Welsh national team.

Our unease with the new setup soon manifested itself on the pitch. Results were dire and so was the organisation. We played Albania in Cardiff in our opening Euro 96 match and reverted to a flat back four, stubbornly eschewing the sweeper system that had served us so well under Terry Yorath. Although we won 2-0 the result didn't reflect the disorganisation of our defence and the huge gaps that Gary Speed and Jeremy Goss had to cover in midfield. Mike admitted afterwards, 'We had four players back marking one.' It was that kind of game.

Things soon got worse. We travelled to Moldova, the impoverished landlocked former Soviet state that sits in a pocket between Romania and Ukraine. They had only been admitted into FIFA five months earlier and had only played one competitive match. The country's poverty was dire. People had nothing and fuel was heavily rationed. But they treated us nicely and as hosts gave us what they had.

But make no mistake, it was grim, a long journey, and preparations weren't the best. Mike had got some sort of video of the Moldovans training, which was meant to be our preparation, but there was absolutely nothing on it of any value. It was just some footballers training, with their kids watching on. When we went to train before the match I'll always remember the fire station next to the stadium, and this little bloke training there. He'd run towards the tower with this little ladder and try and hoist himself up to the second floor. It was truly bizarre.

But despite this backdrop, losing was not an option for our supporters back home. We were roundly humiliated. Gary Speed gave us an early lead, but by half-time we were losing 2-1 to passionate and technically accomplished opponents. Nathan Blake brought the scores level, but we were undone by a late winner. It was the worst result in Welsh football history, though not for long.

A month later we travelled to Georgia. I had been to Tblisi on my first international trip 13 years earlier, when we faced the USSR. Now it was independent and on the precipice of civil war. One hundred thousand people had fled fighting in recent years and the United Nations still classified it as a war zone. We were billeted in the Metechi Palace Hotel, the country's only international hotel. I thought it was a nice place, but apparently it was a gangland haunt with stories of shootings in the bar and drug-dealing in the corridors. I didn't see any of that, but outside on the street it was a different world. People set up impromptu market stalls, hanging up meat as if it was an open-air butcher's.

Because of the distance involved we only arrived in our hotel after midnight. We wanted to get some food and then get to bed, but there'd been a power cut so while that was sorted out Mike announced that we'd go for a training session! I know it was the middle of the night, but as a footballer you tend to just accept what you're told. It was only when we got back that someone said to Mike, 'Why did we go training in the middle of the night?' Mike replied that he didn't realise how late it was! We got to bed around 4.30am and it turned out later that we'd broken a curfew. I suppose we could have ended up in a Georgian prison, but I'm sure they just thought we were a bunch of idiots best left alone.

We had a strong team and eight of the players who had come so close to qualifying against Romania started, including Mark Hughes, Ian Rush, Gary Speed, Dean Saunders and me. But we got absolutely smashed. We lost 5-0 and were probably lucky to get away with that. Why did we get battered? I don't think you can say it was any one thing – the manager, the unusual preparations, the distances travelled, the players – and I still can't put my finger on it. It was demoralising and humiliating though, and the Welsh camp was an increasingly unhappy place.

A month later Mike Smith made a radical attempt to halt the malaise.

Wimbledon's notorious captain Vinnie Jones had found a Welsh grandfather and was called up in place of Barry Horne. Vinnie did okay for us, but I did have my doubts. I knew he was someone who would either come in and do a really good job, or do something stupid and get sent off. There was no grey area. He's one of those of players that people either love or hate, and he had a knack of upsetting opponents and referees. I'm not sure if it's what Wales needed. There was also a constant thought: 'How is he Welsh?'

The selection got a bit of media attention, but Vinnie may never have made it onto the pitch after an FAW official forgot to bring his and Mark Hughes's passports to the stadium. Alun Evans had to enlist the help of a BBC motorcyclist, whose job was to bike pictures of the match to the studios, to go and get the appropriate ID so they could play. Such was the way that Welsh football was run.

Bulgaria were a good team and had finished fourth at the previous summer's World Cup . In the Barcelona forward Hristro Stoichkov they had the newly crowned European Footballer of the Year. Vinnie made no real difference and we got battered again, this time 3-0.

In many minds Smith's position was becoming untenable. But when the FAW council met in January 1995 they gave him a stay of execution. Nobody on the FAW committee asked any of the players their opinions on this. That probably goes without saying.

We were easily beaten in the return match against Bulgaria in Sofia, then recorded a surprise 1-1 draw in Germany. But nobody who paid to watch us was convinced we could turn things around. When we faced Georgia at the Arms Park in June 1995, a couple of weeks after I'd lifted the FA Cup with Everton, just 8,241 turned out to see us lose 1-0. Nine games and six defeats into Mike Smith's second coming he was sacked.

BY NOW I WAS APPROACHING MY 37TH BIRTHDAY and thinking about what I was going to do with the rest of my life. When the Wales manager's job became available again, I put in my application. I had two motivations for applying: half of me really fancied the job; and half of me just wanted to annoy the FAW as much as possible.

To be fair, they called me for interview and I gave a presentation focused on promoting youth. I said that young players should be given a chance in the end-of-season friendly matches, instead of the team going on a pointless tour. I said that there should be better integration between the Wales U-16, U-18 and U-21 teams and the full national team and greater professionalism in preparing for matches. I said that there should be an overhaul of Welsh grassroots coaching. I said that only Welsh coaches should be given positions within this setup.

Obviously they listened to me not one little bit. Instead they appointed the former Wimbledon and Coventry City manager, Bobby Gould. He wasn't Welsh and had no experience of international football as a player or manager, but he had won the FA Cup with Wimbledon's Crazy Gang in May 1988. Without sounding like sour grapes, I don't think Bobby was the right choice for the job. We should have had someone Welsh and someone with some experience of international football.

One of the first things he did was to ask me and Rushy to work as his assistant managers. I thought it was just a gimmick at first. We held a meeting and I said, 'If this is cosmetic, I'm not interested. If you want to do it properly and you want to make a system, I ain't got a problem with that.' Gouldy was his own man and had his own ideas; some of it was strange and some of it wasn't. He gave me some bits and pieces to do, but not an awful lot, and I tended to see myself more as a link between the manager and players. I was never going to do tons of coaching because I firstly didn't have the experience and secondly Gouldy and I didn't know each other from Adam, and so those natural bonds of trust and understanding didn't exist. The best thing he did for me was put me in charge of the Under-16s, which

I thoroughly enjoyed and found to be great experience. Rushy, by contrast, wasn't interested and didn't last.

Gouldy was a good manager, but as with Mike Smith I think it was difficult for an Englishman to come into the Welsh setup. He didn't know how to react to the players who were established and greats for their country and that was a problem. Gouldy still had that Wimbledon mentality, which was fine up to a point. All this 'we're all in this together, we all scrap, we all have a good laugh' can only get you so far and when it came to the better players he struggled, because he wasn't quite sure how to get them on board. He got me onside by making me assistant manager, but not the others, and the supporters never quite took to him either.

At the same time, some standards improved. If the hotel was shit we moved hotels. He wanted a better training ground. He brought in someone to do video analysis and motivation. So he got things up and running that way and things became more organised behind the scenes, but it still wasn't really enough for stars like Giggsy and Sparky.

Barry Horne had dropped out of the Welsh setup in 1996 and we needed a new captain. Bobby asked me, and of course I said I'd do it. Then he changed his mind and said that he was going to have an election for captain. Gary Speed, Dean Saunders and Vinnie Jones all decided to stand. I think from the eleven of us who voted Gary got six votes and Deano got five. But then Bobby announced that Vinnie had won! It wasn't Vinnie's fault, but that kind of thing pissed everybody off.

In fairness he tried certain things to lighten the mood, but even these had a habit of backfiring. We were doing laps of the training ground one day when he suddenly piped up, 'Right, who wants a wrestle?'

We were all a bit perplexed by this challenge, and nobody took him up on it. So he picked out John Hartson.

'C'mon, John, we'll have a wrestle.'

John just laughed at him, but the gaffer was insistent.

'C'mon John, we'll have a wrestle.'

And so they did, in the middle of the training pitch. A middle-aged football manager and a fighting-fit professional footballer. I think John ended up cracking Gouldy's rib, which sent him off into one of his rages.

I don't think the players actively disliked Bobby, but there was no love lost there, either. He was always asking how much we were being paid, which never went down well. He was also a reactor and I think he thought that his best form of defence was attacking someone. When the pressure was on he used to go ballistic at the slightest provocation.

Gouldy tried out a few of the younger goalkeepers, like Danny Coyne, Andy Marriott and Tony Roberts, but when qualifying for the 1998 World Cup in France started with back-to-back wins against San Marino I was still number one. We won those games 5-0 and 6-0, which I suppose was good for morale, but we never took anything from those games. They were lose-lose situations: everyone expected you to win convincingly, so if you did no one praised you for it.

But our limitations and Gouldy's were quickly exposed. We led the Netherlands 1-0 at half-time in a qualifier at the Arms Park, but ended up losing 3-1. Things soon got worse. In the return fixture in Eindhoven in November 1996 our preparations were disrupted because the manager couldn't decide on his team. There was one on Wednesday, one on Thursday, one on Friday and another on the day of the match. Then we got hammered 7-1 and Holland had another 28 chances on top of that. Despite conceding seven goals I won man of the match, I was called into action so often.

I was playing in the World Cup qualifying matches but not the friendlies and it seemed clear that Gouldy was planning for life without me. My 92nd appearance for Wales came at the start of the 1997/98 season against Turkey in Istanbul. We were 2-0 down after just 15 minutes, but by the half-hour mark were leading 3-2. Some of the refereeing left much to be desired and Gouldy was red-faced with rage on the sidelines.

As we came off at half-time, by now drawing 3-3, Gouldy sidled up to me.

'We've got a fucking problem here,' he said.

'Yeah, we have.'

'Yeah, it's fucking you. You've got to come off.'

I just looked at him, dumbstruck. There was nothing I could have done with any of those goals. I'm pretty honest, and if I had felt I was at fault I would have said so. But Gouldy hauled me off and on came Paul Jones. We ended up losing 6-4. It was an inauspicious way to end my international career.

I could have walked away from Wales there and then, but that wouldn't have been me. I love my country and loved being part of the national setup. I also thought I could help Paul Jones who, like me, had come up through non-league football and was belatedly establishing himself in the Premier League at Southampton in his late twenties. I also worked with the Wales youth teams, which I enjoyed, and was allowed to do my own thing with them. So there were some good aspects too.

But things didn't really get better for the national team. Wales's misery under Gouldy continued for another 20 months. During this time I left Everton and ended up at Torquay, but continued to serve as his assistant and to work as a coach for the national youth teams. The end came in June 1999 in Italy, where we played a European Championship qualifier in Bologna. We were having a practice match in the build-up to the game and someone made a misplaced pass. I don't know why, but it triggered a volcanic reaction in the boss. He stood on the pitch, ranting and screaming: 'If you don't want to do it my way, pick your own fucking team and when you've got a team come and tell me and I'll fucking coach you.'

He stormed off the training ground and I went after him to try and calm him down.

'What the fuck's going on?' I asked.

'I'm not having that,' he said. He was furious. He always got wound up near to matches and I think that things had just got completely on top of him by that stage. He probably sensed that he had started to lose the dressing room, and although what had or hadn't happened wasn't any sort of manifestation of it he didn't know how to deal with the developing situation.

'Well, there's no point in us being here then, is there?' I said. 'Let's get on a flight out of here this afternoon.'

He seemed to calm down after that and we managed to cobble together a team, but it was no good. We were losing at 3-0 at half-time and Gouldy just said, 'That's it, I'm going to resign. So long as I get my pay-off I'm going.' He had a go at a few of the players, but it wasn't their fault.

His departure left the FAW with a very immediate problem. Four days later we were playing Denmark at Anfield and there was no manager. Forced into action they asked me and Sparky to take over as co-managers for that fixture, and I was pleased and proud to help. Sparky played and I managed from the touchline. We did okay despite the inevitable lack of confidence and were unlucky to fall to two late goals.

For a second time I applied for the Wales manager's job and this time I was confident I stood a good chance. Phil Pritchard, the new CEO of the FAW, suggested that at the very least I had a very very good chance. Terry Venables, Kevin Ratcliffe, Sparky and Roy Hodgson also applied and I was pleased with the interview. In fact I was told later by someone on the panel that I gave the best interview of the five candidates.

The FAW dithered for a bit, and then one afternoon I was listening to the radio in my car when I heard that Sparky had got it. I was upset and angry, not so much that I hadn't got the job, more that they hadn't even bothered to tell me.

I called the FAW right away and asked Phil Pritchard why they hadn't called me.

'We didn't know where you where,' was the rather lame excuse.

'That's funny,' I replied, 'I was coaching the Welsh youth team in Aberystwyth.'

I don't think, looking back, I ever really stood a chance because I never had an agent, and I didn't play for Manchester United. I suppose I was naive. Sparky took it up another level and in lots of ways was a better appointment than I would have been. I'd rather have had the Wimbledon spirit but with the Man United level of organisation and hotels and travel. I think we would have done well, but in a different kind of way.

# CHAPTER FOURTEEN
# N O M A D

AFTER HOWARD HAD SIGNALLED that my Everton career was over I needed to find a club, any club. It was midway through the 1997/98 season: I was 39 years old, but believed I had another ten years in me. Six months earlier Chelsea had tried to sign me, so it wasn't just me who believed I could offer something at the top.

Looking back I should have remained at Everton until the end of my contract at the end of that season. Firstly, you never know what's going to happen next in football and an injury or change of heart from Howard could have propelled me back into the team. Secondly, it would have given me an opportunity to bide my time, wait for offers to come in, and choose the one that was right for me.

But I didn't see it that way. The rejection by a club I'd given over 16 years' service to hurt me badly. I had no desire to be somewhere I wasn't wanted. There was also the same motivation that had been with me my whole life: I wanted to play. I didn't care where or when, so long as my boots and gloves were on and I was playing first-team football.

I went back to Howard and asked him to help me find a new club. He said he would, but nothing happened; he was too busy running the club, I suppose. Once you're out of the picture you're out of the picture and no one is that bothered with you. I didn't have to go in for training if I didn't want to and could just have stayed away from the club. I was surplus and he didn't want me around being a nuisance. But that wasn't me. I wanted to annoy Howard as much as I possibly could and go in and train as hard as I could just to piss him off. And as I said, you never know what's going to happen next in football.

After some weeks of this, of haunting Bellefield like Banquo's ghost, Howard called me into his office.

'Southend United want to speak to you,' he said.

They were managed by the former West Ham and England defender Alvin Martin, a Bootle lad. We had a chat and he seemed like a great fellow, and he asked me if I wanted to sign on a loan deal. My view was that it was better than doing nothing: I didn't even look where Southend was on the map.

This began a period of my life of long-haul commutes so I could carry on playing football. I was still living in North Wales and would make the four or five-hour journey to the Essex coast midweek, spend Thursday, Friday and Saturday there, and then travel back.

There were lots of good things about Southend and the setup at Roots Hall. I liked Alvin and was grateful for the chance to resume playing, even if it was at the wrong end of English football's third tier. Results weren't great, but there was a good spirit among my new team-mates. But it just didn't feel right. I wanted to play football and I wanted to enjoy it, but I didn't seem to be able to because of what had happened at Everton. No matter how welcome people tried to make me feel, it was never home. It was like a foreign land to me. Because I'd just landed there midseason and wasn't sure how long they wanted me for it felt like I had no beginning and no end. There was no real tie, no emotional connection. And I still mourned the loss of my Everton career.

The only way I can put it to you is that it was a bit like the kids who are let go by clubs when they are 16 or 17. They might have been tied to an academy for two-thirds of their life and have devoted everything to making their way with a club. They go through a period of not knowing what's going to happen next: they're either picked for a club straight away and are really happy, or they don't find somewhere for a while and feel rejected and low, and short on confidence; a bit depressed. That's where I was at in the first days of 1998.

My loan spell at Southend lasted nine matches and then I was back in no-man's land. My agent Peter McIntosh was on the case, however, and had lined up a move to Stoke City, who were at the wrong end of what was then the First Division (now the Championship). Again, the move was a big mistake. I couldn't see past my desire to play, when really I should have bided my time and waited for the right club to come along. I commuted from North Wales, but was in every day and it was a slog. Although it wasn't that far, the M6 always seemed to be a nightmare and I ended up travelling five or six hours a day to get there and back. It soon took its toll.

The atmosphere at the club was toxic too. Chris Kamara signed me and was a really thorough, well-prepared coach. He had that infectiousness and enthusiasm that has translated so well into his subsequent TV career. But it was clear to me that his time as Stoke manager was coming to an end, even though he had only been in charge for a few weeks. You could already see the strain in his relationship with Jez Moxey, the club's young chief executive, and it seemed there were people within the club who had an eye on his job. The previous management team of Chic Bates and Alan Durban had been allowed to stay on at the club when they were sacked, and it created a horrible atmosphere. Chic wasn't a bad fellow, but it was obvious that he didn't like Chris – which was perhaps understandable, because he had taken his job. This wasn't helped by the club being embroiled in a relegation battle; the third one I was involved in that season.

Results were bad. We won just once in 14 games under Chris and the knives were out. Players just didn't perform and I know I didn't play very well. Chris was having a bad time at home and his father died around this time. But there was no sympathy from the Stoke board and he resigned at the start of April before they could sack him. He had been in charge for just ten weeks. I think the lack of empathy and support he was shown by the Stoke board was one of the most disgraceful things I've ever witnessed in football.

In his place Alan Durban was promoted from youth coach to manager. It was an appalling decision. There was no respect for him or Chic and we knew then we were doomed to relegation. I think Chris would have turned things around, and if someone like Paul Stewart or Kevin Keen – who were both very bright and capable and had the respect of their fellow players – had been given a chance we would have been okay. It would have created a bit of atmosphere and we'd have pulled clear of the drop zone. But there was nothing.

Durban pulled me aside on his first day in charge. He was a former Welsh international and had had a good playing career with Derby County, and I had great respect for his achievements in the game. But that quickly evaporated.

'I'll let you manage the reserves, so long as you keep your head down, do whatever I tell you, and I won't tell everybody you're a bad influence.'

A bad influence? I'd never even spoken to the bloke before, and he'd cast me as a bad guy. I have no idea why he thought of me like that, but his dismissive attitude infuriated me.

The training sessions were embarrassingly bad. They were like something you'd see on a Pathé newsreel. They gave us nothing and there was no respect for either of them. Players were just going through the motions. If you think of Chelsea under Andre Villas-Boas, where it was clear that some players just weren't interested in performing for him, well this was ten times worse. Durban wouldn't play Paul Stewart – who was our best player, very talented, a leader and someone who could have produced something from nothing – seemingly because he stood up for himself. He wanted him out. Match days were awful: we won our first two home matches, but deep down all of us knew that we were doomed.

The final day of the season brought Manchester City, now managed by Joe Royle, to the Britannia Stadium. They were in a terrible position as well and, like us, needed a win and for other results to go their way. Everyone was resigned to our relegation. The atmosphere in the stands replicated that in the dressing room: it was torpid, flat and nasty. Eryl and Samantha had travelled down to watch me with Peter McIntosh, but unbeknown to me the club had given them three tickets in the worst part of the ground. Fifteen minutes in there was a massive fight and they left. I simply couldn't believe that the club put my family in that situation.

We lost the game 5-2 and went down with City. Port Vale, Stoke's big rivals but who they dwarfed in size, stayed up by a single point. I'm sure it must have been one of the darkest days in the club's history.

Afterwards nobody spoke to me at all. I gathered my things and left and never went back. One of the worst episodes of my life had drawn to a close.

━┴━

THE SAME DAY STOKE WENT DOWN, Southend were relegated too. A week later Everton faced Coventry City at Goodison, needing to get something from the match to stand any chance of avoiding relegation. There was a very real danger that all three clubs I played for during the 1997/98 season would go down.

Everton had invited me back to say goodbye to the fans that day, but it was probably the worst possible time for me to do so. I would have liked Howard to have given me a run-out in a nothing sort of game; just a final chance to spend some time in the Old Lady of Goodison, to have a run-out in front of the supporters who had followed me through thick and thin during the best years of my life. But it wasn't to be. Everton's predicament was too dire, and in any case it was never Howard's way to be sentimental about anything.

Everton had been terrible through that tumultuous season. Things weren't right in the dressing room and the supporters were furious about the way chairman Peter Johnson was running the club. The atmosphere at Goodison that day was mutinous, but I never thought Everton would go down.

I wasn't sure of the motivation underlying my invitation back to the club. It was a nice opportunity for me to come on at half-time and say a few words and I was moved by the reception that I got. But I wasn't sure whether the club thought it might rub off on the players or raise the crowd.

If that was the case, it probably didn't work. Everton were leading 1-0 at half-time, after a long-range shot from Gareth Farrelly. In the second half they missed a penalty and then conceded a late goal, after Thomas Myhre let a shot slip through his fingers. A draw, however, was enough. At Stamford Bridge, where I might well have been playing had things taken a different turn, Chelsea beat the day's other relegation candidates, Bolton, and Everton stayed up on goal difference. My belief that they would never be relegated had proved true once more.

After the match thousands of supporters flooded on to the pitch to make their displeasure at Peter Johnson known. The pitch was cut up as angry supporters lobbed sods of turf at the directors box and chanted for his resignation.

I'd gone home by then. It was the end for me and Everton; a strange way to conclude a 17-year association with the club. Six weeks later

Howard's time was up as well, after he was sacked by Johnson. The last links with Everton's greatest ever team had ended.

꜀ㅜ꜀

THROUGHOUT MY SIX MONTHS in Southend and at Stoke I had still for the most part been on my Premier League contract, but now that was at an end and I was a free agent.

Despite what had happened over the previous year, I was still as desperate to play as I had always been. I still loved football and knew that I could do a job at whichever club asked me. I felt I had a lot to give the game as a player and although I probably wasn't as quick and agile as I'd been at my peak, my game had improved in other ways due to my experience.

My old team-mate Ian Snodin had taken over as Doncaster Rovers player-manager and he asked me to join on a short-term deal. Doncaster had dropped down to the Conference the previous May, so it meant stepping outside the Football League for the first time in almost 20 years. It turned out to be a short-lived move. Ten minutes into a match against Southport I pulled my hamstring, something that had never happened in my life before. I stayed on the pitch until we were 3-0 down and limped off, and thus ended my Donny career.

I celebrated my 40th birthday without a club. Many players would have given up, but I gave no thought to retiring. About six weeks later I got a call from Wes Saunders, the Torquay United manager, asking if I'd be interested in joining. The money wasn't great and it was about as far away from North Wales as you could get. I thought, 'I don't really want to go to this place.' But Wes was persuasive and so I went to see what it would be like. The first day I got there it was absolutely lashing down with rain. It was a Friday, I hadn't trained. I did what I needed to do to get myself ready ahead of the match, against Hull City.

It was absolutely pissing it down with rain the next day. Just a few minutes had passed when Hull had a corner. I punched the ball away and someone punched me in the nose. I should have expected it, because they're going to test you out to see if you fancy playing at that level, whatever your age. It was fair enough, I suppose, and it woke me up to the challenge ahead. Anyway, I saved a penalty, and we won 2-0. Suddenly it seemed like the right place. I signed for the rest of the 1998/99 season and everything seemed to click.

⌶

IT WAS GOOD THAT I HAD TORQUAY during this time, as just about every other constant in my life was now gone. I'd lost Everton, and after 18 years my marriage to Eryl ended too.

There were many reasons for the collapse of our marriage, mostly due to me. Contrary to the stereotype, the life of a footballer's wife is not always an easy one. I was away all the time in an era before mobile phones and instant communication. I was completely wrapped up in the game, sometimes to the exclusion of everything else. As I've said before, it's a selfish profession anyway and to be the best I believe you need to be extra specially selfish, which is probably not conducive to being a good husband. I'd had a couple of affairs too, and someone had falsely claimed I was the father of their child. In short it was a mess, entirely of my own making. Eryl had stopped trusting me and it was hard to blame her.

Things came to a head after the messy departure from Everton. Looking back, I mourned the end of my Goodison career, although I didn't realise it at the time. My parents had died within a few months of each other a few years earlier and I didn't properly grieve their loss either. There were lots of things going around in my head and it was a difficult time. Deep down I just wanted what was best for everyone.

As well as all this, I'd met someone else; someone who made me very happy. It was a chance encounter at one of the many hotels I'd stayed in. She – Emma – was an aromatherapist and we just got on really well. I didn't see her very often, but it was another variable at a time when I was being overwhelmed by a confusion of priorities and emotions. Although some good eventually came of it, it was a very painful time. It's difficult to put into words how hard that time was. I felt torn in different directions; I wanted Samantha to be happy and I wanted Em to be happy and I wanted Eryl to be happy; although I don't think Eryl was happy with me anyway.

In the end my view was that if there were two happy parents, Samantha would be better off than having two unhappy parents. So Eryl and I broke up, and I got together with Emma, and we're still together and very happy.

But in other ways Samantha did end up with two unhappy parents. For various reasons it took 11 years to get a divorce and this was a trying time for everybody. A few things came out in the media, which were less black and white than the way in which they were construed. I don't think any of this was particularly good for Samantha. With hindsight, I would have done things so much differently, and had a lawyer handle every aspect of the situation properly. I didn't get to see my daughter anywhere near as often as I would have liked. There were times when I would stay in to call her at an appointed time on a Sunday night, and she wouldn't be in. It was soul-destroying; like someone stabbing me. I can't think of anything more hurtful than not being able to speak to your own daughter.

It's difficult for a young girl to actually come to terms with that too. I did think it affected her a little bit at times, but she's turned into a remarkably well-balanced young woman and I'm extremely proud of Samantha. It's sometimes hard to put into words how I feel about fatherhood: when I wasn't a dad I used to think it was an absolute load of old bollocks and take it all for granted that you'd do everything you could for your kids. But then once you're a dad yourself you realise you can't do everything for them; you can't protect them all the time or be there every minute of the day. You have a natural protective instinct, but you'll never satisfy those urges. I did my best and do my best, but I know it will probably never be good enough.

TORQUAY STRUGGLED IN THE LEAGUE that season, but we had a tremendous set of lads and a good team spirit, which counts for a lot. Our captain was Alex Watson, Dave's younger brother, who had played for Liverpool in the mid-1980s and since dropped down the divisions. He was just like Dave, a real robust defender who would stand up for you and the rest of the team, but could also play a bit. Like Waggy senior he was a great asset to his club. There were some good players. There was a hugely talented French kid called Jean Pierre Simb. He could do ridiculous things with a football, but lacked the finishing touches that would have made him a star. He'd take the ball around six defenders and the goalkeeper, and then fall over. You had a lot of players like that at that level. The club was well run and there were a brilliant set of people behind the scenes. The Sky presenter Helen Chamberlain is a Torquay nut and was always around.

Obviously conditions were very different from what I was used to at Everton. The club didn't have its own training facility and would train at a place we called Dogshit Park, the condition of which requires little explanation. It wasn't fun for the goalkeepers, but I mostly got away with it. I was still in Wales, coaching the goalkeepers at Tranmere and Huddersfield a couple of days a week each and travelling down for matches at the weekend. They put me up in the Palace Hotel, where they really looked after me, and I trained on Friday, played the match on Saturday and went home. I loved it.

Life as a big-name player in the bottom division wasn't any different for me than it was for the other players. I certainly never thought of myself as different to anyone else. I was paid the same and treated the same in the dressing room. I just turned up and played the game. Sometimes I was a target for other players and fans, like on my debut. I got a bit of stick at Swansea and Cardiff. At Brentford I went to get a stray ball and a steward lashed it at my face. I had to duck out the way or it would have broken my nose. I went absolutely berserk with him, something which had never happened before. It was a good job there was a fence between us, because I would have beaten him up. But incidents like that were few and far between.

I ended the 1998/99 season as Torquay's player of the year. We finished the season 20th in Division Three, or 88th in the English football pyramid, but I was happy. I was playing well and had found somewhere that I was wanted. It was a good feeling and I signed up for another season.

I trained hard over the summer of 1999. It took me back to the 1980s, where I'd spend the whole summer preparing for the big kickoff and come back fitter than anyone else. But while the team progressed well and ultimately finished just three points off the playoff places, I wasn't so happy. I felt greater pressure to do well and there was more criticism when we fell short. Every time a goal went in the blame was pinned on me, even when it wasn't my fault.

There was also a growing distance between myself and Wes Saunders. I think my name worked against me, which is not untypical for a player who has dropped down the leagues and comes up against people who have never played at a high level. You can either take advantage of someone's experience and pedigree, as he did in his first year, or see it as a danger. He was a nice fellow, but as the pressure increased on him to get promotion he maybe saw me as a threat to his job. He misread me completely, because that wasn't the case at all. I'd have been delighted to help with the coaching had he asked, but I wasn't interested in taking his job.

Things came to a head after we played Chester at the end of January 2000. I went down to block the ball and my opponent caught me in the head with his shin as he went over me. I was badly concussed and seeing double, which meant I would be out for a couple of weeks. In my mind I'd already decided that I wasn't going to go back, so I'm not sure if he called me or I called him, but we agreed to call it quits. It was a shame it worked out like that and I enjoyed playing for Torquay. Even now there's just three results I listen out for at five o'clock every Saturday: Everton, Bury and The Gulls.

———

MY WEEKENDS HAD BEEN FILLED with playing for Torquay, but my weekdays were spent coaching goalkeepers. I'd coached at Tranmere and was now spending a couple of days a week at Huddersfield, where Steve Bruce was manager. I loved working with other goalkeepers and was good at coaching them. If you look at the clubs I've coached at the keepers have always done well.

After leaving Torquay, Paul Jewell became alerted to my availability. He was managing Bradford, who were in the Premier League at the time, and was in the market for a goalkeeping coach, who would ideally still be a registered player in case of an injury crisis. I was pleased to help out, but when I went to talk to Steve Bruce about it – thinking I'd be able to combine it with my duties at Huddersfield – he got in a huff, thinking I was suggesting Bradford were a bigger club than Huddersfield. That wasn't the case at all, and his attitude was ironic given the way that he subsequently leapt between managerial posts as soon as a better one came along.

It was under a cloud that I left Huddersfield, but Bradford was great, a lovely club with brilliant people. Aidan Davidson, Matt Clarke and Gary Walsh were all good goalkeepers and I enjoyed working with them. But less than a month into the job, Matt and Aidan were injured then Gary picked up a knock. It meant that they had a choice of Danny Simpson, a teenager who had never played a senior match, or me for a local derby against Leeds United. And thus, at the age of 41 years and 178 days I became the fourth oldest player in Premier League history.

I was delighted to have another game at the very top. We lost 2-1 to a very good Leeds team that would qualify for the Champions League that season and I was probably at fault for both of the goals. I hadn't trained properly for a while, but I was pleased to have got through the game. It showed me that mentally I was still strong enough to play the game at that level, and there were aspects of my game that were still good – such as my kicking – despite me not being fully fit. But the next day I got slaughtered in the press, people criticising my weight and saying I was too fat to play in the Premier League. Did it hurt? Not really, but it annoyed me. I'd stepped in at short notice, without training properly, and yet people were passing judgement on my suitability.

I carried on doing some coaching at Bradford, who retained their Premier League status on the last day of the 2000/01 season. But I was slightly chastened by the kicking I'd got in the media and had lost some of my enthusiasm for playing. I was focused on a coaching career by now and spent the summer getting myself fit and back into shape. I joined up with York City, where Terry Dolan – who had been reserve coach at Huddersfield – was appointed manager. I did a couple of evenings a week with the club's academy too. There were some good times at York, but the days could be gruelling. I'd get up at 4.30am, leave North Wales at five and be there for seven o'clock. I'd do a couple of hours in the gym, then work with the goalkeepers in the morning. A couple of evenings a week I'd do the academy, which wouldn't end until 9pm, and then it was back to Wales. York held my playing registration and Terry played me in the reserves and used me as a substitute goalkeeper as well. It was nice seeing games from the dugout and I also had my responsibilities at Bradford too.

But in football, as a coach, you're only as good as the man who employs you, and it's a perilous business at the best of times. Paul Jewell left Bradford for Sheffield Wednesday after keeping the club up, and I was kept on by his successor Chris Hutchings, who only lasted five months, then Stuart McCall, who took charge on a caretaker basis. But then the club brought in Jim

Jefferies from Hearts and everything changed. He didn't care for me, or some of the players he inherited, like Stan Collymore. The atmosphere soured and the club was a disaster waiting to happen: there were players like Collymore, Dan Petrescu and Benito Carbone on massive wages; a manager who couldn't really handle them; and results that were getting worse and worse.

Jefferies didn't listen to me at all. Matt Clarke was our best goalkeeper by far and in my view was talented enough to play for England. He was naturally gifted, one of those players you could pull in from the pub or golf course at ten to three and he would do a job for you. But Jeffries simply wouldn't play him.

So strong were my convictions on this that I did something I'd never done before. I pulled Jefferies aside and said, 'You've got to play him. He's the best goalkeeper you've got by miles. If you don't play him you'll get relegated.'

But Jefferies wouldn't listen. He loaned him out to Bolton and Bradford went down, finishing 16 points off safety. There was no point in me working with a manager who wouldn't listen to my opinions, so I left at the end of the season.

⊐⊏

FROM BEING SYNONYMOUS with a single club for more than 16 years, I went to being a football nomad. It sounds strange, but I didn't like being tied down. At the same time I would have loved to have found a place I could have called home, like I had at Goodison. Torquay may have been that place. I loved the people at the club and the area, but it wasn't to be. And so I went on a magical mystery tour of football's outposts that took in Huddersfield, Bradford and York; then Rhyl, Shrewsbury, and Dagenham and Redbridge.

I played for Rhyl at the start of the 2001/02 season, which was a bit of an eye-opener. I'd been approached by their ambitious chairman Pete Parry, not because of my reputation but because he needed a good keeper. I was paid £300 per week, which was a bonus; I viewed it as a bit of a homecoming, a chance to put something back into the area that had made me as a footballer. It was a nice little club, but I found it frustrating: it was slow, which I expected, but not an enjoyable pace. I was still judged on my Premier League reflexes, even though as a goalkeeper you're going to be posed with shots and chances at a decent velocity at any level. A defender might have missed a block, but I would get the blame for conceding even though a shot came in at 100mph because of his defensive lapse. Because of who I was, there was far more scrutiny on me.

We played at home to Bangor City, one of the clubs I'd started out at. I've played in front of crowds of 100,000 in my career on some occasions, but never in my life have I heard anything like the abuse I did from their travelling support, which numbered at most a few hundred. It was unbelievable stuff, from the most foul-mouthed, abusive louts; if I could have met them on the street outside I would have punched them. They were disgusting. I thought, 'I've been a Welsh international, I've come and played in your league, I've played for you, and you treat me like this.' It was absolutely the worst kind of abuse I've ever had, anywhere. They even started on Emma. I don't lose my temper, but if they'd come on the pitch I would have absolutely severely beaten them, and really enjoyed it. I still think I would have enjoyed doing it.

After that I joined Rats, who was managing Shrewsbury, for a while. I was brought in as cover for Ian Dunbavin and helped my old team-mate out with the coaching. It was nice to be reunited with him; he's one of the few people in football who ever took the time to get to know and understand me. If he'd have stayed in the game I like to think we could have worked together at a higher level.

In December 2001 my own managerial breakthrough finally came. Dover Athletic were at the wrong end of the Conference and had had some financial problems. They were run by a supporters trust, but had a good pedigree at that level and there seemed to be some committed and passionate people behind them. I had some conversations on the phone with the chairman and agreed to take over. The experienced Clive Walker, the former Northampton manager, would be my assistant.

It was an eye-opening experience and I learned a lot in my time there, but there were too many institutionalised problems for me to succeed. I was promised a weekly wages budget of £6,000, which would have given me a good platform at that level. But practically overnight I was told it was actually just £1,200 and I'd have to make changes to meet that budget. There was also a former manager, Bill Williams, who was still at the club. He'd been quite successful in the 1970s and early 1980s, managing in the NASL and South Africa, and had wound up in Dover after a few spells in charge at Maidstone United, which had ended up going out of business in the early 1990s. He was a wheeler-dealer, an Arthur Daley type, the sort of person a lot of these clubs need to survive. He was always looking for a deal and reminded me a bit of Barry Fry. But in the end he was undermining my position, swapping players behind my back and not letting me and Clive get on with running the club.

The other thing I learned was that the players couldn't have cared less about preparation. That's completely changed in non-league over the last decade, but it posed me a few problems. I would ask players to come in early, do some set-pieces and we'd have a meal at the clubhouse. But they'd pull faces and weren't interested, even though we were just trying to do things properly. I used to get each set of players in – the goalie, the midfield, the strikers – and talk to them all individually in my office to go through everything that I expected of them. We created a good atmosphere, but things were going on in the background that I wasn't happy with. It looked to me as if people wanted us to lose and wanted to see us relegated. If Dover went into liquidation they wrote off all their debts. My view was that there was a belief that if I got them out of the mire that was great; if not it didn't matter either.

A few months after I took over the supporters trust were replaced by a board representing the club's major shareholders. There was a backroom power struggle going on and I was its casualty. 'This seems a strange time for the club to make such a decision, which does not send the right message to either players or supporters,' said Simon Harris, who chaired the supporters trust after I was sacked. I'd barely been in charge for any time at all. It needed a lot more time, patience, resources and sorting out, but I believe we could have played league football. Unfortunately football casts people as failures, even when your inheritance is deeply unstable and all sorts of things are happening that are beyond your control. The magazine *When Saturday Comes* referred to the task facing me as 'similar to turning a local pantomime into a successful West End musical'.

I was now aged 43, but I still wanted to play. I made cameos at Dagenham and Redbridge, Canvey Island and Moseley. I played for the pub team, the Bull Fossils, in the second division of the Dover & District Sunday League and scored in our championship-winning match against Norfolk Line.

My next posting as manager came at Hastings United in the Ryman First Division. I arrived in December 2004 – they always changed their managers just before Christmas, as I was to find out to my cost – and we did just fine. It was a part-time posting and I was combining it with my other work, but it was actually a full-time commitment. It was quite full-on, dealing with agents, bringing players in, letting players go; all on a limited budget. I didn't really miss league football, it was back to my roots and, again, I learned a lot. But I never played the political game and ended up falling foul of the chairman over something as stupid as the training schedule. Come December 2005 he was looking for a new manager again.

Besides a brief period in caretaker charge of Margate that was the end of my day-to-day involvement in professional football.

I write this without a trace of bitterness, because I'm happy with who I am and the life that I lead. But I found that football management is based on a combination of fear and cliques. People are scared of being told what they don't want to hear, of having their authority challenged. I think it's healthy to have a backroom debate, but I constantly fell foul of people because I voiced opinions and said what I believed. What's the point of being a yes man? Why should I be ashamed of not saying yes when I mean no? There's also chronic instability in the game. Changes are made midseason and people are expected to come in and make a difference while all sorts of backroom shenanigans go on. The lower you drop the harder this all becomes to deal with. You're judged on your results, but all sorts of things can be happening behind the scenes.

There is also an 'old boys' network in play. Football isn't a meritocracy. The same people get the same jobs and bring the same backroom staff. You look at someone like Steve Bruce who has recently taken on his eighth managerial job at Hull. Good luck to him, but has he ever actually achieved anything? These people bring the same backroom staff and the same ideas to each club. Everything stays the same; insulated to new ideas and new people. Because of the way I was as a player I probably cast myself outside those cliques and thus never had that sort of network to fall upon.

I'm proud of my coaching record and look at the goalkeepers who progressed under my charge. I did some difficult jobs in difficult places and sometimes things didn't work out. I believe that if anyone gave me the chance I still would do a good job. But I don't think it's going to happen. No one has bothered to sit down and listen to my ideas about football. They have a preconceived idea that I'm a bit grumpy, a bit idiosyncratic, a bit bonkers. It's one of the reasons I decided to sit down and write this book, to show that I'm a more nuanced and complex character than they could ever have imagined. But it may have come too late.

# CHAPTER FIFTEEN
# TEACHER

SOMETIMES FOOTBALL CAN TAKE YOU UP the most unexpected paths. I was at Dover Athletic for just a short time, but it led me into something I've now been doing for nearly nine years.

Shortly after leaving the club I became involved in a community scheme called Soccer Skills, which basically entailed taking local kids off the dole and teaching them the skills they needed to make them a football coach. This wasn't some sort of massive initiative and we had seven kids from a variety of backgrounds. All of them had fallen out of mainstream education: some had learning difficulties, others had got in with the wrong crowd or been kicked out by their parents. All had some sort of unrealised potential and it was up to us to release it. After coming onto our scheme I think six finished up in decent work; one drifted. I enjoyed it a lot. There were some battles and challenges, but underlying it all was a great camaraderie that reminded me of the football dressing room.

From there, I went to work at Ashford Special School.

We had some interesting kids and it was something of an eye-opener. What I liked about them was that they were not 'Yes sir, right away sir' types. They had attitude. They messed around. They didn't listen. Some of them were genuinely bonkers – we'd go on trips in a minibus and the girls would be flashing their tits at other drivers. They were probably most teachers' idea of a nightmare, but I liked them for that fact. They gave us dogs' abuse and we gave them stick back. I never got angry and never held grudges; I just took the piss. It was our way of building up a rapport. I treated them like adults. I didn't demand they asked us to go to the toilet, have a drink or food, or listen to music, I just let them get on with what they had to do. Once you had built an element of trust and mutual respect, then the learning tended to follow.

There was one lad that was hyperactive and no matter what you did with him it was impossible to wear him out. I used to send him off running, and no matter where he went and how far and fast he'd run he'd still come back full of energy. Some of them lacked even the most basic knowledge and skills. It was sad, really. I remember sitting with one girl in front of a diagram of the human body and asking where the heart was: she didn't know. We worked around that, and she progressed well, but then parents' night came along. We were going through her work and the progress she'd made and she suddenly professed her love for me! Which was a bit of a shock, to be fair.

Other kids were talented in different ways. One boy was severely autistic and used to have conversations with his hand, but if you gave him a musical instrument he was transformed. He lacked what most people would consider practical or social skills, but was brilliant in other ways. We had a project where we went to this forest and they gave us so much earth to move so we could plant a load of bulbs around this lake. All the other kids were humping around old logs and wheelbarrows full of earth, but this kid was bringing one twig at a time. He'd got it into his head that that was all he was going to do, and that was the limit of his contribution. I got a bit fed up with this, so I told him there was a crocodile in the lake. He dropped everything and legged it.

Later he came back meekly and said, 'There can't be crocodiles in that lake. There's no crocodiles in this country.'

'That's a good point,' I said. 'But they've come up the plug from Australia.'

I think he believed me for a minute, before he realised I was pulling his leg. I know it sounds cruel, but piss-taking is just part of the way you build up trust and rapport with these young people. Conventional educational methods have failed them, so you have to think outside the box all the time. I like to create something of a dressing-room atmosphere in the classroom.

Some of them you encounter and you wonder if they ever have a chance at all. I've seen cases of 16-year-olds being kicked out of their homes, so that the parents can foster younger children and claim benefits from someone else's child. The mind truly boggles. Other kids had parents who were not cruel, just a bit stupid. One lad came in and told me one Monday morning that his dad had taken him to a stripper.

'Was it good?' I asked, trying to humour him.

'Yeah, it was really good.'

'What was she like?'

'It was a fella.'

From there I joined an alternative curriculum company called Voices that operated throughout Kent. The names Craig Vaughan, Matt Fogg, Amanda Mountjoy, Toni Bates, Heather Bar and Lyn Turner will mean little to most people reading this, but they were my colleagues and the atmosphere and rapport that they created among themselves and with our students was wonderful, something I can only compare to the Everton or Wales dressing room.

This was one of the best experiences of my life and the happiest period I've had since leaving Everton. We achieved a lot, laughed a lot, and I learned a lot.

Because it was alternative curriculum there was a lot of thinking outside the box. You had to try methods that transcended the usual textbook approach and would benefit the kids. There was no point in giving anybody homework because they'd never dream of doing it. There was one young lad who had real difficulty with multiplication. He could understand, say, '7x2', but he was not able to get his head around '2x7'; the idea that the sum produced the same result just defeated him. It sounds silly given that it was something so simple, but it was just soul-destroying for this poor kid. In the end I brought my dartboard in, and we'd spend the mornings chucking darts at it. It was as if a mist lifted. Suddenly this lad who couldn't get past such a simple problem could do anything. He was transformed.

I worked on a variety of these projects for a couple of years and really enjoyed the work. There were frustrating times and hard times but there were rewarding times too, and I think that we helped a lot of people.

At this stage I had no formal qualifications at all. I'd left school when I was 16 without any O Levels and although I was always a great and voracious reader, everything was self-taught. I was told that if I wanted to develop my career in education I should get a teaching qualification. At this time I was at Hastings United and I used to study during the day at Canterbury and then race across Kent to Sussex to make training. Sometimes we didn't finish until after 6pm and I'd be like a Formula One driver, racing across the counties. It was very interesting, and again, it made me think about coaching differently, because of the different learning styles and methods. It stood me in good stead; it was handy with the coaching, and obviously the education was a benefit for me. The qualification I undertook was meant to take three years, but I did it in two.

⌶

UNFORTUNATELY KENT COUNTY COUNCIL DECIDED to close down Voices and merge their services with others. Not for the first time, I was out of a job. They called me and asked me what I would like to do; it was like that moment all those years earlier when I was redeployed by Llandudno Council as a binman.

'I don't care,' I said, 'so long as it's interesting.'

'Okay,' they replied, 'we'll get back to you.'

They did, in fairness, get back to me. 'We're sorry, Mr Southall, but we don't have any interesting jobs,' they said. So that was that.

But I liked working in that area of education and enjoyed working with kids. I felt I had something to offer and liked giving something back to the community. I worked in a few other roles here and there, but nothing matched up to the brilliance of life at Voices, so I decided to go it alone. As you might have gathered by now, I'm a free spirit and have always sought to shape my own destiny rather than rely on others to do it for me. So I set up my own educational consultancy, that specialises in working with NEETs (young people Not in Education, Employment or Training).

We work in partnership with Brooklands College in Surrey, offering 26-week apprenticeships that use football at their core. We offer an NVQ in activity leadership, which is the hook, and build a range of other skills around it. The kids come out with seven qualifications; get paid a weekly wage, without which most, frankly, wouldn't come. I dish out fines for poor punctuality and indiscipline, the same as a gaffer would in a football dressing room. There are sticks as well as carrots; there have to be.

One massive misconception people have about NEETs is that because they're naughty kids they don't like boundaries. In fact they absolutely love boundaries; they love them because they know how far they can go, whereas in school they never know. We tell them exactly how we expect them to behave and if they don't they can go and do something else. But at the same time I've got no problem with someone not turning up because they claim their mum's ill, or they've got to stay in to wait for something stupid like a washing machine to be delivered. A school would give a kid a bollocking for something like that. But that's not going to work with one of these kids, so we treat them with a bit of respect. So long as they keep continuous contact with us, and they tell us things and talk to us as if we're all adults and basically don't take the piss, we'll let something like that pass.

We assess these kids when we think they're ready. We don't set deadlines that we know they won't be able to keep, even if they might sometimes suit the further education colleges better. Our approach is always gradual and we build up the learning slowly, starting, for instance, in the coaching module with easy things like warm-ups and warm-downs, which are straightforward, and we take it from there. Most of them mess it up first time around, although some are really good. But they all get their confidence and eventually we get them to do free sessions, where they've got to check all the equipment at both ends and make sure the pitch is ready, and oversee an entire training session. It's a process that we take them through and at the end of it hopefully they'll be able to go right through it, without forgetting anything, and know what they're doing. Some of them take to it quite quickly, but most of them get there after some practice.

It's good work, challenging; full of highs and lows, but with a great group of people. It's not football and it will never replace keeping goal for Everton or Wales. But there are moments when, in very different ways, the level of satisfaction garnered from my job comes close.

# CHAPTER SIXTEEN

# SAGE

WHAT DO I THINK ABOUT THE MODERN GAME? There's a danger when espousing your views on the Premier League that you fall into the trap of every old pro and sound bitter or angry or jealous. That's not me. It really isn't. I don't have any strong feelings, for instance, about the amount of money players earn today. Good luck to them, I say; although I do feel that they have become inherently detached from the public that pays to watch them. How can any ordinary bloke relate to someone who's a multi-millionaire, lives in a gated community and has his own security entourage?

What I will say is that when I look at the top level of English football and that which is played in European club and international competition, it's started to become a completely different game. Football, at the highest level, is ceasing to be a contact sport. I believe we'll have to rethink the refereeing as well, because referees don't have a clue. The very top ones have a naturally good instinct, but it's becoming harder and harder for them because the game has been manipulated to the point where any contact is deemed a foul.

I think English football has suffered because of the creeping influence of Europe and the internationalisation of the game. What I mean by that is there's hardly any distinction between different football styles. If, like me, you were a player for an English club in the 1980s and played a German or an Italian team midweek, you knew that there were certain things that were going to be different; that some things were less likely to get past the referee, or that certain players were more likely to go down for a foul. That distinction has been eroded. There's been a homogenisation of football, and the physical contact that was a big part of the English game even 20 years ago has now gone.

Now they're saying players can't defend and defensive players can't practise their art. They can't get in people's faces and rough them up. They can't tackle properly. In fact, tackling has become a dying art, which is ridiculous, because most people go on a Saturday and want to see 100 per cent effort and 100 per cent contact at all times. But fans are now coming away frustrated because they're just not seeing that. People go and watch football to get the frustrations out of their system, but they just can't do that now. They're quicker to boo; they lose patience more easily. Still the biggest round of applause goes for big tackles – albeit when they're still allowed.

In my opinion the professionalisation of referees has compounded the problem. Because they're now paid to do their job they're expected to be perfect, but fallibility is inevitable in any profession, particularly football. The problem is that when they get something wrong, they don't say they're wrong. In 99 out of 100 cases they don't say anything, or are protected by somebody else behind the scenes. All this breeds a disdain towards referees and instils among referees themselves a deep insularity. Referees are similar to the police. Lots and lots of people hate them, but they are a necessity. Un-fortunately the same distrust and entrenchment characterises both professions.

I'd like to see the referees train with the teams, or actually have players – or former players – come and talk to them about how players will try to bend the rules and what they're actually thinking.

My favourite referee was Keith Cooper. You could absolutely slaughter Keith and he'd slaughter you back; we had a good rapport. You'd tell him he was having a nightmare, and he'd say, 'Yeah, I know, that makes two of us.' At the end of the game you shook hands with him and that was the end of it. There was no grudge, there was nothing. I see him now and he's stayed the same, we just take the piss out of each other. And that's how it should be; but Keith's successors are just not allowed to communicate any more. They don't build up relationships with players like they used to, and that's a problem. It shows the level of their insularity.

The erosion of football as a contact sport makes a goalkeeper's job easier too. Through my career you had to constantly be aware that opponents would be looking to smash you. There'd be stray elbows, boots going in and players challenging you for the ball. It was part of the game. But how often these days do you see a centre forward going up to challenge a goalkeeper? They can't because it's not allowed. Goalkeepers are massively protected by the referees, which – so long as they're not placed in a dangerous situation – I just can't understand. It's one of the reasons that I don't believe goalkeeping is any better than it was back in the day.

A huge part of every keeper's game now is concentration. They're certainly less busy and can go for long spells without touching the ball, which wasn't the case when I played. Or rather it was when Everton were doing well. I don't know if anyone has done any statistical analysis about this, but it would be interesting to see how many times the keeper touched the ball in the 1980s – before the back-pass rule was implemented and physicality was all but forced out of football – and how often they touch it today. I bet it's not half as much.

That's one of the reasons why I look at today's current crop of keepers and think to myself, 'What do they do?' Do they make a difference? How many points a season do they earn their teams? Would they be missed if they had to move on or were forced out? There are, clearly, some very good goalkeepers in the Premier League. But world class? Pepe Reina probably comes closest to filling that criteria, although Joe Hart isn't far behind. He looks like he has the hunger and desire to improve and improve, so that he becomes completely essential to Manchester City and England. I also admire Shay Given and Brad Friedel and believe that in Tim Howard, Everton probably possess the best goalkeeper they've had since I left.

When you look beyond England, the two stand-out goalkeepers for me are Gianluigi Buffon of Juventus and Italy, and Manuel Neuer of Bayern Munich and Germany. Buffon is on his own level and has been so outstanding for so many years that he stands alone at the top of European football. Neuer, by contrast, is really at the start of his career, but just has that indefinable quality that tells me he's going to become a great, great footballer.

━━

THE BIGGEST THING that has changed in the Premier League in recent years is the massive influx of money at Manchester City. I know it happened at Chelsea and Blackburn Rovers, but never to this extent and never with the same broad implications for football. You look at where Everton were in 2008 and where Manchester City were. My old club had been managed brilliantly by David Moyes, who had built a young, attractive team with very little money. They just needed a little something at the time to press on and challenge for honours. City, by contrast, had been badly managed for years and were nowhere. Then someone with no links to the club or the city came and emptied his bank account into Manchester City's and suddenly the complexion and dynamics of the club and the whole league changes.

How is a club like Everton – which tries to be sensible and live within its means – supposed to compete with that?

In a world with some natural justice this wouldn't have been allowed to happen. But then natural justice has never really applied to football, has it? I don't think too many Manchester City fans are moaning about what's happened and I don't think Everton fans would complain either if it happened to them. It's just what goes on in football now.

If an oil sheikh or Russian oligarch came in at Everton and put £1 billion into the club it would be far bigger than anything that has happened in Manchester. Everton are a bigger club with far more history. If this sort of takeover happened at Goodison it would be massive. But would it be better? I'm not so sure. I think you've got to be careful what you wish for because there's always a risk of losing your identity, who you are and what makes you special.

The biggest consequence of a takeover would be that it would inevitably involve a new stadium, which has good and bad implications. Good because you get a nice new ground, but bad because I find these new stadiums quite cold and austere places. There's warmth at Goodison now because it's an old stadium with history that comes from everything that's gone on there. Would you want to say goodbye to that? For the most part clubs that have relocated to new stadiums – Arsenal, Southampton, Middlesbrough, Coventry City – have struggled. It takes a long time to get used to new surroundings.

When a takeover happens there are also bound to be people that don't understand the people or the club, and that inevitably creates a gap. Manchester City are brilliant in doing what they do for the community. I've watched them now and they do try and cater for everybody. But that was set up before the money came in and I suspect there's a constant battle between those who want to uphold the club's tradition and values, and those who have come in and don't know the first thing about them.

My own view is that I would sooner see Everton continue to adopt a gradual approach and add two or three key players than have some outsider come in and tear apart the squad that David Moyes has built up over a decade.

I think there's also got to be more of an understanding of the business of football among some of the supporters. If Bill Kenwright were to say, 'Tell you what, we'll spend another £30million and raise the club's debt,' what would the outcome be? Do Everton players or supporters particularly care if the club's debt is £45million or £75million? They don't. They just want some results on the pitch. But at some level someone's got to balance the risk involved. That's what people don't understand and they get upset and angry when players aren't signed. It's not really fair when the club's owners and the banks are merely trying to be realistic about the situation.

For all the talk about Everton's financial predicament, I don't actually think they're far away from challenging for trophies. I know everyone just looks at them and thinks, 'Oh well, they're short of money,' and that's the end of the story, but there's more to it than that. They are short of money but I think the goalkeeper is decent; the back four is decent; the midfield is decent. In Nikica Jelavic they've signed a top-class centre forward, which is something they've lacked for a few years. I'd like to see another playmaker in midfield, somebody who can actually make things happen, and they need some pace and some more strength in depth up front.

I reckon if David Moyes was able to bring in two wingers and two forwards, just to beef up the squad and give him some more options, they'd have half a chance of winning things. If you got those four players I think they would do well. Sometimes it's not big names that win you things; sometimes it's the players like Kevin Richardson or Alan Harper who are the key to it. You've got your players that play, but you've got other people that can do their jobs for you, and I think it's the unsung people that win you things. It doesn't take an awful lot of money: Everton are three-quarters of the way there; they just need a little extra punch and momentum.

The danger, of course, in modern football is that Manchester City will come along and just buy your best players if you pose a threat to them. That's what they did with Joleon Lescott, of course. A lot depends on the strength of your board. I guarantee that if Everton were second in the league and going for the title, they wouldn't sell anybody because they wouldn't need to. If the team were challenging for Champions League qualification the board would look to that pot of money and brush away covetous attention. If they got to second in the Premier League you can also bet that they'd have investors coming out of their ears.

How far are Everton away from that day? Not far, if they get the breaks. But their predicament is such that they're constantly walking a high wire. They're not far from reaching the end, but it's also easy to trip and fall into the mire.

⊐⊏

ON THE MORNING OF SUNDAY 27 NOVEMBER 2011 I was driving back to my home from Wales when an old friend I hadn't heard from in a while sent me a text message. Its four words struck me cold: Gary Speed is dead.

At first I thought it was the cruellest joke that anybody had ever played on me. But then other text messages started to come through and before long it was leading the radio news. I was devastated.

I still find it really difficult to believe that he's gone. When I'm at Wales matches I think Gary's going to walk into the room or lead the team out. He's still there for me in some form and I think that the players he managed feel that too.

Five weeks after Gary's death another one of my old team-mates, Gary Ablett, died after a long and courageous battle against cancer. I'd known Gary long before he played for Everton and knew his dad, a policeman, too. Again, it was very hard for me to take.

People seem to look on footballers as superhuman, but we're not. We're ordinary men who are – or were – good at our sport and lucky enough to be paid to do it for a living. We are elevated to the status of icons, but frankly when you think of British soldiers in Afghanistan, or firemen, what we do is pretty ordinary. We live life and we have the same fallibilities as the next man. Some of us get cancer or depression, or our marriages break down, or we leave the game and do what some people would consider ordinary jobs. Within our sport we may have done some extraordinary things, but we're only human. I think for all footballers and former players, the deaths of the two Garys were reminders of our impermanence.

Most recently, one of my predecessors in the Everton goal – Gordon West – died too. Every time one of these players passes away, you've lost something from the club. It eats a little bit away from Everton's fabric. Yes, they're part of its history, but while they're alive they're a living part of it too. Gordon, for example, was a popular and well-known face to everybody on a match day, as was his best friend, Brian Labone, who died suddenly in 2006.

One by one these giants of Everton's past are fading away. There will be heroes in the future, of course, but it will be different. There was a sense of humility and normalcy among previous crops of players. You can't get bigger giants in Everton history than the late Brian Labone or Howard Kendall, but they were – and are – always there for everybody. Dixie Dean was too. Until the last decade footballers were genuinely of the people. But the game has changed inexorably and I think that the top players have grown away from the public. It's a massive issue.

I, of course, am deeply aware of my own mortality. Losing two of your friends and team-mates brings that into sharp focus. I've had a few issues with my health, as many men in their fifties do, and not long after the Garys passed away I went to a solicitor to put my affairs in order. It was easy, really, because I only had one great wish: that when I go, wherever I am in the world, my body is brought back home and buried in Welsh soil. That's all that matters to me. But hopefully that's many, many years in the future, because this old goalkeeper has still got plenty of living to do.

APPENDIX

# Q & A

In the final stages of writing this book I took questions from some of the football fans who saw me play during my long career. Here are the answers I gave to the best ones posed to me.

**What was the funniest incident you have ever witnessed during a match you have played in?** *Jason Russell, Sevenoaks*
One of the funniest things was right at the end of my time at Everton. We played Chelsea away and Howard Kendall wanted to make a substitution. So he said to Tony Thomas 'Go and warm up'. Tony said nothing. After five minutes, nothing had happened and he said, 'Tony go and warm up'. Again, Tony said nothing and nothing happened. Five more minutes passed, and Howard yelled, 'Tony will you go and fucking warm up.' Finally Tony spoke up: 'Gaffer,' he said, 'I'm in my suit, I'm not even sub'.

**Since retiring, who's been the best keeper you've seen in an Everton shirt?** *Lee Marshall, Auckland, New Zealand*
I think Tim Howard by a mile. I think Timmy's been really consistent, and everybody trusts him. I think it was a toss up between him and Nigel Martyn. Tim's been here longer so I think, they're both similar ability, don't make mistakes, and everybody trusts them. I think for pure length of time you've got to give it to Tim.

**Who's the player you love playing alongside at Everton and also at international level?** *Michael Stewart, Crosby*
Probably Kevin Ratcliffe because I knew his game inside out and he knew mine. I missed him when he retired because nobody defended like him. He had a thing where he knew he could let the opponent shoot because he knew I had it covered. That's what he always says anyway; whether he was just fucking slow or not I don't

know. I knew he was as quick as anything so I didn't have to go charging out all the time; I knew he'd recover. Some of the others afterwards, they weren't as quick as him and they didn't have as good a brain as him, so you know you might have to sweep a little bit more. But with Rats you could drop off a little bit because he'd actually tackle and play sweeper, and if you made a mistake he could recover as well.

**What was the greatest moment in your career?** *Lee Dunne, Liverpool*
Bayern Munich semi-final. Not because there was any medal at stake; not because of anything else, apart from the people. I've said earlier in the book that it was the only time the people ever won a game. You can say what you like about all the other games put together, there was nothing to touch the atmosphere there. It was the one night I think I've ever seen Merseyside spirit win the game, or Evertonian spirit win the game. I've never seen it anywhere else in all fairness; it reminded me of Rocky. The crowd can lift everybody, but it's very rare isn't it? It's very rare that the people make a difference in sport. Generally if you concentrate on what you're doing, you don't hear the fans. That night was different. It was a different atmosphere from when we got to the ground, and it was people power really. For me it was as good as pulling the Berlin Wall down. It was that significant for Everton that kind of spirit.

**What was more enjoyable – winning the FA Cup in 1984 or 1995?** *Thomas Regan junior, Liverpool*
1984 in one way because we proved we could win it, and prove we were a good team. 1995 because it was my last one, I knew it was my last one. I think they're both equally important for different reasons; and they're at both ends of my career aren't they? So the first one it was fantastic because we actually achieved that and it was the first time I'd won something at Wembley; and then the second time it's because I knew the club was on the verge of trying to push me out the door; so I relaxed and really enjoyed it. From a personal point of view, the second one. From a professional perspective the first one, because we proved we could compete at that level and win the Cup.

**In terms of personal form, what was your best ever season?** *Paul Owens, Hull*
To me it was when Colin was there. If I was going solely on what I did, I think that period. When I played well in, I suppose, late '83 to '86-ish, when I got my injury, I was in a really, really good team. With Colin I think the team wasn't as good as that team, so it was harder. I think I also played better because I was at an age where I

knew exactly what I was doing. I felt ridiculously fit and strong as anything. I always felt that was my best.

**What was it like as a goalkeeper when playing away, and yet being so close to the home crowd, and did it affect you?** *Andy Edwards, Wallasey*
I loved it; absolutely loved it. Most of the time if we got there early, I made sure I walked down to the home end, so they could have a go at me. It used to motivate me going out to play. But I loved it to be fair; the comments you get and all that is brilliant. That's the best bit about it. I used to hate it when the crowd were miles away. If we went abroad somewhere, there was usually a running track at the ground and I don't think there's anywhere with the same atmosphere. When you get all the people around you that's when you perform better, I think.

For me, when all the new stadiums are built, it's too far away from the players; and I think even at Wembley the pitch should be a lot closer. It should be as if you're on top of the people. That's how you make an atmosphere. I think the further away you go the worse it is. I loved playing at West Ham, the old West Ham, when it was right on top of you; Leeds, brilliant; Liverpool brilliant; Manchester was too big; Old Trafford for me is too big. I like the grounds that are really compact and really tight. Everyone moaned about Millwall; I loved playing ay Millwall, it was brilliant. Alright, it was a hostile crowd; so what? It was brilliant. If it intimidates you you shouldn't be playing in the first place, should you? The more stick they gave me the better I wanted to play against them.

**Old Wembley or new Wembley?** *John Kenny, Wallasey*
In some ways, old Wembley, because the pitch was softer, the atmosphere was better, and it had tons of history. I played on the new Wembley funnily enough and it's rock hard. It's a great stadium, but it doesn't have the history. I think if you look at new stadiums in general, I can only think of one team that's got a new ground and been successful and that's Man City. All the other clubs who've had new grounds have struggled. Leicester, Middlesborough, Coventry. I don't know why – whether they lose a bit of impetus or a few fans

That's why I'm a little bit more sceptical of moving from Goodison, because I think you will lose something. I think some places, the history lives in the walls; it lives in the building itself, and Goodison is one of them places. Sll the other historical teams have that sort of atmosphere. You go to a new thing, it's bland isn't it? I think everyone feels like an outsider; I think that's what it is.

You know when you go to Goodison and you get in your normal seat? That's home for you, isn't it? It's like leaving your armchair in your house to go to your armchair in the ground. I think you lose that with some of the new grounds because you don't tend to sit where you normally sit; you have a different view; normally you're sat by different people. So you have to build all them links again.

**Which of your medals meant most to you?** *Alan Davies, Kindle Bay, Rhyl*
I suppose the first one I ever won in the Milk Cup Final, even though it was a runner's-up one, because it proved I could actually play at that level. And we shouldn't have lost it and I think the first one you get is always a stepping stone if you're really a good team. A lot of players have gone to one Cup Final and never had another one. We were lucky because that one game gave us the belief to go and play the others and be successful. I loved the first League one because that proved more than anything else we were the best team in the country. Over a period of games we showed a consistency. I loved that one.

**In which game was your best performance in an Everton shirt?** *Karl-Yngve Lund, Sundsvall, Sweden*
I do think everybody goes on about Spurs and all that. But actually I think Tony Cottee's second game, we played Coventry away. I think I played brilliantly. That was the one I most enjoyed. There was a couple of Southampton's away, nil-nil, where we always got murdered.

**Who outside the football world inspired you, and in what way?** *Brian Lane, Llandudno*
That's quite a difficult one, to be fair. My uncle Johnny Roberts, because he just let me go and play, and believed it didn't matter what the score was. Gwyn Williams at Conwy United. Then Johnny Williams at Winsford. There was a fellow called Mr Coe, who had a Sunday League team, and to be fair I don't think he knew much about football, but again he was there and he made sure all the teams went out and he was a really nice fellow. Those kind of people really. I know they're sort of in football but they're not in football. It's a really difficult one; I tried not to look at anybody apart from myself.

**What was your favourite save, and why?** *Paul Hill, Leeds*
I tried not to have a favourite one, because I was hoping I'd make a better one the next game. And then I finished my career and I didn't make one! I suppose that is my answer really.

If I look back I suppose there are a couple. There's a penalty from Brian Kilcline and for years I've tried to figure out how I saved it. He smashed it, and I don't know how I stopped it, so he hasn't got a clue either. That one was probably one of my favourites. I suppose above all else the Sheffield Wednesday one [v Imre Varadi], because he thought he scored and went away to celebrate. I suppose that was as near to perfection as I could get

**What was your most memorable game in a Wales shirt?** *John Connor, Wigan*
My debut would come close, because obviously it's the first one. Probably the 7-1 defeat in Holland, because even though I let in seven, I saved 28 chances too and that was the busiest I've ever been in a goalkeepers' shirt, ever. That was like playing for Llandudno Swifts again. I loved playing in Holland because I thought the fans were absolutely brilliant, and the atmosphere was great; the whole game was brilliant. It was brilliant for me personally because I can't think of many games where you come off as Man of the Match and you've let seven goals in. That was unique really, wasn't it?

**Who was the best amateur or semi-professional footballer you played against, or with?** *Craig Joel, Liverpool*
There was a lad who I liked, he played for Winsford– John Price; I think he's in New Zealand now. And as a left-back he reminded me so much of Bails, he was just brilliant to play with. Proper Scouse sense of humour. He wasn't an out-and-out smasher; he had a real good bit of quality on him as well. John was probably as close as I'd get I think, if I had to name one.

**As the best goalkeeper in the world during the 1980's, were you tempted to follow some of your team mates to play for some of the top teams in Europe?** *Mark Richmond, Liverpool*
No, because I never thought about it. To be fair it would have been a nuisance if someone came and hassled me. I hated contract negotiations; I hated anything to do with speculation like that, because it just detracted from what I did. I wasn't tempted, no, because mainly I never gave it a thought, and at that time it was well known that all the European clubs hated British goalkeepers, so I was never going to go anywhere.

**If Pat Van Den Hauwe hadn't been in the way would you have saved Norman**

**Whitseside's shot in FA Cup Final?** *Paul Miller, Bury*
I don't think so. Norman said he used Pat as a shield but then maybe I should have done better, anyway.

**Why did you keep the moustache for so long?** *Stephen Gladwin, Neath*
Because I couldn't be arsed shaving it off. Sometimes I did when I was away with Wales because it used to annoy anybody who was in charge – they used to come down and I'd only shave one half of my face. So sometimes I'd leave it on and shave right round it; just do half my face. It's amazing how many people just don't notice it.

**Out of all the defensive line-ups you've played with, which did you have the greatest understanding with?** *Chris Schofield, Nelson*
Gary Stevens, Dave Watson, Rats and probably Bails. Those I could read the best.

**You were the best keeper in the world for a good few years; who in your opinion is the current number one?** *Mike Chubb, Penrith*
I'd narrow it down to three, which would be Pepe Reina, Gianluigi Buffon and Manuel Neuer. I still think everyone can get better. I think Joe Hart is just class. But I also like Shay Given and Brad Friedel, because their level of consistency is brilliant. But Buffon is probably the best in the world. He's like a Rolls Royce; he's been around a long time, knows exactly what to do, when to do it.

**What system did you use for stopping penalties?** *Shane Woods, Longford, Ireland*
Gut instinct. And maybe a little bit of information if I was given it. I might have found someone to tell me what way they put the ball, but that tended to distract me. A lot of the time I had a gut instinct where I thought the ball was going to go and I dived that way. I just picked up visual clues really, the body shape and what way they looked. It also depended for me what minute of the game it was. If it was the first minute, then I think it's 50-50 whether I save it and he misses it, because he hasn't got his aim, and I haven't got my aim. If it's towards the end of the first half and he's having a really good game then I think the odds are on him because he's got the confidence. If it's towards the end of the game there's a lot more pressure and I think it goes back to 50-50.

The only thing I did was to just walk off. If there was a penalty I just walked as far away as I could and then gave him as much time to think about it as I could. A lot of it depended on the timing and the size of the game. If it's a friendly and nothing in it, then the odds are in his favour because he's more relaxed. If it's a semi-final or an FA Cup or something and it's the last minute, the pressure is all on him to score.

There's a million other factors that come into it; if you just do a straight penalty competition, then I think if you go the right way for the first one, you've got a chance of going the right way for most of them. If you go wrong for the first one they've got the advantage because you're always trying to play catch up. The onus swings back to you then to actually guess, because if you go the right way the first one, they then think that you can read it so there's doubt in their mind.

**Who was the best coach you've worked with?** *Terry McGrath, Warrington*
I'd say Colin Harvey. Colin and Willie Donachie were on par with each other. Colin because of the ridiculously high standards he demanded of himself in training, never mind anybody else. And Willie was very, very similar. But I think Willie was a little bit different; he tried to fix the whole mind, body and soul, where Colin wanted your ability to shine through and your footballing skills to shine through.

**Out of all the football grounds you've been to, which one do you enjoy the most when playing on?** *Ryan Primrose, Chester*
I loved West Ham, Leeds, Southampton, and Arsenal, because people were close. I didn't mind Millwall at all. I liked playing at Liverpool, obviously. Best ground is always going to be is Everton though.

**What do you consider to have been your biggest mistake in your career?** *John Waddington, Suffolk*
Listening to Mike Walker I suppose! Seriously, it was joining Stoke. I should have stayed where I was. Actually, it was staying at Stoke when Alan Durban took over. That's probably the worst one.

**As the golden generation of Welsh footballers have now retired, do you think Wales will ever make it to a major football championship?** *Antony McClafferty, Flint*
I'm positive they will. I'm positive because they've got really good players. My one fear for the current crop is the lack of strikers, or lack of strikers that are playing the Premier League, let's put it that way. That could be the only thing that stops them, because I think they've got a really good goalkeeper, defence is solid, midfield is good; they've got Bale, they've got Ramsey; if Bellamy continues that'll be great. I think there's some really good players. My only problem is their lack of cutting edge.

**What was the defining moment that you can say it was the make-or-break point of becoming a professional footballer?** *Gary Bundy, Barrow-in-Furness:*
I always thought I could play. I suppose taking the initial step from leaving hod-carrying to join Bury on less money was a massive risk. I think that was the defining moment, and after making my debut, I thought, 'Yeah, I can do this'. But I was lucky because I had decent steps. I went from getting beaten every week with Llandudno Swifts to a bit more professional at Bangor City; then I left there, went to Conwy United where I really flourished because it was a really good atmosphere and we paid our subs to play and there was a real togetherness. Then I went from there to Winsford and a team of Scousers and had a really good time with a bit more of a crowd; so that led me to believe that I could play again. By the time I got to Everton, there was never a question in my mind that I could play, so each time I had a stage. I was lucky really that there wasn't one defining moment; I think it was just a combination of steps. Rather than looking for a single moment as a young player, the question was always how good did I want to be and where did I want to end up.

**What was the pivotal moment when you felt Everton was your club and somewhere that you could spend most of the rest of your career?** *John Guy, Hever*
The proudest moment of my life is probably when we got beat by Liverpool in 1984 in the Milk Cup replay. I just knew then that we had a team. I was really, really proud of all of them. I've never said that to be fair; so it was a really funny feeling to say yeah, actually we know we can win something now, because we've come this close; there was nothing in it really.

I don't think when you feel proud of other players unless it's your club, do you? But from day one I just loved training at Everton anyway. The training ground felt like home, from the second I stepped through the door.

**What is the worst mistake you've ever made on the pitch?** *Michael Lam, Wirral*
Probably playing Norwich away, I think. Someone had a shot and I let it in through my legs. I thought 'Bollocks; that's in'. I didn't know it stuck in the mud behind me. Someone ran in behind me and scored. Probably if I had turned round and dived on the ball I would have saved it. But Norwich wasn't a happy place for me, ever. The first time I went there somebody spat in my face, which I didn't really expect. Then I made a couple of mistakes, then I dislocated my finger and had stitches in my finger. Then I walked in their dressing room.

**How frustrating was it sitting out the end of the 1986 campaign and Cup Final, and would Everton have won the double if you had not got injured?**
*Martin Rampton, Liverpool*

I don't think I'd have changed it. Bobby Mimms did really well, to be fair. I don't think I'd have made a difference in that. I couldn't criticize Bob for anything he did at the time. How frustrating was it? Once I'd done the injury and knew how serious it was, I found it quite easy really. If it had been a short-term one, or I had a chance of getting back earlier, it would have been really frustrating; but because I knew I was going to be out – they told me six months, nine months, to maybe a year – then I got it in my head that it was a long job and there was nothing I was going to be able to do about it. If it had been a short, niggly injury I think I would have stabbed somebody, or killed somebody, or hacked somebody; but because of the way it was, it was a long one and it was easier probably to digest.

# ACKNOWLEDGEMENTS

To ALL Evertonians, wherever you are - Thanks for showing me trust, respect, loyalty and love. I will never forget you.

To the city of Liverpool - Thanks for taking me to your heart.

To all the clubs I have ever played for - Thank you for the opportunity I will always be extremely grateful.

Deal Town FC & Ramsgate FC - Just a big thank you.

The Football Association of Wales - Thank you for letting me represent the country I love.

Dave & Michelle - For being some of the very few people I would trust with my life, thank you for all your support and help.

Les Reed - (Mr Crocs) Thanks for all your help over the years and wonderful memorabilia.

Ade Danes - Thank you for always thinking about me.

Dawn Griffiths - For all your patience and hard work in writing my qualifications.

Peter Griffiths - Thanks for putting up with me.

Kristian Smith & the PFA - For all your advice and guidance.

To my closest friends - Sue, Brad, Oliver, Aimee & Benjamin, Quags, Ruth, Francesca, Katerina & Raffi, Viv & Al, Vinnie, Tracy, Abbie & Neville, Gary & Jen - who know the real me and are still my friends.

My family - Steve, Jeff, Teresa and Alan thank you for always being there.

Margaret, Tony, Dai, Rach, Ieuan, Ella, Roger, Karen – thank you for letting me into your family.

Allen Mohr and Thomas Regan – For your fantastic cover designs

Kate Highfield and Sabahat Muhammad – For your important roles in the production of this book.

Graham Bateman – For coming up with the brilliant title of this book.

James Corbett - For showing great patience, drinking loads of tea and coming up with something sensible from my garbled rubbish, a massive thank you.

Anna Corbett - For keeping James in check.

Samantha & Emma - without whom my life would be incomplete.

# INDEX

## A

Ablett, Gary 257
Adams, Neil 134
Amokachi, Daniel 188, 195–197
Angell, Brett 182
Arnold, Jim 40, 46, 50, 55, 73, 79
Atkinson, Ron 149

## B

Bailey, John 58
Ball, Alan 149
Bangor City FC 24
Barmby, Nick 206
Beardsley, Peter 174
Berry, George 93
Biley, Alan 47, 54
Billing, Peter 143
Bodin, Paul 169
Borrows, Brian 67
Bruce, Steve 80, 238
Bury. *See Southall, Neville: Bury*

## C

Carter, Philip 75, 77, 82, 155
Chamberlain, Helen 236
Charles, Jeremy 92
Clarke, Matt 238, 240

Clinkard, John 130, 133
Clough, Brian 36, 149
Connor, Dave 31, 33
Cottee, Tony 141, 142, 150, 172, 188
Curtis, Alan 96

## D

Dalglish, Kenny 149, 172
Dave Connor 31
Davidson, Aidan 238
Davies, Alan 161
Davies, Dai 40, 95, 96
Dublin, Dion 180
Durban, Alan 230
Durrant, Iain 192

## E

Eales, Peter 25, 26
Ebbrell, John 143, 194, 197
Elliot, Dave 24, 26
Ellis, Alfred 93
England, Mike 90, 91–93, 99, 102–104, 129, 160
Evans, Alun 93, 94, 99, 104, 160, 220
Everton. *See Southall, Neville: Everton*

## F

Ferguson, Alex 156
Ferguson, Duncan 192–194, 197
Ferguson, Mick 47, 56
Football Writers' Player of the Year
    114
Forrest, John 35, 40
Fortuna Dusseldorf 17

## G

Gabriel, Jimmy 180
Gerrard, Paul 201, 204
Giggs, Ryan 158, 166
Gould, Bobby 167, 221
Gray, Andy 75, 76, 81, 113,
    124, 209
Greenhoff, Jimmy 71
Greenwood, Jim 44

## H

Hansen, Alan 83
Harper, Alan 74, 115, 136, 174
Harvey, Colin 45–46, 75,
    139–141, 147, 150,
    156–157, 170
Heysel Stadium Disaster 122–123
Hill, John 169, 214
Hillsborough Disaster 145, 147
hod carrier 26, 32
Horne, Barry 178, 194
Howard, Bob 71
Hughes, Mark 3, 96, 149,
    159, 219

## I

Iley, Jim 33–35, 41, 43

I Love My Wife, T-shirt 126
Injury, ankle 129–131, 133–135

## J

Jefferies, Jim 239
Jennings, Pat 18, 96
Jewell, Paul 238
Jim Iley 39
Johnson, David 61
Johnson, Peter 187, 190,
    209, 232
Johnston, Mo 176
Jones, Andy 159, 161
Jones, Joey 19, 29, 95
Jones, Paul 224
Jones, Vinnie 220, 222

## K

Kanchelskis, Andrei 200
Kendall, Howard 44, 48, 56,
    60, 70, 73, 75, 77, 78,
    80, 82, 124, 133–134,
    138–139, 171, 174,
    180, 210, 212
Kenny, Billy 178
Keown, Martin 151, 153,
    157, 178
Knill, Alan 162

## L

Langley, Kevin 134
Lineker, Gary 3, 124, 125, 132
Liverpool 27, 43, 192
Liverpool FC 64, 65, 122,
    131–133, 146
Llandudno 5, 7, 8, 13, 17,
    19, 22, 41, 147

Llandudno Swifts 13, 13–15
Llandudno Town FC 24
Lyons, Mick 58–60, 116

**M**
MacGregor, Jim 44
Martin, Alvin 228
Martin, Jimmy 187
McCall, Stuart 141
McDonagh, Jim 46
McDonald, Neil 141, 150
McGrath, John 70, 71
McGuinness, Wilf 36–37
McIntosh, Peter 229
McMahon, Steve 59
Mimms, Bobby 132
Moss, Ernie 71
Mountfield, Derek 119–120, 133
Murray, Joe 131

**N**
Nevin, Pat 5, 141
Newell, Mike 150, 152
Nicholas, Peter 91, 96
Niedzwiecki, Eddie 20, 133
Norman, Tony 161
Norwich City 145, 181, 190

**P**
Parkinson, Joe 183, 194
Philips, Dave 159
Platini, Michel 91
Power, Paul 134

**R**
Ramsgate FC 2

Ratcliffe, Kevin 57, 97, 175
Rehn, Stefan 151
Reid, Peter 76, 147
Richardson, Kevin 59, 115
Rideout, Paul 178, 197
Ritz Café 22
Roberts, Gareth 19
Roberts, Johnny 13, 14, 16–18
Roberts, Stan 20
Robson, Bobby 101
Rous, Sir Stanley 114
Royle, Joe 170, 190, 201, 203, 208
Rudge, John 70
Rush, Ian 3, 91, 97, 100, 125, 219

**S**
Samways, Vinny 187
Saunders, Dean 165, 169, 174, 219, 222
Saunders, Wes 233, 237
Sharp, Graeme 3, 56, 104, 172, 173
Sheedy, Kevin 61, 74, 118, 136, 157
Shreeves, Peter 161, 214
Smith, Mike 217, 220
Snodin, Ian 233
Southall, Eryl (nee Williams, wife) 88, 234
Southall, Fred (father) 7–9, 18, 25, 88–89
Southall, Jeff (brother) 9, 10
Southall, Neville
  As a MANAGER 241–242, 243
  As a TEACHER 238

BURY 5, 32–42, 88–90
CHILDHOOD 7–12
DONCASTER ROVERS 233
EVERTON
  5-0 derby defeat 65–67
  1984 - 85 Season 106–120
  1986-87 League Championship
    135–137
  Debut 51
  Early Interest 41–42
  End of Everton Career 203–213
  FA Cup Final (1984) 85–87
  FA Cup Final (1985) 119–120
  FA Cup Final (1989) 146
  FA Cup Final (1995) 196–198
  League Cup Final (1984) 83
  Port Vale loan 70–71
  Reserve team football 68, 75
  Signing 43
  Sit in v Leeds United 155
  v Bayern Munich (1985)
    114–116
  v Liverpool (1991) 172
  v Tottenham Hotspur (1995)
    195–196
  v Wimbledon (1994) 184–186
FATHERHOOD 147, 235
NON-LEAGUE CAREER 13–18,
  27–29
SOUTHEND UNITED 228–229
STOKE CITY 229–231
TORQUAY UNITED 233, 236–237
WALES 90, 158–161
  1988 European Championships
    qualifying 159–162
  1994 World Cup qualifying
    166–169

Assistant Manager to Bobby Gould
  221–222
Interview for Manager 221, 225
v England (1984) 98
v Georgia (1995) 219
v Germany (1991) 164–168,
  166
v Iceland (1984) 91–92, 99,
  100
v Moldova (1995) 218
v Netherlands (1996) 223
v Northern Ireland (1982) 96
v Romania (1993) 168–169,
  214
v Russia (1981) 94–95
v Scotland (1985) 100–101,
  102–105
v Spain (1985) 101–102
Southall, Rose (mother) 7–9, 20
Southall, Samantha (daughter)
  147, 196, 199, 231, 235
Southall, Steve (brother) 9, 10
Speed, Gary 158, 167, 169,
  201, 204, 211, 218, 219,
  222, 257
Speedie, David 104, 127
Sproson, Phil 70
Stevens, Gary 57
Steven, Trevor 3, 74, 113, 147
Stoke City 73

T
Teaching 1–2, 12, 245–250
Toshack, John 216
Turpin, Randolph 10

## V

Van Den Hauwe, Pat 58, 101,
    111, 136–137, 147

## W

Wales. *See Southall, Neville: Wales*
Walker, Mike 181, 187, 189,
    190
Walsh, Gary 238
Walsh, Mick 47
Warburton, Peter 27
Ward, Mark 174
Warzycha, Robert 179
Watford 86
Watson, Alex 236
Watson, Dave 133, 189, 208
Whiteside, Norman 150
Wigan Athletic 31, 36
Wilkinson, Paul 125
Williams, Bill 242
Williams, Dave 189, 217
Williams, David 182
Williams, John 30
Wimbledon 144
Wright, Billy 60
Wright, Richard 204

## Y

Yorath, Terry 161, 166, 215
Youds, Eddie 143